HOW TO CHOOSE AN
Adventure
Vacation

D0720420

Fodor's Fodor's Travel Publications
New York, Toronto, London, Sydney, Auckland

How to Choose an Adventure Vacation

Editor: Diane Mehta

Production/Manufacturing: Robert B. Shields

Creative Director: Fabrizio La Rocca

Text and Cover Design: Guido Caroti

Cover Photo: Robert Bossi/Stone/Getty Images

Copyright

Copyright © 2003 by Fodors LLC

Fodor's is a registered trademark of Random House, Inc.
All rights reserved under International and Pan-American
Copyright Conventions. Published in the United States by Fodor's
Travel Publications, a unit of Fodors LLC, a subsidiary of
Random House, Inc., and simultaneously in Canada by Random
House of Canada Limited, Toronto. Distributed by Random
House, Inc., New York.

*No portions of this book may be reproduced in any form without writ-
ten permission from the publisher.*

First Edition

ISBN 1–4000–1213–9

ISSN 1541–2873

Important Tip

Although all prices, opening times, and other details in this book
are based on information supplied to us at press time, changes
occur all the time, and Fodor's cannot accept responsibility for
facts that become outdated or for inadvertent errors or omissions.
So always confirm information before you book a trip.

Special Sales

Fodor's Travel Publications are available at special discounts for
bulk purchases for sales promotions or premiums. Special editions,
including personalized covers, excerpts of existing guides, and cor-
porate imprints, can be created in large quantities for special needs.
For more information, contact your local bookseller or write to
Special Markets, Fodor's Travel Publications, 1745 Broadway, New
York, NY 10019. Inquiries from Canada should be directed to your
local Canadian bookseller or sent to Random House of Canada,
Ltd., Marketing Department, 2775 Matheson Boulevard East,
Mississauga, Ontario L4W 4P7. Inquiries from the United
Kingdom should be sent to Fodor's Travel Publications, 20
Vauxhall Bridge Road, London SW1V 2SA, England.

PRINTED IN THE UNITED STATES OF AMERICA

10 9 8 7 6 5 4 3 2 1

Contents

About Our Writers

Georgia de Katona, who updated the Archaeological Digs chapter, has a background in anthropology and has worked on archaeological digs in northern New Mexico.

Bill Strickland, editor of *Bicycling* magazine and original writer of the Cycling and Mountain Biking chapters, pedals his way to work every day and races mountain bikes frequently. In more than 10 years of riding he has toured every corner of the United States. **Joe Lindsey** is a contributing writer for *Bicycling* magazine. He rides road and mountain bikes, races, and in 15 years of riding has ridden in much of the American West, Canada, Belgium, and Italy. He updated the cycling and mountain biking chapters.

Paul M. Konrad, who wrote the Birding chapter, is a professional ornithologist and the previous editor of *Wild-Bird* magazine. New Jersey bird lover **Andrea Lehman** updated the chapter.

Fishing camps and Fly-Fishing Schools writer **Bud Journey** has won outdoors-writing and photography contests and claims to have caught a 10-pound, 9-ounce walleye. Updater **Carol Bareuther** grew up fishing off the New Jersey coast, south to the Carolinas and

Florida. She lives in St. Thomas, U.S. Virgin Islands, and contributes to *Marlin* magazine for big-game tournaments and *All at Sea,* a Caribbean newspaper, about regional tournaments. She enjoys fly-fishing for bonefish on the coral flats with her husband, 12-year-old son, and 9-year-old daughter.

Manager of Editorial Projects for the Golf Digest Companies and editor of the popular *Golf Digest's Places to Play* book, **Sue Sawyer,** updater of the Golf Schools chapter, is an avid golfer who has won several amateur-level championships, sports a single-digit handicap, and is the Web master for the Southern New England Women's Golf Association Web site (www. snewga.org).

Adventurer and writer of the Hang-Gliding chapter, **Erik Fair** is the author of *California Thrill Sports* and winner of the 1991 Max Karant Award for Excellence in Aviation Journalism. He has taught hundreds of folks how to fly a hang glider and wrote a book for them called *Right Stuff for New Hang Glider Pilots.* Updater **Jim (SkyDog)**

Palmieri has been flying hang gliders since 1992. He's on the editorial staff of *Hang Gliding Magazine,* to which he has contributed many articles. He and his wife, Maggie, have edited three books on hang gliding and run their own publishing company, Sky Dog Publications. Jim has towed hang gliders behind trucks, boats, trikes, and ultralights, and he combines these skills with his love for flying the mountains of Virginia and Tennessee.

Outdoors writer **Peter Oliver,** who wrote the Hiking and Backpacking chapter, has hiked all over the United States. His favorite destinations are New Hampshire's White Mountains and grizzly country in Montana. Writer and editor **Cindy Hirschfeld**—who updated the chapter—has hiked on four continents, but her favorite outings are the trails near her home in Aspen, Colorado, in the company of her golden retriever.

Dennis Stuhaug, a contributing editor of *Canoe & Kayak Magazine,* is a former white-water and flat-water instructor and a longtime sport and recreational paddler. He wrote the Canoeing and Kayaking in White Water and Flat Water chapters. Freelance writer **Julian Tonsmeire,** who updated both chapters, is a recovering river junky, an avid Class V white-water kayaker in the western United States, and an international river guide. He has completed a 400-mi canoe expedition down the Nahani River in Canada's remote Northwest Territory.

Although writer **Melanie Sponholz** loves Manhattan, urban life has taught her to truly appreciate her escapes to areas of natural beauty—she wrote the Nature Camps chapter. **Marilyn Haddrill,** of Las Cruces, New Mexico, updated the chapter. In her 30-year career, she has been a newspaper reporter, photographer, novelist, and television news correspondent. As a New Mexico native, she has written many articles about the desert and wilderness habitats of her rural homeland. Her work has been in the *Dallas Morning News* and other publications. She's a contributing editor for *EyeWorld Magazine,* an ophthalmology trade journal.

Outdoors writer **Lee R. Schreiber,** the founding managing editor of *Golf Illustrated and Backpacking Journal* and author of seven books, wrote the River Rafting chapter. Freelance writer and updater **Julian Tonsmeire** is a former river guide on the Arkansas, Colorado, Green, and Blue rivers of Colorado.

Outdoor writer **Michael B. McPhee**—who wrote the Sailing Schools chapter—has logged more than 10,000 mi of offshore passages and has owned boats ranging from a Hobie Cat to a wooden Norwegian 8-meter sloop. **Carol Bareuther,** the chapter updater and a writer in St. Thomas, U.S. Virgin Islands, enjoys cruising in a 28-ft O'Day. She has narrated live radio broadcasts from major northern Caribbean sailing events, such as Puerto Rico's Heineken International Cup, the International Rolex Regatta, and British Virgin Islands Spring Regatta.

Scuba Diving chapter writer **Lisa Skriloff** holds a PADI Advanced Open Water certification card and has logged more than 100 dives. Updater **Priscilla Burgess** has spent her entire life in, on, under, and around California's Pacific

Coast. She has PADI Open Water certification.

Peter Potterfield, author of *Selected Climbs in the Cascades and Chimney Rock* and the original writer of the Climbing and Mountaineering chapter, was formerly the editor of *Pacific Northwest Magazine* and has contributed to *Condé Nast Traveler, Summit, Outside,* and other magazines. **Cindy Hirschfeld,** updater of the chapter, has had a lifelong passion for the mountains. She lives in Aspen, Colorado, and travels the world in search of additional peaks to climb while also working as a writer and editor for such magazines as *Skiing and Back Country.*

Susan Farewell, a travel and fitness writer who wrote the chapter on Tennis Camps, has an eclectic style of play that comes from a dozen years of visiting tennis camps and resorts the world over. Updater **Brad Weiss** was deemed the "tennis court baby" by his parents, who regularly left his stroller at mid-court as they played. He grew up to be an avid tennis player and traveler and has written chapters in Fodor's guides to Brazil, Argentina, Costa Rica, and Los Cabos, Mexico.

New Jersey resident **Andrea Lehman** credits a youth full of camping in downpours as great preparation for life. She has dug her own latrines, built fires the old-fashioned way (with matches), and has gone on 24-hour solo sojourns in the woods. She wrote the Wilderness and Survival Schools chapter.

Elizabeth Gehrman windsurfs at Kalmus Beach in Hyannis, Cape Cod, and gravitates toward seaside destinations around the world. She wrote the Wind-Surfing chapter.

Freelance writer **Rena Zurofsky** has paddled the waters of Maine, Central America, and the Canadian coasts. She wrote the chapter on Sea Kayaking. **Chris Cunningham,** who updated the chapter, began building and paddling kayaks in 1979 and has been the editor of *Sea Kayaker* magazine since 1989.

Surfer and Fodor's vet **Rob Aikins,** author of the Surfing Schools chapter, has been immersed in the southern California surfing culture and industry since the late 1970s. He has taken his quest for the perfect wave down the Pacific Coast from

California to Panama, as well as to Australia, Brazil, the Philippine Islands, and the requisite pilgrimage to Oahu's legendary North Shore. When not traveling, he attempts to plan his schedule around his surfing rather than his surfing around his schedule.

Rosemary Freskos and **Jonathan Wiesel** wrote the Nordic Skiing chapter—she has been writing about snow sports for several decades, and has skied at most of the world's major ski resorts. Jonathan has visited more than 300 North American cross-country ski areas. Rosemary also wrote the chapter on Ski Schools. **Gregory Benchwick,** a frequent Fodor's contributor, updated both the Nordic Skiing and Ski Schools chapters. He works as a ski instructor in Vail, Colorado, and Spain's Sierra Nevada Resort, and has written extensively about outdoor-adventure sports and travel. His first experiences with Nordic skiing came in Colorado's Rocky Mountains, where he grew up—he started skiing at the ripe old age of three. Since then he has skied in many areas and mountain ranges around the globe.

Revving Up

by Diane Mehta

Full-tilt adventure shakes your life up in ways you'd never expect. Skid across a lake on a Windsurfer, zigzag your way down powdery slopes high up in the Rockies, or lift off terra firma in a hang glider, and you experience a kick of adrenaline that's like nothing else in the world. There are countless ways to turn a vacation into an adventure, but sorting through the activities available and finding the right outfitters are no minor tasks. This book will make both jobs easier.

All the adventures in this book are, in essence, safe bets—the schools and programs we list are suitable for novices or athletes. Many multiday programs are geared to people who are jumping in feet first. If you're curious about a sport but haven't tried it, you'll find all the information you need here, including an assessment of the risks involved. Most physical activity or exploration involves some risk, but the risk decreases when you know what you're in for and you plan accordingly. In return for your gumption you might get the chance to see a different part of the country from a different angle—looking up from underwater, for example, or down from the summit of an icy peak. Then, of course, there's the private, incomparable thrill of doing something not everyone has the nerve to undertake.

More and more people are taking to the outdoors—America, after all, has always been a place of exploration, with a varied, dramatic landscape. From the stark Southwest to the looming peaks of the Rockies, the landscape here is as fine as—and probably more diverse than—any other place in the world. There are plenty of established schools to take you wherever you want to go and to teach you whatever you want to learn, and there are more new outfitters than ever before. Family trips and women-only expeditions are increasingly popular, and many outfitters customize trips to groups of people with similar interests—such as a rafting trip for aficionados of bluegrass music or a cycling trip to Civil War sites in the South. Fitness, the outdoors, and educational adventures are *in* and are available to anyone with a little spirit or, for the more demanding adventures we include, daring.

Everyone's idea of an adventure naturally differs: while you may be looking to improve your mountaineering or backcountry skiing skills, someone else may find a deeper sense of adventure scudding the surf or excavating an Anasazi settlement—or sharpening a killer serve on the tennis court. And some people want to rough it while others prefer a more comfortable adventure. Some outfitters and schools take you camping; plenty of others treat you like royalty.

Something for Everyone

This guide will help you figure out what kind of adventure you're looking for—and whether in fact you're up to it. In each chapter we explain what the sport involves and what kinds of programs are available, and supply you with a list of essential questions to get you started. All sports are for both beginners and athletes. In the last chapter of this book, "Resources," we list top outfitters for each sport and the programs they run. Under each listing we describe either the range of trips available and the techniques or activities in which that particular outfitter specializes, or we highlight a particular trip or several popular trips. It's up to you to inquire with the outfitter about additional trips.

The trips or expeditions we list mainly include scheduled group trips and courses in the United States that last anywhere from a few days to several weeks. In addition to all-inclusive multiday programs, we sometimes list guide services that base their total fees on day rates—so we help you calculate costs based on what's most appropriate to the sport.

Essential Questions

Each chapter in this guide contains a checklist of questions to help you choose the right trip. But for every outfitter, you should make some general inquiries. First and foremost, always ask for references. It's a reliable way to get the lowdown on the real nature of the course or expedition. If the outfitter refuses to give you a reference, or shies away from it, think twice about booking a trip with them.

On the financial end, know how much of a deposit is required and when the balance is due. Ask about the cancellation policy—how far in advance must you cancel to get a full refund, and do special conditions apply? If the outfitter offers cancellation insurance, always take it. You'll receive a full refund if for any reason you can't make the trip. Also make sure you ask whether taxes and tips are included (generally they are not). Find out who gets tipped and how much that tip should be, as that can add substantially to your costs. If you're traveling solo, ask about the single occupancy policy. Most prices we quote are per person based on double occupancy. Almost all companies will charge you a single supplement if you request a single room.

Also make sure you let the outfitter know before you sign up if you have special dietary or health needs. If you're traveling with your family, check to see if youngsters are permitted or discouraged. Some programs are just not suitable for children—they're too hard or too dangerous or require too much sitting still—and other trips are more family-oriented, or fine for teenagers.

Every care has been taken to ensure the accuracy of the information in this guide. All prices and dates quoted here are approximate ranges, based on information supplied to us at press time, but trips and pricing may change, and calling to ask about details is prudent.

We want to hear about your travel experiences, both pleasant and unpleasant. When a school or outfitter fails to live up to its billing, let us know and we'll investigate the complaint and revise our entries where the facts warrant it. Send your letters to editors@fodors.com or c/o Fodor's at 1745 Broadway, New York, NY 10019.

Archaeological Digs

Updated by Georgia de Katona

No matter how much dirt you move to get to it, there's nothing like the moment you find your first relic. Whether it's a yucca sandal in a remote corner of the Southwest or a tool used by an early European in the Northeast, archaeology was made for people who understand that good things come to those who wait.

The rituals and rewards of archaeological digs can be as mundane as bowls and bones or as exciting as Indiana Jones, minus the Hollywood aspect. Archaeology is not just about collecting artifacts; it's about understanding people from times past. It is by examining ordinary objects used in daily life, that archaeologists learn about how people lived. The programs below allow you to work alongside professionals at archaeological sites, helping to excavate some of the same types of objects you see on display in museums—pottery, stone tools, and religious artifacts.

Most archaeological programs don't require any previous dig experience or knowledge of archaeological techniques. In fact, most, as part of their mission, teach the public about archaeology and its methods, and how to conduct research and document, preserve, and protect sites threatened by weather, development, looters, or vandals. You need to be able to perform basic physical activities: hiking, shoveling, lifting, carrying, or pushing a wheelbarrow.

A typical day at an excavation begins early, especially if you're staying at the site. (Some sites are so remote that you must hike in and camp there. With others you can drive to the dig.) Once on location, you'll be briefed on what you're looking for and what you should aim to accomplish that day. Each site varies, as do excavation techniques. The basics include surveying a location to determine possible excavation sites, laying out a grid over a site you want to explore, carefully removing topsoil without disturbing artifacts, sifting to find small items, logging and recording the position of artifacts in the grid, removing pieces, and, finally, cleaning and storing them. Good programs rotate you through the tasks so you can experience them all.

Participants typically range in age from teens to senior citizens, though most programs have a minimum age of 17 or 18 (and don't provide day care). Groups are usually small (5 to 25), which helps create camaraderie. Expect to be in the field, and sometimes the lab, for eight hours a day. Projects that run throughout "the season" start in the spring, as early as the weather permits, and continue into the fall; others last only the short sessions that faculty, trip leaders, or volunteers are available.

The biggest difference between programs is the peoples they study. Digs cover all types of cultures, in all types of places, and at all points in time. The representative ones we list at the back of this book are just that—if you're interested in a particular aspect of history (or prehistory), there's a good chance you'll find a program out there for you. Other significant differences between programs include the weather, the physical demands, and the "comfort factor." Remember: what's challenging and fun for one person may be daunting and miserable for another.

CHOOSING THE RIGHT DIG

If you don't mind getting down and dirty, and slowing your pace, working on an excavation can be rewarding and educational, not to mention fun. A dig isn't just a dig—you'll find that programs vary drastically. Here's a list of questions to get you going.

What's the subject of the excavation and the site?
Archaeological digs are as different as the sites at which they're located and the cultures they're attempting to uncover. Especially in western states,

many excavations focus on prehistoric or historic-period Native Americans. For more recent American history, other, typically eastern, excavations take place at such locations as Colonial villages and Civil War–era plantations.

What types of activities are offered? Chances are if you're looking for an archaeological dig, you're interested in, well, digging. But most programs also offer activities that put excavating in a broader context—lectures, tours of other historic sites, and trips to museums. Some also teach you other archaeological skills, such as cleaning, analyzing, and cataloging the artifacts you discover. Decide whether you want to be out in the sun, trowel in hand, as much as possible, or if you want to sample different facets of the field.

Where's the dig and what are the conditions like? Most digs are hot, dry, and dusty. Many programs are in the South, Southwest, Midwest, and West, and most are offered in summer, the prime research time. You're outside much of the day, far from the comforts of soda machines and swimming pools. You'll quickly learn to look forward to sunshades and ice water, afternoon lab breaks and afternoon thundershowers. For many, hot weather is no big deal, but if you can't stand the heat, stay out of the Sun Belt or opt for spring or fall sessions. Ask for suggestions regarding appropriate dress for the time of year you'll be on-site; it could make a bigger difference than you realize.

What kinds of experience or skills are necessary? In most cases, the answer is none: no previous dig experience, no knowledge of archaeology, and not even any particular physical skills. The only requirement is the desire to learn. If the work is strenuous and you're out of shape, or if most of the other participants will have a level of knowledge you don't, you might want to reconsider.

How long has the program been in operation? Older doesn't necessarily mean better, but it can mean more organized. A few years of working with volunteers can help staff fine-tune how to train them.

What's the cost and what's included? Roughly speaking, archaeological digs come in two varieties: full-service and self-service. The programs we list, which are sponsored by government agencies, universities, museums, and archaeological societies, tend to be the latter. Open to volunteers, they generally charge nothing, except the occasional small fee for supplies or association membership. The drawback is that nothing is included. For self-service digs, you are responsible for your own meals, lodging, and transportation unless otherwise noted. Ask about transportation from the nearest airport to the site; sometimes it's supplied. Also ask whether there are camping fees.

Full-service digs, on the other hand, charge a fee for participation ($500–$1,800 for several days to several weeks); unless otherwise stated, digs of this kind listed in this book include accommodations, meals, and transportation to the site from a nearby airport or other rendezvous point. Part of the fee covers the cost of the research project itself. These programs are usually operated by national organizations, most nonprofit, that are in the learning-vacations business, offering a variety of projects beyond digs. In either full- or self-service digs, the program generally supplies the equipment and materials needed in the research.

Many programs, however, fall somewhere in between full- and self-service. It's always best to check exactly what is and what isn't included, especially if particular items, such as tents and sleeping bags, are concerns.

What are the accommodations like? Most volunteer programs encourage or at least make arrangements for you to camp out. It's part of the experience: just pitch a tent and pitch in. As a rule, you're closer to the site if you camp, so you can participate in evening activities. However, programs almost always provide lists of reasonably priced local motels or even bed-and-breakfasts and finer hotels, especially at sites near cities or popular tourist attractions. Many bigger and more established programs have arrangements with nearby colleges to provide low-cost accommodations. Ongoing research sites often provide lodgings near the excavation, though they tend to be rustic.

What's the food like? If you camp, your food is likely to be what you cook yourself; if you stay in a motel, you'll probably be eating in restaurants. Programs that offer lodging usually provide meals in a common dining hall. If meals are provided and you have any special dietary needs, ask whether they can be accommodated.

How long can I stay? If you have never done anything like this before and want to try archaeology on to see how it fits, perhaps as part of a longer vacation, a program that lets you stop in for a few days is ideal. For more than a taste, you need a good week or longer. Programs that are designed in one- or two-week sessions have a learning curve and some flexibility built in. You not only have more time to perfect excavation techniques, but you also can learn more in the lab and at lectures and possibly develop your own small projects based on special interests. Some projects allow you to work a month or all season, staying over a number of sessions (where formal sessions are offered).

How far in advance do I need to book? Check the literature you receive for application deadlines. Most programs don't have them and take applicants as long as space is available, so try to sign up two to six months in advance. For programs with fees, make sure you check for cancellation deadlines and policies.

SOURCES
Organizations

At Boston University, the **Archaeological Institute of America** (656 Beacon St., Boston, MA 02215-1401, 617/353–9361, www.archaeological.org), also known as AIA, has served both the public and the scholarly community for more than 100 years. It encourages and supports archaeological research, informs the public about archaeology, and helps protect the world's cultural heritage. **State archaeologists** and **state historic preservation offices,** often under the jurisdiction of a department of cultural resources and historic preservation, are excellent sources of information.

Periodicals

The AIA (www.archaeological.org) issues two newsletters, two catalogs, and two magazines per year. The magazines do features on everything from efforts to catalog the disappearing cultural artifacts of Afghanistan to fieldwork opportunities. The outfit's *Fieldwork Opportunities Bulletin,* issued annually in January, has a comprehensive directory of education opportunities in the field for students and amateur archaeologists. Among the many publications that list upcoming excavations are Earthwatch's self-titled magazine, *Earthwatch Journal* (680 Mt. Auburn St., Box 910, Watertown, MA 02272-9924, 617/926–8200, www.earthwatch.org), which is available gratis to members. Also free is "Passport in Time Traveler" (U. S. Forest Service, Box 18364, Washington, DC 20036, 800/281–9176); the newsletter is published every spring and fall by Passport in Time.

Books

The Guide to Cultural Travel (Shaw Guides, 800/247–6553, www.shawguides.com) contains extensive information about academic learning vacations sponsored by schools, colleges, museums, educational and cultural organizations, and travel companies.

Internet

Check on-line for field schools associated with major universities (the University of Arizona, Stanford, UCLA, UC Berkeley, University of Florida, Northern Arizona University, Southern Methodist University, and University of Texas at Austin have world-class programs) or nationally recognized organizations.

Birding

By Paul M. Konrad
Updated by Andrea E. Lehman

Watch large numbers of migrants alight for a stop on one of their immense biannual journeys. Rise long before sunrise to see birds that go into hiding after dawn. Listen for birdsong as night settles. Hike through spectacular mountain, coastal, forest, desert, or wetland scenery in search of that elusive species. A common bond unites people of all ages and types to birding tours: a serious interest in birds and a broader love of nature.

You can set off bird-watching on your own just about anywhere, but on a guided group you'll benefit vastly from the experience of group leaders and other birders. Not only will you get to explore an area you're unfamiliar with, but, conveniently, someone else takes care of the less thrilling, nonbirding aspects of the trip. Tours cover every region of the country, but most travel to known and renowned birding hot spots—often in Alaska and Texas.

There are three major U.S. bird-tour operators. They plan the itinerary, arrange lodging and at least some meals, and provide transportation during the tour (and, on request, help you with your pre- and post-trip transportation needs). All employ dedicated, knowledgeable, and personable guides. Tours are generally limited to 9 or 10 participants with one leader, or 16 with two. In addition to the big three companies, some nature-tour packagers cater to birders, and smaller, local outfits offer limited tours, including one-day pelagic (offshore) trips to see seabirds and mammals.

There are three points to consider when planning a birding trip: when to go, what to see, and where to see it. Not surprisingly, these issues are all connected, because certain species tend to be in certain parts of the country at certain times of the year. As a result, it's not unusual for several outfitters to offer trips to the same place at roughly the same time, allowing you to comparison shop.

Though daily activities may vary—some trips take limited time for mammals, other natural wonders, or sites of cultural or historic interest—most concentrate on hard-core birding. You may pass much or all of a day visiting every inch of a wildlife refuge or bird sanctuary at a leisurely pace, or you may pop in and out of the van for short stints at a number of birding spots. Most tours provide some time for photography, but if that is your focus, try a nature-photography tour instead. Nearly every tour has some predawn or after-dark birding, but often these excursions are optional, unless the group does not plan to return to the hotel for breakfast before going back into the field. Since tours usually stay far from commercial development, the only nightlife you're likely to encounter is owls. Recently, tours concentrating on both birds and butterflies have cropped up, as many birders are avid watchers of these other winged wonders.

Tours generally run from 5 to 14 days, with most going to readily accessible areas. Though terrain varies, the walking and hiking involved are usually comfortable for young and old alike, as long as you're in relatively sound physical shape. Since noise levels in the field need to be kept low, tours tend to exclude children under 14.

Costs range from under $200 to almost $400 per day, depending on the destination, but none of these tours are luxurious. You stay at moderately priced hotels and motels, eating in modest restaurants (many with intriguing local fare) for most breakfasts and all dinners; lunches vary from sit-down affairs to stops at a sandwich shop to picnics.

For transportation, most companies cart you around in 15-passenger vans, which carry up to 10 birders plus their luggage and the driver in relative comfort.

CHOOSING THE RIGHT TOUR

Because there are so many birding tours to choose from, when you are trying to pick one, it is best to ask plenty of questions. Start with these.

What birds do you aim to see on this trip? Tours are often planned around particular species, but leaders happily stop for a look at any interesting birds you come across. Itineraries are usually set up to see the maximum number of the region's specialty birds, although all birds are looked at once. Some tours also specialize in migration spectacles. Ask for a list of the birds seen on the tour in the last year or two so you'll know what you're likely to see.

How long has the company been in business? Stick with an outfit that has been around for several years. The big three we list in this book have all been in business since the early '70s to the mid-'80s.

How long has the company conducted this tour? If the company has not done this tour before, scrutinize the credentials of the tour leader.

What are the guide's qualifications? Guides tend to be very knowledgeable birders who know the area well. They don't need to be locals, but they should be well informed about the ecology of the area you're visiting and the birds you're seeking out.

What's the cost and what's included? Most operators include lodging and meals in the price of tours, but some don't cover all meals. You generally must room with another birder or pay a single supplement for a private room. Transportation between birding destinations once the tour is under way and other en-route expenses, such as park entrance fees, are included.

What are the accommodations like? Because what most birders want from a lodging are clean sheets, a comfortable bed, and plenty of hot water, most tours use reliable national chain hotels and motels or comparable local establishments that are clean and comfortable. Sometimes tours go to areas with inns and bed-and-breakfasts. National parks tend to have lodges and cabins with charm and character.

What is the food like? No operator provides fancy dining, but most try to find restaurants that serve good food, including regional dishes. Many operators arrange for picnics so you don't have to leave your birding spot at midday.

How difficult are the hikes? Generally, the pace is moderate enough to be comfortable if you're in good health—any truly strenuous hiking is spelled out in advance. On trips with more than one leader, you might split up into faster and slower groups. On some trips, walks last up to four hours; others require nothing longer than a stroll. Uneven or wet terrain and high altitudes are not unusual. Count on regular early risings—and corresponding early turn-ins. Some tours allow for midday breaks, especially when it's hot, while others keep on trekking. If you want a more low-key tour, you probably won't see as many birds.

How far in advance do I need to book? Most outfitters ask you to reserve several months in advance, but you may want to book even earlier to make sure you're not left out of a popular tour. Signing up early for less-popular trips can help ensure that they actually run;

tours that are under-enrolled about two months prior to departure may be canceled. However, don't be shy about inquiring as late as a few weeks before a trip.

SOURCES

Organizations

The **American Birding Association** (Box 6599, Colorado Springs, CO 80934-6599, 800/634–7736) is the major national organization for serious birders. It has about 22,000 members, acts as a clearinghouse for information of interest to birders, and offers multiday birding workshops at various locales.

Many states have ornithological societies and bird clubs that have regular meetings, publish newsletters and journals with information of local interest, and schedule field trips. Local Audubon chapters also run field trips and other bird-related functions.

Periodicals

Birding, published bimonthly, is the magazine of the American Birding Association (*see* Organizations, *above*). It's geared to active recreational birders of all levels and emphasizes identification, bird-finding, and reviews. Members of ABA also receive the monthly newsletter "Winging It." The ABA also publishes *North American Birds,* with quarterly summaries of bird sightings and articles on bird distribution. *Birder's World* (Kalmbach Publishing, 21027 Crossroads Cir., Waukesha, WI 53186, 800/533–6644) is a bimonthly magazine featuring articles of general interest to birders. *Bird Watcher's Digest* (Box 110, Marietta, OH 45750-9977, 800/879–2473) is a small-format, general-interest birding magazine published six times a year; it's designed for beginner to intermediate and backyard birders. *Living Bird* (159 Sapsucker Woods Rd., Ithaca, NY 14850, 800/843–2473 or 607/254–2473) is the quarterly publication of the Cornell Lab of Ornithology. The monthly *WildBird* magazine (Box 5060, Mission Viejo, CA 92690, 949/855–8822) is also for beginning to intermediate and backyard birders.

Books

The Field Guide to the Birds of North America, a portable single volume to all of North America published by the National Geographic Society (updated 1999), and *The Sibley Guide to Birds,* by David Allen Sibley (2000) are favorites with intermediate and advanced birders. The Sibley guide has large numbers of incredibly detailed artwork but very little text, and the trim size is slightly larger than most field guides. Roger Tory Peterson's *A Field Guide to the Birds of Eastern and Central North America* (updated 2002) and *A Field Guide to Western Birds* (updated 1998) use arrows and in-flight drawings to help you identify birds. For beginning birders in the East, *Eastern Birds: A Guide to Field Identification of North American Species,* by James Coe (Golden Press), contains superb artwork and leaves out most of the rarer species. Also used mostly by beginners but containing photos are *Birds of North America* (Kaufman Focus Guides), by Kenn Kaufman, which uses computer-enhanced photographs and facing-page text and map, and the *Stokes Field Guides,* by Donald and Lillian Q. Stokes. Various states and regions have their own bird-finding guides; check in your library or a bookstore that has a regional or local section.

Canoeing and Kayaking in Flat Water

By Dennis Stuhaug
Updated by Julian Tonsmeire

French voyageurs in the 18th century and the Inuit of the extreme north of Alaska and Canada covered miles of rough territory in canoes and kayaks, just as modern-day adventurers use these same craft to explore the wilderness. Flat water can be serene or nervy—sometimes you drift across a lake, other times you maneuver your way down the bend of a river. The boats carry lots of gear, which means camping, later, can be downright luxurious.

If you've never done any canoeing or kayaking, start with a short guided trip on a nearby lake or river. Unlike white water, paddling flat water requires very little advance training. A few days of professional instruction will teach you much of what you need—paddle strokes, low-impact camping, and rescue skills.

Alternatively, if you feel confident that you can travel safely in the wilderness without a guide, consider using an outfitter. An "outfitted" trip is generally customized for you and includes many of the same services as a guided trip—except for a professional guide. Typically, outfitters will plan a route to suit your tastes and abilities, and equip you with a map, canoe or kayak, paddle, personal flotation device, and camping gear (tents, sleeping bags and pads, stoves and cookware). They'll also supply you with fresh and freeze-dried food and the necessary permits. Most outfitters can provide guides, too. Guides act as instructors, safety consultants, navigators, cooks, and naturalists. On a gentle river trip a guide may seem unnecessary, but you might reconsider if you're planning a week or longer in a remote area that requires multiple portages and difficult route finding.

On most expeditions, outfitters generally start out with a rendezvous at an inn or local paddling center, where they introduce you to the craft you'll be paddling in, fit you for paddles and life jackets, and discuss what to expect on the journey. You'll also discuss your route, your gear, and your food packs. Then it's off to the embarkation site or, in paddling terms, the put-in (the end of the trip is called the take-out). Some outfitters shuttle you to the put-in; others ask that you provide your own transportation.

Multiday paddling trips—from three days to three weeks—have a predictable rhythm. The first day is hectic: you discover how to pack the canoe, you master new strokes or relearn old ones, and you get accustomed to your paddling partner.

Don't expect smooth going all the way. There will be rapids, beaver dams, shallows, and occasional dry spots that must be hiked over to get to the next patch of water; the boat must be carried around the obstacle, in a maneuver known as the portage, from the French word *porter* "to carry," used by the French-Canadian voyageurs who first explored the continent's inland waterways. Helping hands are not only appreciated but usually expected—paddles and packs need to be transported, in addition to the boats; the sooner they are moved, the sooner you're back on the water.

More and more flat-water outfitters use kayaks as well as canoes (seldom are both used on the same trip). Often equipped with seats with adjustable backrests, kayaks are more comfortable than canoes. However, they're harder to portage, since they weren't designed to be carried. Canoes can be hoisted onto the shoulders of a single schlepper with relative ease, but kayaks take two people to carry. That's why kayaks are typically used on long river trips rather than on lake-to-lake itineraries.

Expect to pay about $100 per person per day for scheduled group trips and about $175 a day for custom expeditions—costs vary depending on the number of guides, the quality of provisions, the lodging (camping or inns), and the permits required, as well as whether the shuttle service takes you to and from put-in and take-out.

CHOOSING THE RIGHT TRIP

Before you open your wallet, always ask questions.

How long has the company been in business? Stick with an outfitter who has been in business for several years—it is more likely to have worked out the kinks. Ask about its current operating license and the professional organizations it belongs to. It should be an active member of America Outdoors or the North American Canoe Liveries and Outfitters Association (NACLO), umbrella organizations that set minimum standards to which members must agree. Know also that canoe outfitters in particular are an independent lot, and they concentrate on serving the rivers near their home base.

How experienced are the guides? Your guide, whether paddling canoes or kayaks, should be certified by the American Canoe Association (ACA) or the British Canoe Union (BCU) and be able to administer emergency medical aid, including CPR. The certification process ensures that the instructor can teach the right strokes the right way and has the necessary wilderness skills, such as route-finding and navigating on a river. An ideal guide will also be able to identify plants, animals, and geological phenomena.

What about safety and insurance? Mostly you paddle at your own risk. On-water liability insurance is not mandatory for NACLO members, although if an outfitter is operating on state or federal property, it is required to be insured as part of the permit process. NACLO distributes a safety video that most members show prior to the trip. It's always a good idea to check your own insurance coverage, too.

How strenuous is the trip? Some trips involve a leisurely float and the likelihood of being waited on hand and foot. On others you may be expected to help with portages, pitch in while making camp, and grab a paddle to power the boat. Mileage doesn't count as much as hours on the water and paddling conditions, so be sure to ask about wind, waves, and weather.

How many people are in the group? Ten is typical, but even 20 can be companionable, and you'll get more diverse socializing off-river.

What is the ratio of paddlers to guides? Four or five paddlers per guide is typical, but on trips with a support crew, the ratio may be lower.

What's the cost and what's included? Make sure the costs are precisely spelled out and that you understand exactly what's included. Unless otherwise noted, the prices for all trips listed in this book include a guide and basic instruction, canoes or kayaks, life preservers, all meals, and accommodations while you're canoeing. Unless we state otherwise, sleeping bags and pads are included in the cost of custom trips—but not in that of scheduled group trips.

What are the meals like? There's enough room in a canoe to pack a cooler, so you can usually expect a good supply of fresh fruits and vegetables and frozen meat or chicken. Breakfasts are typically hot cereal, granola, or pancakes. Lunches "on the paddle" (in which your paddle doubles as a serving platter) are often a smorgasbord of cheese, peanut butter, and fruit. Some outfits are ambitious about dinner; others prepare basic food. Ask to see sample menus.

What are accommodations like? Most canoe trips involve camping; if you don't supply your own equipment, make sure the outfitter's gear is up to snuff. Are the sleeping bags made of down (which loses its insulating properties when wet) or of a synthetic material (which keeps you warm even if it's had a dousing)? Are the tents modern and easy to set up?

What do you do when you're not paddling? Few river trips involve more than six hours per day on the water. Find out whether hikes or wildlife watching is planned and what the countryside is like off the river.

Is the trip suitable for singles? Most canoes and many flat-water kayaks are powered by two paddlers, and a single person may not always be matched with an appropriate partner. If you're solo, find out what the policy is in advance. On camping trips, ask whether you'll get your own tent.

How far in advance is booking required? Most outfitters prefer that you book at least 90 days in advance so they're sure of having enough participants before planning a trip.

SOURCES
Organizations
Membership organizations set standards for river guides and outfitters and are good sources for referrals and for checking references. Among them are **America Outdoors** (Box 1348, Knoxville, TN 37901, 615/524–C4814, www.americanoutdoors.com), the national association for river guides, and the **National Association of Canoe Liveries and Outfitters** (NALCO; U.S. 27

and Hornbeck Rd. [Box 248, Butler, KY 41006], 606/472–2205). Another good source for information about guides and outfitters and listings of local clubs, the backbone of paddling-sports today, is the **American Canoe Association** (7432 Alban Station Blvd., Suite B226, Springfield, VA 22159, 703/451–0140, www.aca-paddler.org), which publishes the *American Canoeist* newsletter.

Periodicals

Canoe and Kayak Magazine (Box 3146, Kirkland, WA 98083, 800/692–2663, www.canoekayak.com) has an up-to-date list of local paddling clubs, and covers flat and white water. The quarterly *Paddler* (Box 775450, Steamboat Springs, CO 80477, 970/879–1450, www.paddlermagazine.com) covers canoe and kayak trips and runs product reviews and tips on paddling skills.

Books

Canoeing Made Easy, by I. Herbert Gordon, is a manual for beginners. *Canoeing & Rafting: The Complete Where-to-Go Guide to America's Best Tame and Wild Waters,* by Sara Pyle, is a state-by-state list of canoe and kayak waters, with notes on difficulty and optimum paddling times; it's valuable despite its somewhat dated livery and outfitter information.

In the summer of 1930, a pair of Minnesota teenagers paddled a canoe from Minneapolis to Hudson Bay, 2,250 mi away. *Canoeing with the Cree,* by Eric Sevareid, is a great yarn—it describes their four-month journey on the wilderness waterways made famous by fur traders. *The Complete Wilderness Paddler,* by James West Davidson and John Rugge, is a ripping tale of a great adventure, paddling down the Moisie River in

Labrador. It's a must-read if you're interested in canoe tripping. *A Guide to Big Water Canoeing,* by David Alan Herzog, is an introduction to the techniques of paddling North America's large lakes, bays, and saltwater. *Pole, Paddle & Portage: A Complete Guide to Canoeing,* by Bill Riviere, distills the experience and Northeast viewpoint of this respected outdoors writer and former Maine canoe guide into a readable introduction to canoeing. *Rivers Running Free: Canoeing Stories by Adventurous Women,* edited by Judith Niemi and Barbara Wieser, is an anthology. Necessary reading if you're planning on an Everglades trip is *A Guide to the Wilderness Waterway,* by William G. Truesdell.

Canoeing and Kayaking in White Water

By Dennis Stuhaug
Updated by Julian Tonsmeire

With a powerful stroke, you slip from a calm eddy and point the bow downstream, into the white water. Leaning forward and stroking, you ride a long wave train down the center of the river channel. As waves break over the bow, you let out a nervous, gleeful yelp. Whether you're piloting a canoe or kayak, this is classic white-water river paddling. The rhythm of silence, punctuated by a glittering rush of water, thrills.

This thrill is available to virtually anyone. Under the guidance of a seasoned instructor, the art of maneuvering your way down a river is easily acquired. In just a few lessons, you can master the strokes and combinations of strokes that allow your boat to move forward, backwards, or sideways, or to turn. You can find a route through a boulder garden, do an Eskimo roll (using your paddle to flip your kayak right side up when it overturns), or slide yourself to the upstream side of your canoe if it fills up with water—and hang on as the canoe runs the rapids.

What's the difference, practically speaking, between canoes and kayaks? Canoes are usually open on top; you kneel or sit relatively high in the craft and power the boat with a single-bladed paddle. Kayaks are enclosed, and the paddler sits low and propels the craft with a double-bladed paddle. Unlike long, stable sea kayaks (a.k.a. touring kayaks), which average about 17 ft in length, white-water kayaks are short, typically under 10 ft, with a low center of gravity so that they respond instantly to the paddler's command—a responsiveness that in the hands of a novice equals extreme tippiness.

Instruction is available both on learn-as-you-go group trips down rivers across the country and in organized white-water paddling schools. Typically, the former involves a classic wilderness camping-trip format, with guides who teach paddling skills and handle camp chores; the cost includes food, equipment, instruction, and lodging (usually a tent) at about $125–$200 per person per day.

During organized classes, you spend from three days to a week in a single location, usually at the school's base camp or headquarters, and learn strokes, ways to read the river, and methods of getting out of the water if you get in; the cost runs about $75 a day per person, including equipment and lunch but not breakfast, dinner, or lodging.

On a typical first day, you meet early in the morning and get a brief description of the course itinerary, followed by a detailed description of what you'll learn that day. Then it's down to the water for step-by-step demonstrations of the techniques you'll need to master, and lots of practice. Many schools videotape you in action and play the videotapes at the end of the day, after you shower, clean up, and have dinner.

You can undertake white-water boating in canoes or kayaks. A few programs are geared exclusively to kayaking or canoeing; others use one or the other depending on the preferences of whoever has signed up. Instructional programs use canoes and kayaks with equal frequency nationwide. If long wilderness travel is your ultimate goal, a canoe is a better option—it's more comfortable and it carries more equipment. If you want to run challenging white water, go with a kayak. Once you master the Eskimo roll, a swamping that would ruin your day in a canoe becomes an easy fix as you roll your kayak upright.

The opportunity to travel in the company of a professional guide who not only knows how to get you down the river but can also point out the natural features of the landscape is reason enough to sign up for a group white-water trip rather than strike out on your own. Being able to lean back after a day on the river in anticipation of a superb meal, without having to do the cooking, is another. And facing the challenge of a complex rapid—and accomplishing the last mile into camp—is a pleasure that quickly turns new paddlers into die-hard enthusiasts.

CHOOSING THE RIGHT TRIP

Before you leap to sign up, start asking questions—the more, the better. A reputable outfitter or school will be glad to tell you anything you want to know.

On certain multiday trips, you may be waited upon hand and foot. Alternatively, you may be expected to help with portages and making camp. In terms of sheer toughness, mileage doesn't count as much as the number of hours on the water and paddling conditions, so be sure to ask about wind, waves, and weather. Intense heat or cold can make a day much more difficult, so ask questions about seasonal weather and water temperatures. Similarly, numerous challenging rapids in succession will drain you much more than one extremely difficult rapid on a given day, so inquire about the spacing of rapids. River conditions are not static. A change in water level and river flow can transform a stream. In some cases, a very challenging rapid may disappear when higher water floods a channel. In others, a simple section of river at low water may turn into a cauldron as the volume of water increases.

Know before you sign up that not all trips are for all paddlers. Learning to kayak is much harder than going rafting for the day. Most of the schools we list have three- to seven-day programs because it takes that long to become an advanced novice or beginning intermediate.

The key to a pleasurable white-water experience is selecting a course that gives you thrills and frills but which is also appropriate to your abilities. The following questions will help you find the company that's best for you.

How difficult is the river? Familiarize yourself with white-water classifications, the shorthand code that paddlers use to describe the relative difficulty of rivers. The classification goes in increasing order of difficulty from Class I to Class VI. The class system describes the difficulty (skill and experience required) as well as consequences of a mistake; the higher the class the more likely a mistake will result in serious injury.

Class I connotes moving water with small waves, runnable by practiced beginners. Obstructions, if any, may be easily avoided. Class II signals easy rapids with waves up to 3 ft. Channels are wide and clear, and the routes may be easily identified from a boat without scouting. Some maneuvering is required. Swamping a canoe or swimming out of a kayak shouldn't be too frightening. Class II waters are runnable by intermediate paddlers. Class III waters contain narrow passages and high, irregular waves capable of swamping an open canoe. Complex maneuvering and scouting from shore may be required. You need experience, and the consequences of a mistake become more severe. Class IV rapids are long and difficult, with constricted passages, often requiring precise maneuvering in turbulent waters. These waters are generally impassable for open canoes. A high degree of paddling skill is essential, and injury is very possible if you make a mistake. Class V rapids are long and violent, nearly always requiring scouting from shore. Rescue conditions are difficult, and any mishap causes a significant hazard to life. Only a team of experts should undertake these waters. Class VI waters approach the limit of navigability; they are nearly impossible, very dangerous, and suitable only for teams of experts and only after close study and with all precautions taken.

How long has the company been in business? If you're a beginner, stick with an outfitter or school that has been in business for several years. Ask about the outfitter's current operating license, and find out which professional organizations the company belongs to. At the very least, it should be an active member of such professional groups as America Outdoors, the National Association of Canoe Liveries and Outfitters (NACLO), or the American Canoe Association (*see below*). These organizations set minimum standards for the profession.

How experienced are the guides and instructors? The better the guide, the better the trip. Instructors and guides should be certified by either the American Canoe Association (ACA) or British Canoe Union (BCU). The certification process ensures that the instructor can teach the right strokes the right way and that the guide knows the necessary wilderness skills. Also ask whether guides are experienced naturalists, and find out how well they know the region. One guide in each group should be able to administer emergency medical aid, including CPR. A knowledge of plants, animals, and geological phenomena is a decided plus—after all, you'll be in the wilderness.

What about safety or insurance? Mostly you paddle at your own risk. On-water liability insurance is not mandatory for NACLO members, for instance. If an outfitter is operating on state or federal property, though, he or she is required to be insured as part of the permit process. NACLO distributes a safety video, which most members show prior to the trip. It's always a good idea to check your insurance coverage—medical or home owners/renters for personal articles—before any trip.

How many people are in your group? Ten is common on group trips, although even 20 can be companionable (especially off-river).

What is the ratio of paddlers to guides or instructors? Usually there are four or five paddlers per guide, but when there's a support crew to do chores and cooking, the ratio may be higher. In instructional setups, more guides mean more personal attention

How much time do you spend on the water? This is especially relevant when you're signing up for a clinic or school. The usual range is five to six hours; you may get tired after that if you don't start out in great shape.

What do you do when you're not paddling? Few river trips involve more than six hours or so on moving water. Ask what happens the rest of the time, and find out whether there are plans for hikes, nature walks, wildlife watching, or photography.

What's the cost and what's included? Make sure you understand exactly what's included. Typically, and for the operations we list in the back of this book, unless otherwise noted, paddling schools include instruction, equipment, and lunch only, with accommodations, breakfasts, and dinner extra. On point-to-point trips, the price includes instruction and guiding, all meals while you're on the river, boats, life preservers, wet suits if you need them, and camping equipment, including tents but not sleeping bags and pads. Anything not supplied is usually available for rent. Find out if you'll need wet suits and ask whether it's included.

What are the meals like? For point-to-point trips, ask for sample menus. Because there's enough room in a canoe to pack a cooler, you can expect lots of fresh fruits and vegetables, as well as frozen meat, fish, or chicken. Breakfasts are standard camping fare: hot cereal, granola, pancakes. For lunch expect cheese, peanut butter, fruit, and perhaps something canned. Dinners may be simple—lasagna and pasta—but can sometimes be mouthwatering. In some parts, river guides informally compete over who makes more elaborate meals.

What are the accommodations like? If accommodations are not included, ask about what's available nearby; then call the properties themselves to find out about rooms and facilities. If the outfitter is providing camping gear, make sure it's of decent quality—you don't want a sleeping bag that isn't warm enough or a tent that you have to wrestle with to set up. Also ask about the campsites and shower and latrine arrangements.

Is this program suitable for singles? Most canoes are powered by two paddlers, and a single person may not always be matched with an appropriate partner. Check the outfitter's policy before you sign up. Similarly, most camping trips put two people in a tent. If you're solo, ask whether you get your own tent.

How far in advance do I need to book? Count on a week to several months ahead, depending on the season, the type of program, and its location. Summer is prime paddling season in much of North America, so book these dates a few months in advance. Specialty trips, such as those that feature celebrity chefs or instructors, often fill up early as well.

SOURCES

Organizations

Setting standards for the outfitters and guides are several organizations: **America Outdoors** (Box 1348, Knoxville, TN 37901, 615/524–4814, www.americanoutdoors.com), the association for national river guides; the **American Canoe Association** (7432 Alban Station Blvd., No. B226, Springfield, VA 22150, 703/451–0140, www.aca-paddler.org), which publishes the *American Canoeist* newsletter; and the **National Association of Canoe Liveries and Outfitters** (NACLO, U.S. 27 and Hornbeck Rds., Box 248, Butler, KY 41006, 606/472–2205). For lists of paddling clubs, the backbone of paddling sports today, contact *Canoe & Kayak Magazine* (800/692–2663, www.canoekayak.com) or the American Canoe Association.

Periodicals

Canoe & Kayak Magazine (Box 3146, Kirkland, WA 98083, 800/692–2663, www.canoekayak.com), the leading paddle-sports magazine in North America, focuses on both flat- and white-water canoeing and kayaking, on both rivers and lakes. It covers both international and North American canoeing and kayaking destinations and provides a look into the nooks and crannies of local paddle-sports trips. Regular columns have tips and techniques for all levels of paddling. Each bimonthly issue includes sections listing paddling schools and major outfitters. The quarterly *Paddler* (Box 775450, Steamboat Springs, CO 80477, 970/879–1450, www.paddlermagazine.com) covers a broad spectrum of both major and easily accessible canoe and kayak trips and includes product reviews and pieces on paddling skills and techniques.

Books

Canoeing & Rafting: The Complete Where-to-Go Guide to America's Best Tame and Wild Waters, by Sara Pyle, is a valuable state-by-state compendium of canoe and kayak routes, with notes on degree of difficulty and the best time to paddle; the information on equipment rentals is a little dated. The ultimate reference guide for river running nationwide, *The Complete Whitewater Sourcebook,* by the Boat People (408/258–7971), lists phone numbers, water levels, regional guidebooks, access points, and permit requirements; the book is a must if you're planning a trip on your own and need a reliable source for names of outfitters. In *Whitewater Canoeing,* William Sandreuter reflects on his 35 years of white-water canoeing.

Climbing and Mountaineering

By Peter Potterfield
Updated by Cindy Hirschfeld

You don't have to be among the elite of the physically fit to experience the many pleasures of climbing: the satisfying bite of the ice axe as you crampon across a steep glacier beneath towering peaks; the solidity of a smooth rock face as you reach for a hold on its warm granite, adrenaline pumping, confidence high; or the tranquillity you feel when you're deep in the wilderness en route to a remote alpine peak or standing atop a high, quiet summit on a clear summer day.

By taking a course or two on basic rock climbing or mountaineering, almost anyone who is moderately fit can experience the excitement of this sport. In just a couple of days, a quality climbing school can have a beginner climbing pretty well or put a climber of medium abilities on harder routes. The schools we list introduce you to a range of experiences, from New York's Shawangunk Cliffs to alpine programs that include ascents of major peaks such as Mt. Rainier.

Each climbing course concentrates on a different facet of the sport; some address several. Rock climbing can be done in much of the country, not necessarily in the mountains; many towns and cities have cliffs, quarries, crags, or even indoor climbing walls where beginners can learn and experts can practice. It's an activity that you can pursue after work or on weekends, since you have to travel only as far as the nearest steep, rocky surface to be able to do it. When you take a rock-climbing course, you learn to recognize hand- and footholds in rocks that may appear quite smooth and to use these holds to ascend rock faces of anywhere from 20 to 3,000 ft. Many of the skills you acquire in a rock-climbing course are used in ice climbing and mountaineering.

Ice climbing involves climbing frozen waterfalls, traveling on glaciers, or ascending steep slopes covered with snow or ice, using special equipment (and additional skills). Snow and ice techniques are a must in Alaska and the higher elevations of the Rockies, the Cascades, and the Sierra. Few beginners start out learning to handle ice; it's a skill that climbers acquire as they gain experience.

Mountaineering involves traveling on foot to a summit in mountainous terrain, then heading into the alpine zone, the area near and above timberline. This may require skills in both rock and ice climbing, so thorough mountaineering courses will cover the basics along with other skills you need to spend extended time in the wilderness. The wilderness experience is one of the rewards of mountaineering, but to get it, you must live near the mountains or travel to them.

To choose among America's hundreds of climbing programs, decide what you want to learn and where you want to learn it. No two climbing areas are quite alike. The landscape and weather are different, and—more to the point for rock climbers—the terrain is different. The quality of the rock also varies from one area to another, requiring you to master different skills. Where you find cliffs of fractured or broken rock, you acquire a repertoire of ways to grasp the protrusions. Where the local rock is smoother, you may learn crack techniques—different approaches to sticking your hands and feet into cracks in the rock—or you may concentrate on friction climbing, which involves using your weight and balance to ascend a smooth rock face without holds. Basic skills, such as rappelling and belaying, are standard elements of any curriculum.

Most U.S. climbing schools operate in their home region, but some offer courses nation- or worldwide. Many operate year-round, changing their location with the season and their curriculum with the location.

CHOOSING THE RIGHT TRIP

While there are some questionable operations in the mountain-guiding game, most climbing schools are run by competent climbers and guides. However, you can't be too careful, since you could be injured or even killed while learning to climb. These questions will help you find a school that's right for you.

Is the school accredited by the American Mountain Guides Association (AMGA)? It's not necessarily a bad sign if it isn't, since accreditation is a relatively new function for this organization, which is dedicated to developing and maintaining high standards of mountain guiding and climbing instruction (*see* Sources, *below.*) However, AMGA accreditation does assure you that the school's safety practices are appropriate for its activities. All of the outfitters we list in the back of the book are AMGA accredited. If the school you're interested in is not accredited, ask about their safety record.

How long has the school been in business? Longevity provides some assurance that it's not a fly-by-night operation.

What are the instructors' qualifications? If you're serious about acquiring climbing skills, go for a program whose instructors are experienced teachers *and* experienced climbers. If you're told where the instructors have climbed, don't be impressed before you ask: "But can they teach?" If all you want is a taste of the sport, you may prefer to hang out with a hotshot climber who can regale you with sagas of climbs in the Himalayas and other exotic locales.

What's the cost, and what's included? Most programs have a range of rates; the deciding factor is the number of clients. Unless otherwise noted, your fee for courses we list in this book includes instruction, transportation between course venues, and any necessary technical climbing equipment (such as ropes, helmets, and harnesses). Meals, accommodations, and camping gear are often not included. Ask whether the outfitter provides special rock shoes, crampons, ice axes, and double plastic boots (climbers' standard footwear, resembling ski boots, in snow and ice environments). When equipment is not included, outfitters may rent it to you.

What are food and accommodations like? When you attend most courses, you lodge and dine in nearby mountain towns. Motels and restaurants tend to be basic. On backcountry trips, ask about the menu.

What experience is required for the course? Beginner courses don't require previous climbing experience, but you should be at least moderately fit. It will quickly become obvious if you're out of shape. As one wise man observed, climbing would be great, a truly wonderful thing, if it weren't for all that damn climbing.

How far in advance do I need to book? Sign-up dates range from two weeks to six months before the course begins.

SOURCES
Organizations
The **Access Fund** (Box 17010, Boulder, CO 80308, 303/545–6772, www.accessfund.org) is a nonprofit advocacy group that works with land management agencies, environmental groups, and others to keep climbing areas open and accessible to climbers and to help formulate climbing-friendly land-use policy. The **American Alpine Club** (710 10th St., Suite 100, Golden,

CO 80401, 303/384–0110, www.americanalpineclub. org), founded in 1902, is a national nonprofit organization that serves as an information clearinghouse, educational promoter, and advocacy group for climbers and mountaineers. The **American Mountain Guides Association** (710 10th St., Suite 101, Golden, CO 80401, 303/271–0984, www.amga.com) can provide a list of members and accredited schools and guides. You can also contact local climbing shops in areas where you want to climb.

Periodicals

Climbing (0326 Hwy. 133, Suite 190, Carbondale, CO 81623, 800/493–4569, www.climbing.com) and *Rock & Ice* (1101 Village Rd., UL-4D, Carbondale, CO 81623, 970/704–1442, www.rockandice.com) cover this sport exclusively. *Outside* (400 Market St., Santa Fe, NM 87501, 505/989–7100, www.outsidemag. com) and *National Geographic Adventure* (104 W. 40th St., New York, NY 10018, 212/790–9020, www. nationalgeographic.com) occasionally publish articles on mountaineering.

Books

Fifty Favorite Climbs, by Mark Kroese, contains descriptions of routes chosen by 50 well-known climbers and highlights of North American climbing history. *Mountaineering: The Freedom of the Hills* (6th ed.), edited by Don Graydon, is the essential reference on climbing techniques, equipment, ethics, and more.

Cycling

By Bill Strickland
Updated by Joe Lindsey

See the country by bike and you see it as no one else can. Cycling brings you closer to the landscape and wildlife. When cycling, you notice hills, dips, and rough roads; you pay attention to the weather. You travel slowly enough to spot unusual flowers and birds, and quietly enough to happen upon deer and other animals. Cycling also brings you closer to people—locals will wave or stop to chat while you're refueling at the country store.

Still, you can travel long distances on a bike: you see more and cover more ground than you could on foot. A laid-back bike tour might cover 150 or 200 mi in less than a week. Big-ride sessions can go 600 mi. Yes, you can do it. Bike touring is easy on the body. Modern bikes are more comfortable than ever and have more gears for easier pedaling. On the right terrain, even an out-of-shape noncyclist can cover 30 mi or more before lunch.

The existence of commercial touring companies makes it possible for just about anyone to tour by bike. These organizations supply the expertise. There's no need for you to know how to plot a bike-friendly route, arrange food and lodging, customize your bike to carry equipment and luggage, or fix a flat tire. You don't even have to own a bike. You simply choose an area of the country you'd like to see, identify the companies that offer tours there, and ask a few questions to make sure you and the trip are a good match. And, of course, you do have to pay: a bike trip with an outfitter can run from $130 to $250 per day, not including bike rental. To cut costs, opt for a camping trip instead of an inn trip.

A typical touring company offers a selection of 2- to 10-day trips with preplanned routes and usually provides at least two guides for every trip: one rides with the cyclists, and the other drives a support van along the route. This van transports your luggage to each destination and patrols the route, carrying water, snacks, repair equipment, and even tired cyclists. Most companies also rent bikes.

These organized trips have from 6 to 20 riders and range from daylong pedaling marathons to casual jaunts with many stops, in which the bike is mainly used to travel from one point of interest to another. Will you ride too fast or too slow to remain with the group? It doesn't matter. Most tours offer multiple options for each day's ride. You can go short or long, flat or hilly, difficult or easy.

Whichever option you choose, you won't be alone. Just as there are no atheists in a foxhole, there are no enemies on a bike tour. Sharing physical challenges seems to bond people. Participants tend to cheer each other on during the day and gather at night to share tales from the road. It seems that at least one close, lasting friendship is formed on every trip, and it's not uncommon for riders to meet a mate.

Traveling as a group can, of course, be a drag. You're tied to a common schedule for everything from waking in the morning to eating dinner. Sometimes your meals must be selected from a limited menu. If the weather stinks, you can't hide in the lodge for another day. If you need a rest day, it's more often than not spent in the back of the support van—not exactly the best way to explore the country. See an inn you'd rather stay at, or enjoy a village so much you'd like to tarry there an extra day? Too bad.

Most tour veterans agree that the advantages of commercial trips outweigh these inconveniences. You may have a bad experience if you choose a trip that doesn't match your cycling ability. But if you'd still rather gather a group of friends and create your own itinerary, most bike-touring companies will be glad to guide you.

While it's true that anyone can complete a bike tour, it's not true that anyone can complete any bike tour. Perhaps a weeklong trip that covers 850 mi is just your speed. Plenty of people, however, prefer a 30-mi-per-day bike-and-shop through quaint New England towns. Maybe, instead, you're in excellent shape but don't want to grind out 100-plus mi per day—you'd prefer biking yourself senseless with 50 mi of Colorado mountain passes every morning.

It's important to match your physical ability and ambition to the trip. Don't sign up for the toddler trip along beachfront and then complain that you aren't getting enough training miles at your target heart rate. Nor should you let your aspirations outweigh your common sense and land you in a West Coast hammerhead tour with ultrafit riders when you just wanted to spin a few miles between sips of wine.

In the trip descriptions, we've tried to give you an accurate picture of how tough the riding will be. Don't judge toughness by mileage alone. Plenty of riders have been toasted senseless by 20 mi of hilly Pennsylvania roads, or have walked away from 65 flat Florida mi whistling and wishing for more. Pay attention to other factors, such as terrain description, number of off-bike activities (the more detours, the less strenuous the trip is likely to be), and even the time of year. Rolling Kentucky hills in September? Fabulous. Same territory in summer's dog days? Ugh.

The classic touring areas are New England (especially Vermont and the Massachusetts coast), Pennsylvania, North Carolina and Virginia, and California. They all deserve your consideration, but pay attention to the other listings, too. Tour companies have branched out in the past few years, and some of these gambles have led to the discovery of amazing new areas for bike touring. Any region seems fair game these days.

Also be honest about your level of comfort. Rugged camping trips sound admirable, but it's okay to spoil yourself on a pampered tour of plush resorts. Hey, it's a vacation.

Finally, there's food. Fuel. You burn a lot of calories on a weeklong tour—up to 2,000 calories per day—so you must take in a lot simply to replace your energy stores. This means you get to eat and eat and eat and not feel one bit guilty. Gaining weight on a bike tour is almost impossible. Indulge: spicy Mexican meals, fresh seafood, hearty midwestern dinners, heaps of family-style Amish fare, campfire-grilled anything, home-made soups and breads. The secret's out. Sure you must eat to ride, but you can also ride to eat.

See you on the road. And, as the pros say, keep the rubber side down.

CHOOSING THE RIGHT TRIP

To be included in the listings in the back of this book, a touring company has to offer trips along preplanned, established routes; provide at least two mileage options each day; furnish some type of support (such as motorized route patrols, "sag" service for tired or injured riders, and luggage transport); provide or assist in arranging lodging; supply at least some meals; and require the use of helmets (you never appreciate a skid lid until you need it).

But before you make your decision, take some time to learn about the company and the specific tour you're interested in. Don't be shy about asking questions. If the organizers seem too busy to respond, that's a kind of response in itself.

How long has the company been in business? You take a trip with an outfitter in order to capitalize on its experience. Make sure it has enough, or at least that the people running it do.

Should I go with a large or small outfit? When it comes to touring companies, bigger is usually better, although many small organizations run fine programs. The difference between small companies and the major players is scope. Where the small tour operator offers 6 yearly trips, the large organization runs 30. The small operator works within a state or a small multistate area. The major companies span whole geographic regions, coasts, maybe even the entire country. If one tour is booked, they can offer another (and another) with approximately the same flavor.

Who are the leaders, how old are they, and how are they trained? Sound a little nosy? Hey, you're putting your whole vacation in these people's hands. Make sure they're fit to hold it.

How tough is the trip? Find out as much as you can. Describe your riding experience and physical condition, and then ask if the organizer thinks you can do the trip (or if you'll be bored). You'll get an honest answer: a miserable guest is not a repeat guest.

How much can the mileage be increased (or decreased)? Most companies will go beyond their stated limits.

What's the weather like when I want to tour? Some folks like it hot; others think cold is "fresh." In any case, you will have to bring the proper clothes.

What are the accommodations like? Be specific or be surprised. Some impressive bed-and-breakfast inns, for example, require you to share hallway bathrooms or telephone lines. If it's a camping trip, find out if you'll be in a campground with hot showers or in farmer Joe's field.

What are the meals like? Same idea. Also, most companies skip at least one lunch or dinner.

Will laundry service be available? This could make the difference between one suitcase or two.

What's the cost and what's included? Costs vary from outfitter to outfitter, depending on the type of accommodations, the quality of the food, or simply the remoteness of the area where you'll be biking. Prices in these listings are per person and include double occupancy, lodging, meals, gratuities, entrance fees to parks and attractions, and, when applicable, camping fees.

Always ask whether there are extras: $75 for that hot-air balloon trip or $50 for the massage that was added shortly before the tour. Airfare, the cost of shuttle service between the airport and the trip starting and ending points, and the cost of renting bikes or other equipment are not included in prices we quote, unless we note otherwise.

What is the makeup of the touring group? You can find out the size of the group and the participants' ages, gender, marital status, and home states. This will keep you from being a third wheel in a couples-only tour.

Is this same tour available for singles (or families, senior citizens, or women)? You may prefer to pedal with your peers. Some companies offer reduced rates for kids and families.

How extensive is the support? Some companies make only one or two runs along a route; others patrol constantly. Find out how many guides work each trip. The more the better.

Can the leaders handle minor mechanical repairs (and is there a charge)? Something will break. Something always breaks. If it's just a wheel that needs minor truing (straightening), you should expect a freebie. But be reasonable: if your bottom bracket and hubs must be overhauled, cough up a tip even if the guide doesn't charge you for two hours of labor.

What is the rental equipment like? Find out what brands of bikes are used, how many sizes they offer, and how old the fleet is. Between the sleek road bike and thrasher mountain bike lies an ideal touring compromise called a hybrid, or cross bike. These are equipped with flat bars (for an upright sitting position and more stability) and semi-wide tires (for a cushy but easy-spinning ride). Ask if the company has these. If you want special equipment—gel saddles or mixte frames—make sure you can get it. Ditto for camping equipment. Prices quoted in the listings for rentals get you a two-wheeler for the duration of the trip.

Is helmet use free? If you're renting a helmet, make sure it fits properly—buckle the chin strap so it's snug but you can open your mouth (the side yokes should fit high on your jaw, just below your earlobe). Grasp the helmet and move it forward, low on your forehead. Then rock it back and forth a bit to make sure it doesn't come off—you should not be able to roll it off your head. Many cyclists tip theirs back, unnecessarily exposing themselves to injury. If you're bringing your helmet, pack it between soft items in your luggage so it won't be damaged; if you're flying you can buckle it to your carry-on. Also ask the tour company about children's helmets for rental; if they don't have them, you'll need to buy one (it fits the same way).

What extras are included? Many companies offer T-shirts, sweatshirts, water bottles, and other freebies.

Are any local events happening before or after the tour? Some cyclists only take tours when they can piggyback big events such as the Kentucky Derby or wine-harvest festivals with their trips. Others just want to ride.

How far in advance must I book? The most popular trips may fill up a year in advance; others can be booked just a month before. Always call if you want to make a last-minute booking; cancellations are common.

SOURCES
Organizations

Adventure Cycling Association (Box 8308, Missoula, MT 59807, 406/721–1776, www.adventurecycling.org) runs long tours, sells cycling maps, and provides information about touring. **American Youth Hostels** (Box 37613, Washington, DC 20013–7613, 202/783–4943, www.hiayh.org) runs long tours and provides inexpensive accommodations. **League of American Bicyclists** (190 W. Ostend St., Suite 120, Baltimore, MD 21230–3755, 410/539–3399, www.bikeleague.org), an organization of cycling enthusiasts, runs events, provides touring information, and publishes *Bicycle USA*. **Rails to Trails Conservancy** (1400 16th St. NW, Suite 300,

Washington, DC 20036, 202/797–5400, www.railtrails. org) promotes conversion of abandoned railroad land to cycling paths and provides touring information.

Periodicals

The League of American Bicyclists publishes *Bicycle USA* eight times per year, which it distributes to members. Every issue contains at least one touring feature and lots of rides and events. *Bicycling,* a how-to magazine, features numerous touring articles throughout the year and a special touring issue. It's published 11 times annually (Rodale Press, 33 E. Minor St., Emmaus, PA 18098, 610/967–8093 information; 515/242–0286 subscriptions; www.bicycling.com). Adventure Cycling Association (*see* Organizations, *above*) publishes *Adventure Cyclist* magazine nine times annually; every year it also publishes *The Cyclists' Yellow Pages*—which lists sources of touring information and maps—and distributes it to Adventure Cycling members. *California Cyclist,* published 11 times per year, lists rides and events for the northern part of the state (490 2nd St., Suite 304, San Francisco, CA 94107, 415/546–7291). *Northwest Cyclist* catalogs rides and events in the Pacific Northwest. It's published 10 times per year (Box 9272, Seattle, WA 98109, 206/286–8566).

Books

Pick up a copy of *500 Great Rail Trails* (Living Planet Press) to discover the U.S. rail-trail system, a series of abandoned rail lines that have been converted to bike trails. Researched and written by one of the country's preeminent cycling-guidebook authors, Dennis Coello, the *Bicycle Touring Series: Arizona, Colorado, Utah* (Northland Publishing) maps out the best routes in each state, pointing out attractions along the way. Some of the best touring books available are those in the *Bicycling the Back Roads* series: Puget Sound, Northwest Washington, Southwest Washington (The Mountaineers Books, www.mountaineersbooks.org). Each book is compiled by local experts, with detailed route directions, sightseeing tips, and lodging and food recommendations. Two other series, *The Best Bike Rides* and *Short Bike Rides* (both published by Globe Pequot, www.globe-pequot.com), are 200- to 300-page comprehensive handbooks to touring various regions. The *Bicycling America's National Parks* series (Countryman Press, www.countrymanpress.com) has editions for California, Oregon and Washington, Utah and Colorado, and Arizona and New Mexico. Dennis Coello wrote the introductions.

Fishing Camps and Fly-Fishing Schools

By Bud Journey
Updated by Carol Bareuther

It's no cinch to cast a bulky line, a flimsy leader, and a featherlight fly between trees, against the wind, away from the back of your neck, and into position just in front of a fish's nose. The fly must land without frightening the fish and must look natural, or the fish will see it for what it is: a deceitful attempt by an antagonist to entice it into ingesting a bundle of feathers, fraught with peril, containing no food value at all.

Therein lies the allure of fly-fishing: it's a challenge that's rewarding when you succeed and that teaches you humility when you fail. Spin-casting, trolling, and bait-fishing have a similar attraction, and the type of angling you choose has nothing to do with a right method or a wrong method. It has more to do with personal preference and what's available.

If you want to spend a week learning to fish, a fishing school can teach you the rudiments, supply the equipment, and see that you get a chance to practice your new skills on nearby streams or ponds. A two-day course runs from $225 to $650. If you're a seasoned angler, you can sign up for an advanced class, or choose one of the camps, charter boats, or guide services.

Fishing schools and fishing camps are not always discrete entities—elements of each often overlap. The operators of most fishing schools also usually offer guide service for a day's fishing or can recommend local guides. You can fish by yourself, but guides know all about the local waters and the best ways to extract their inhabitants; some even provide equipment. They charge hefty sums ($150–$350 per day) for their expertise, but many anglers feel they are worth it. With a guide, you also get the benefit of learning exactly what you want and, in general, a more casual experience. People who hire guides typically get a few friends together and hire a guide to take them fishing for up to a week. In this book we list both schools and guides, but we specify daily rates for guides—since you decide how many days you want to fish—and all-inclusive rates for schools.

Camps often house and feed you but don't supply equipment; most anglers prefer to use their own. Most fishing schools furnish all or most of the necessary gear while you're in class, and they frequently provide lunch, but for other meals and lodging you're usually on your own (but operators will help you make arrangements). Guide services and charter boats, which usually charge by the day, can put together a five-day or weeklong package for a vacation, but you often have to forage for nearby food and lodging.

Most fishing camps are independently run, as are most fishing schools, although some are set up in conjunction with a manufacturer or a merchant such as Orvis or L.L. Bean. Bigger is not necessarily better. Book a school in an area you want to visit—don't go out of your way to attend a school with a big-name sponsor.

If you have a limited budget, it might be best to forget the school altogether and look for a fishing camp that can provide a few minutes of instruction before you go out onto the water. Some camps cost less than $100 per day. Be forewarned, however, that if you're fly-fishing, those few minutes of instruction are not likely to make you more than barely competent. If it's what you can afford, though, go for it; a crash course in the fishing camp may be enough.

Whether you're at a school or camp, you'll soon become familiar with the concept of catch-and-release. Because the populations of some species have been diminished by overfishing, short growing seasons, low reproduction, loss of habitat, and other factors, most schools and camps encourage the practice of carefully releasing uninjured or slightly injured fish. At some, this practice is mandatory.

Although fly-fishing skills are generally considered the hardest to master, you must know a few basics for any kind of fishing. Consider the following: you must (1) get a lure in front of a fish and (2) entice that fish to take the lure into its mouth. The fish will do so because (1) it wants to eat the lure or (2) it wants to attack the lure, sometimes both.

A fly fisherman almost always tries to simulate food for the fish. A bait fisherman actually offers the fish real food. Anglers who cast artificial lures (cast-and-retrieve) or who troll, slowly dragging a lure behind a boat, are trying to imitate food or provoke an attack. It's the same with jiggers, who sit over their quarry in a boat or on a bank and bounce their lures up and down, and also with little children who fish with safety pins on the end of a string. Their varying degrees of success depend on their skill and on the willingness of the fish to take the lure. As all anglers learn, the disposition of the fish can be affected by weather, barometric pressure, water temperature, pH factor, fishing pressure (the number of people fishing a particular area), the food supply, and just plain cussedness.

For some, the allure of fishing is in the challenge. Making a perfect cast into a tiny pocket of open water, amid weeds, willows, and overhanging limbs; fooling a wily game fish into striking; then deftly guiding it to the net through an underwater labyrinth of weeds, roots, and rocks is the ultimate satisfaction. For many others, fishing is renewal. It recharges you after the pressures of the modern world have sucked out your vigor. Sometimes you may catch fish and other times you may not. But it's not the catching that counts, it's the process: a renaissance that only a fisherman knows.

You'll have to try it to understand. It's an old truth that if you're too busy to go fishing, you're too busy.

CHOOSING THE RIGHT OUTFIT

No matter how well you check out a school or a camp, it may not meet your expectations. You can minimize that possibility, however, by asking the right questions.

On which species do you focus? Different fish inhabit different parts of the country, and anglers have their preferred species. If you want trout, you might go to the Rockies; for bass, try the South. Northern pike lurk in Minnesota lakes and in much of the West and Midwest; salmon stay on the coasts.

What method do you teach? Ask schools whether they teach just fly-fishing or can also instruct you in other methods, such as jigging, spin-casting, and trolling. Remember that learning a method of fishing is just the beginning. A school can give you a glimmering of these skills, but you must go fishing again and again to refine them. A school can teach you to read water—to recognize the kinds of places fish like to stay and feed—but only by hunting a species time after time do you discover its ways and habits.

Do you provide actual on-site fishing opportunities for real fish in natural conditions? That's a question that's essential to ask any fishing school you're considering. Casting and fishing on a stocked or sterile pond are a far cry from fishing in the wild for wild fish on a swiftly moving stream, surrounded by vegetation and other obstructions.

What's the cost and what's included? Unless other-wise noted, the cost of camps includes food and lodging but not guiding; schools' prices include instruction only; and guide services provide guiding only. All prices are per person.

Schools typically provide tackle, but not for the time you spend fishing on your own afterwards. Camps and guides seldom provide tackle but may lend or rent it to you. Boats may cost extra.

When accommodations are not provided, most outfits can steer you to a variety of lodging in a range of prices. The cost of your fishing license is almost always extra.

How do I get there? Some fishing camps are very remote, and getting there can be pricey and time-consuming. Some operators have shuttles; in remote areas you'll often be transported by riverboat, airplane, floatplane, horseback, and the like. Check to see if this is included in the rate.

What are accommodations like? If you're staying at a fishing camp, ask what the guest quarters and public spaces are like; they could be stylishly rustic and sturdy or they could be cheap motel rooms with paper-thin walls. If you're camping, find out about the campsites and the shower and latrine arrangements. Before you sign up to use the outfitter's tents or sleeping bags, make sure they are suited to the location.

What's the food like? Although ambitious cuisine is unusual, plain American fare, which you are most apt to find, can seem extraordinarily tasty when your appetite is sharpened by a day in the fresh air. Still, some outfitters and camps do better in the kitchen than others. If what you eat matters to you, make sure you know what to expect.

What is the fee for a guide? How many guests per guide? Guides' fees can often be split by as many as three people, although with fly-fishing, two anglers per guide is the most you want.

What equipment is required? Make sure your equipment matches the requirements of the camp or school you are considering. For fly-fishing in streams you probably need waders, which are not always provided, although in hot weather in some waters, you can wade in sneakers and shorts or jeans.

In a fly-fishing camp, are fly-tying facilities available? You might want to try to "match the hatch" of insects that are emerging while you are there.

What is the weather like? Is it buggy? The weather can range from snowstorms in the Rockies in June, though they're rare, to hot and humid days in Florida, which is usual. Mosquitoes are always around in woods and swamps, but some seasons are worse than others.

What is there for nonfishing companions to do? Many schools and camps are near cities large enough to have the usual complement of amusements. At schools in the wilderness, you'll have to be content with such rural pursuits as hiking, bird-watching, and identifying wildflowers.

How long have you been in business? Longevity should not necessarily be the deciding factor. Everybody has to start sometime, so if other things are favorable, don't let the operator's lack of experience discourage you. It's best to get a word-of-mouth recommendation from an independent source, whenever possible. Chances are if other anglers are satisfied, you will be, too.

How far in advance must I book? You can ordinarily sign up anywhere from a month in advance to a year ahead. The more famous and the more remote locations tend to fill up faster. If you have your heart set on a specific location or program, however, call and see if you can snag a cancellation.

SOURCES
Organizations

American Bass Association, Inc. (402 N. Prospect Ave. Redondo Beach, CA 90277, 310/376–1126, american-bass.com) is an advocacy group that works on improving bass fisheries and sponsors fishing tournaments. It publishes the monthly *American Bass News*. The **Federation of Fly Fishers** (Box 1595, Bozeman, MT 59771, 406/585–7592, www.fedflyfishers.org) focuses on conservation, education, and restoration and publishes *FlyFisher*. The **International Game Fish Association** (300 Gulf Stream Way, Dania Beach, FL 33004, 954/927–2628, www.igfa.org), an advocacy group, also maintains a book of fish records and publishes *World Record Game Fishes*. The **National Fresh Water Fishing Hall of Fame** (Box 690, 10360 Hall of Fame Dr., Hayward WI 54843, 715/634–4440, freshwater-fishing.org), an advocacy group, keeps track of record fish and publishes *Official World and U.S. State Fresh Water Angling Records*. **North American Fishing Club** (12301 Whitewater Dr., Minnetonka, MN 55343,

800/843–6232 or 952/936–9333, www.fishingclub.com) publishes *North American Fisherman*. **Trout Unlimited** (1500 Wilson Blvd., No. 310, Arlington, VA 22209, 800/834–2419 or 703/522–0200, www.tu.org) is "dedicated to conserving, protecting, and restoring wild trout and salmon and their habitat throughout North America."

Periodicals

How-to magazines include *Bass Fishing* (88 Moors Rd., Gilbertsville, KY 42044, 502/362–4304), *Bassin'* (Natcom, 15115 S. 76th E. Ave., Bixby, OK 74008, 918/366–4441), and *Crappie Magazine* (8530 Russell, Overland Park, KS 66212, 913/302–4528). *California Angler* covers where-to and how-to (all species, all techniques) for California and Baja (1921 E. Carnegie, Suite 3N, Santa Ana, CA 92705, 714/261–9779). *Fishing Holes* (17021 N.E. Woodinville–Duval Rd., Woodinville, WA 98072, 206/489–2919) is about where-to, how-to, and personal experience (all species, all techniques) in the northwestern United States. *Fishing & Hunting News* (511 Eastlake Ave. E, Seattle, WA 98109, 206/624–3845), about where to fish in the West (all species), is published weekly. *Fishing World* (700 W. 47th St., No. 310, Kansas City, MO 64112, 816/531–5730) is a magazine on destinations in the United States, Canada, Mexico, the Bahamas, and the Caribbean. *Fly Fisherman* (4 High Ridge Park, Stamford, CT 06905, 800/435–9610) is a how-to, where-to (all species), and personal experience magazine. *Fly Rod & Reel* (Box 10141, Des Moines, IA 50340, 800/888–6890) covers how-to and where-to for all species. *In-Fisherman* (2 In-Fisherman Dr., Brainerd, MN 56401, 218/829–1648) is all about freshwater fishing for all species, all techniques. *Salt Water Sportsman* (280 Summer St., Boston, MA 02210, 617/439–9977) is about sportfishing (all species), including fishing boats and tackle.

Books

National or even regional guides to fishing resources are scarce. (Most such guides are done by states, and good sources for them are the state agencies that administer fishing, for example the California Department of Fish & Game, Vermont Fish & Wildlife Division, Washington Department of Wildlife, and the Virginia Department of Game & Inland Fisheries.) However, how-to and where-to guides are not nonexistent. *Chris Batin's 20 Great Alaska Fishing Adventures* (Alaska Angler Publications), by Christopher Batin, is on glossy paper, with lots of color photographs of the author and friends fishing. *Fishing Montana* (Falcon Press Publishing), by Michael Sample, is a text locating species and type of water. *Fly Tying Made Clear and Simple* (Frank Amato Publications), by Skip Morris, is a large-format book with step-by-step photographs in color. *Joan Wulff's Fly Fishing* (Stackpole Books), by Joan Wulff, is a good book on the fundamentals, with photographs, by the co-owner of the famous Wulff School of Fly-Fishing. *Knee Deep in Montana's Trout Streams* (Pruett Publishing), by John Holt, is a where-to and how-to book with humor. *Presentation* (Scientific Anglers), by Gary Borger, is a hardcover reference book that covers the art and science of fly-fishing from choosing equipment to casting and catching.

Golf Schools

By Sue Sawyer

How's your golf game? It's a humbling question, but even pros rely on teachers when their game goes south. Imagine an entire week devoted to you and your game—a week in which you're forced to confront some of your greatest personal weaknesses: slicing, hooking, shanking, the yips (missing short putts). But you get the game's best teachers, a plush setting, and golf all day—that part sounds good, doesn't it? So what are you in for?

There are a few things you can expect no matter what golf school you attend. Whether the school is part of a large franchise or independently operated, the instruction will almost always be excellent. That's because it's rare to find faculty at a school that isn't made up entirely of Class A Professional Golf Association (PGA) types. Almost all schools are at or near an upscale resort with a quality golf course. Return students and word-of-mouth are essential to a school's business, so accommodations are often quite fine. The food will likely be good, and you can probably expect a pool, tennis courts, and a health club on-site or nearby. All this, of course, costs money: golf school is pricey, so chances are your fellow students will be established businesspeople. Don't be surprised to see plenty of business cards change hands over lunch during your stay. But most importantly, you're at school to spend a lot of time with a golf club in your hand, perhaps more time than you ever have.

Most schools spend four to six hours a day covering all aspects of the game, from driving to putting. A typical day consists of breakfast, then warm-up at the driving range. If the class size is more than 10, students usually are divided into two or more groups, usually based on handicap. For example, a group of 18 will be divided into three groups. All three groups participate in a warm-up, led by the instructors. After the preliminaries, Group 1 works on full-swing fundamentals, Group 2 on chipping and pitching, and Group 3 has their swings videotaped and analyzed. By mid-morning, the groups rotate stations; after lunch, they rotate again. In the late afternoon, students are then given the option to play and practice what they have learned out on the course. The process starts over on day two, except now the stations are trouble play, sand shots, and your mind-set. By the end of the week, students have been immersed in every possible aspect of the game. It's a lot of golf and a lot of work. Expect to get blisters.

Not all schools are alike. There are plenty of distinguishing factors; it just depends on what you're looking for. If you're willing to spend more money you can get higher-end accommodations at some of the country's most exclusive resorts. If you're concerned with activities geared toward the nongolfer, choose a location where golf is not the focal point. Most schools have a minimum student–teacher ratio of 4:1 but some go as low as 2:1, so you get significantly more attention. Some have packages that include everything, including transportation to and from the airport, all meals, and all golf—so you don't have to worry about money while you're there. Specialization is also becoming popular. You can find schools that offer a short game clinic or help you with the mental game. You can even find women-only sessions.

Now, what *not* to expect: don't think that you'll magically cut five strokes off your handicap by the end of the week. Many students look back at their golf experience months later and realize, with disappointment, that their scores are no better than before they attended. There are no quick fixes to your golfing ills. You will pick up a number of fundamentals at golf school that provide clues to some of the game's mysteries, but they will do you no good unless they're applied through consistent practice. Truly dedicated students will consult a local PGA professional before choosing a school, so the experience fits in smoothly with regular lesson plans. Make your choice carefully.

Do your homework before you plunk down those hard-earned dollars. Determine what type of school best meets your needs. Above all, don't be afraid to ask questions before you sign up.

CHOOSING THE RIGHT SCHOOL

Is this school suited to my playing style? Is there a specific swing method taught? If your pro teaches a big-muscle method, it might be a mistake to go to a school with a small-muscle philosophy. If you've taken any lessons, it's important that you find a school that complements the method that you've been using.

Will the instructor want to change my swing? Some instructors will only teach one type of swing and will try to get you to change. Others will work with your existing swing and help you improve your game without major changes.

What is the maximum class size? Most people prefer a smaller class because you get more personal attention. Many schools limit the size to 18, but some don't, so make sure you check.

What is the student–teacher ratio? This actually is more important than the class size. You don't want to have a ratio higher than 8:1. The lower the ratio, the more attention you're going to get.

Are the groups broken out by ability or gender? You will want to be in a class with people of similar needs. For example, if your group is largely beginners, the instructor will probably work on grip, stance, and swing. For a group of advanced students, the instructor will probably focus on specialty shots.

Do you need your own clubs? If you are a beginner and haven't purchased a set of clubs, you may want to rent clubs from the school or nearby golf facility. This is an excellent way to try clubs before buying them and gives you one less bag to tote through the airport.

What percentage of instruction time is spent on the golf course? Is the bulk of your day in a classroom, on the range, or on the course? As a general rule, the more on-course work the better.

How extensive is the practice facility? Questions to bear in mind: how big is the driving range? Is there a putting green—and if so, how big is it? Is there a short-game area? Is there a bunker? All of these facilities enable you to concentrate on different parts of your game.

Are there indoor facilities in case of rain? What alternatives does the school offer if you're rained out? Are you entitled to any type of refund or rescheduling if the entire school gets washed out?

What is the cost and what is included? Prices vary depending upon the length of the classes and the amenities included in the various packages. Schools are more varied now—to better accommodate the needs of their pupils. Find out if carts and greens fees are included in the package price. Most schools don't provide transportation between the airport and the hotel, so you may need to rent a car or take the hotel's airport shuttle.

What are the accommodations like? All multiday schools put their guests up in hotels, although the degree of luxury of the rooms and the facilities can vary quite a bit.

What is the food like? Is the restaurant full-service, including room service, or is it only operational during specific times of the day? Does the menu offer you enough variety? If there is no on-site facility, how far will you have to drive to the nearest restaurants?

Is there a dress code? Will laundry service be available? This could save you that extra suitcase or allow you to take a much smaller one.

What social activities are planned for off-hours? What activities are available for nongolfing guests?

Is there a spousal or nongolfing guest rate?

How long has the school been in business? If the school is new, be particularly careful to find out about the people in charge and their plans for the program. Make sure that their teaching experience is credible and that the instruction seems well conceived and well organized.

SOURCES

Listed below are golf-industry leaders who have either rated golf schools or who maintain data on golf schools. They can be a great resource when trying to make a final decision.

Organizations

The **National Golf Foundation** (407/744–6006, www. ngf.org) isn't golf's governing body, but it is golf's largest research resource, and it has its collective finger on the pulse of just about everything that's happening in the game. It also happens to publish a list of the country's golf schools.

Before you commit to any golf school, be sure that those teaching the golf swing are members of the **Professional Golf Association of America** (407/624–8400, www.pga.com). Class A certification by the PGA of America indicates that teachers know what they're doing. This is important not only in choosing a golf school but also when taking individual lessons. Your local PGA chapter has a list of certified pros in your area.

Periodicals

The leading golf magazines, *Golf Digest* (www.golfdigest.com) and *Golf Magazine* (www.golfonline.com) will, on occasion, run school listings, but many of the best teachers appear on their mastheads and contribute monthly to their instruction pages. Both magazines have conducted their own ratings of the top teachers in the nation and list them monthly in their publications. Several of the instructors on these lists also teach at the top schools.

Books

Once you've completed your instruction and are ready to hit the links you may want to check out *Golf Digest's Places to Play* (Fodor's Travel Publications), the results of the magazine's reader survey, which chronicles more than 6,500 courses in the United States, Canada, Mexico, and the Caribbean.

Hang Gliding

By Erik Fair
Updated by Jim Palmieri

Hang gliding is the flyingist flying there is. Hang-glider pilots eschew the confines of cockpit or cabin and hang out in the breeze. They feel airspeed with their skin and hear its whisper in their ears and revel in the silent, swooping sensations they feel when in flight.

Believe it or not, relaxation is the heart and soul of hang gliding. That's because a hang glider literally follows your spine. Hang gliders only weigh 50 to 75 pounds, and they're the only fabric-and-frame aircraft light enough to be foot-launched by a human being. With your body hanging in a hammocklike harness attached to the glider's center of gravity, you pull your weight forward to fly faster and push it backward to slow down. Nudge yourself to the right or left and the glider will follow your lead. When you relax your grip and just hang there, the glider flies straight and level, just above the minimum speed required to sustain flight.

There are two safe, enjoyable ways for you to try hang gliding for the first time. One option is bunny-slope training, which typically costs from $85 to $140 for a half- or full-day lesson. You spend the first few hours running around on flat ground, learning how to control the glider as it floats overhead. After you develop a feel for the friendly way the glider tugs up at your pants, you try a takeoff on a gentle slope. Gravity and lift work their magic and suddenly you're moonwalking, then *really flying,* just a few feet off the ground. Several heartbeats later, you gape at your feet, knowing—though not quite believing—they actually left the ground. You need at least average strength, aerobic capacity, and flexibility to enjoy slope training. Avoid it if you have leg or back problems that keep you from running.

If the bunny slope sounds a little tame, you may want to go for a tandem flight. For $100 to $200 you'll spend half an hour in ground school practicing launch procedures; then, safely under the wing of your instructor, you'll trot off a mountaintop or cliff for a high-altitude dance with blue space. A tandem flight gives you ground clearances of several hundred to several thousand feet, plus 10 to 60 minutes of air time on your first excursion. Experienced tandem pilots turn the glider over to you following launch. With your pilot in the "driver's ed" instructional position, you're suddenly in command. Modern towing techniques fix the problem of taking off in flat regions—you and your instructor can safely launch, via towrope and winch, from the back of a boat or truck. Tandem is great if you weigh less than 200 pounds; some pilots will, however, fly 200- to 225-pound passengers in strong wind conditions.

Vicarious thrill-seekers can have fun just watching others carve circles in the sky. Observation is free. Call the nearest hang-gliding school, ask where and when the flying is, get directions to the LZ (landing zone), and show up an hour early. If it's a cliff site, just start asking questions and watch. If it's a mountain site, offer to serve as a driver and notice how popular you become. Hang-glider pilots gladly befriend anyone willing to ride with them to the launch site and drive their car back to the LZ. You'll get a great taste of hang gliding and make a new friend, too.

The size of the hang glider (often called a wing) varies according to the pilot's weight. Solo pilots fly wings with 130 to 175 square ft of sail area; tandem pilots require 180 to 220 square ft of sail to support the weight of two people.

One common misconception is that a hang glider is powered by fickle wind. The wings are actually powered by gravity, which causes them to fly downward through whatever air mass they are in. A hang glider can climb away from the ground only if the air mass is rising faster than the glider is flying downward through it. Hang gliders can stay aloft in the wide band of air that is deflected upward when wind strikes the face of a cliff. They also climb away from the ground in masses of hot air (thermals) that rise faster than 200 ft per minute.

Wind direction, velocity, and degree of turbulence affect safety during launch and landing. Most pilots don't fly in winds greater than 25 mph, and experience teaches them how to predict and avoid turbulence. A beginner's inexperience at judging wind conditions is one of two main reasons why professional instruction is a must. The other is that trial-and-error learning is especially stupid in any form of aviation.

If you want to fly solo, you'll need to train—at minimum—a few days a week for several weeks. You might learn the skills necessary to fly by yourself during a two-week vacation, but you won't develop the judgment needed to fly safely without professional supervision.

To earn a United States Hang Gliding Association (USHGA) Hang I (beginner) rating, you must demonstrate the ability to perform three consecutive smooth launches, followed by three soft landings on your feet into the wind. You will also have to demonstrate the ability to fly straight with good airspeed control. Some folks can do this in a single half-day lesson, but most require two to four lessons. A Hang I rating simply means you can launch and land on a bunny slope under professional supervision. To earn a Hang II (novice) rating—which allows you to fly under your own supervision in mild conditions—you also have to perform precise, linked (consecutive) 90- and 180-degree turns and land within 100 ft of a target. Naturals have been known to accomplish these feats in 3 lessons, but most people require between 4 and 12.

Fortunately, it's quite easy to incorporate two or three days of hang gliding into a weeklong vacation. California, particularly southern California and the Bay Area, offers the best year-round conditions and training areas. But there are a number of good seasonal places in New England, the Southeast, the Southwest, and the Rocky Mountains. And developments in towing technology (launch via truck, boat, or ultralight airtug) have opened up the vast flatlands of the Midwest to hang gliding.

Because many hang-gliding sites are threatened by development or liability considerations, secure locations are the sport's most treasured commodity. A secure site is one where the landowner formally acknowledges and permits hang gliding. These sites usually have bathrooms, launch ramps, picnic areas, and other conveniences.

Most schools will have you sign a liability release form, which says that you are willing to assume the risks associated with leaving the ground under your own power. A good school will make sure you clearly understand this document before you sign it.

CHOOSING THE RIGHT SCHOOL

You should choose a hang-gliding school primarily on its adherence to the regulations that govern the sport. The certification of a school's hang gliders by the Hang Glider Manufacturers Association (HGMA) ensures that they are strong, sophisticated aircraft, thoroughly tested for structural strength and aerodynamic stability. Certification of a school's instructors by the United States Hang Gliding Association (USHGA) guarantees that they are experienced hang-glider pilots who have taught at least 10 days on a training hill under the supervision of a certified instructor, attended a four-day training-and-certification seminar, and passed a written test. Ask these questions before you pay money or sign a liability release form:

Are your instructors certified by the USHGA? The only acceptable answer is yes. The schools we list in this book employ only certified instructors.

Will I be flying a glider that is certified by the HGMA? Don't take no for an answer, unless the glider has been specially modified for use on a bunny slope. HGMA-certified gliders are about five times stronger than they need to be to withstand normal flight loads in normal weather conditions. Since instructors of first- and second-day students teach only in very mild conditions, they will sometimes install lighter frame parts in a training glider. Even then, the glider is twice as strong as it needs to be and will save you 5 to 10 pounds of extra weight on the hill.

Is this a secure site? Avoid schools who use "bandit" sites, where there's a good chance that a badge-toting "smokey" (cop) will run you off mid-lesson.

What kind of instruction do you offer? Whether you are interested in tandem flights or slope training (or some combination of the two), make sure the school you choose offers what you want. All the schools we list offer both tandem flights and bunny-slope training.

How long has your company been in business, and how long have you been teaching? Experience means a lot. It's the only way you learn to read the wind.

What is the best time of year to hang glide here? With the exception of California—where blue skies, sunshine, predictable wind flows, and varied terrain make for some of the world's best year-round hang gliding—most places have definite gliding seasons.

What other attractions are in the area? This is especially important if you're traveling with nonpilots.

How far in advance do I need to book? Although some schools accept walk-in students when not fully booked, it's best to make reservations at least two weeks in advance. In the listings in the back of this book, we include chamber of commerce telephone numbers for assistance in finding accommodations near the schools.

SOURCES
Organizations
United States Hang Gliding Association (Box 8300, Colorado Springs, CO 80933, 719/632–8300) provides general information on ratings, services, certification, and membership. Its official monthly publication, *Hang Gliding Magazine,* features an annual New Pilot Edition for beginners.

Periodicals
Hang Gliding Magazine (6950 Aragon Cir., Suite 6, Buena Park, CA 90620, 714/994–3050) has articles and

photographs of interest to hang-glider pilots of all skill levels.

Books

Right Stuff for New Hang Glider Pilots (Publitec Editions), by Erik Fair, is primarily aimed at people already enrolled in hang-gliding lessons, but it also gives outsiders an inside look at some of the zanier aspects of hang gliding's offbeat culture. Peter Cheney's *Hang Gliding for Beginning Pilots* is thorough and well illustrated—it's the best written resource available to the novice hang-glider pilot. Both can be ordered through the United States Hang Gliding Association (*see* Organizations, *above*).

Hiking and Backpacking

By Peter Oliver
Updated by Cindy Hirschfeld

If horse racing is the sport of kings, hiking is the sport of the populace. So elementary and plodding is hiking that you can do it without *any* experience or preparation. No special skills are required, no extraordinary physical conditioning, and no snazzy gear. You can get by with walking or running shoes, but if you're in the mountains—and particularly if off-trail scrambling is involved—you'll need a sturdy pair of hiking boots.

Hiking demands only one thing: reasonably solid ground to walk on. Perhaps it's because hiking involves the most rudimentary of human motor skills that it can be recast under so many different headings: trekking, walking, backpacking, tramping, scrambling, rambling, and so on. Let's just call a hike a hike.

Although hiking is something you can easily do under your own guidance, and most hikers do just that, organized trips are sometimes appealing. Some hikers toil with expeditionary zeal to select a route, plan an itinerary, get the right gear and maps, organize meals, and make other preparations. If you simply sign up with a trip organizer, all you need to do is decide where to go and how strenuous you want the trip to be, and then choose a trip to match.

A backpacking trip conjures up the popular image of hiking as sport—trekking into the wilderness while lugging your housing and food on your back. This is hiking at its most demanding, where you earn your reward—say, the blissful solitude of sunset in some remote wilderness. Then again, the weather can be miserable or the bugs unrelenting, your equipment could fail or your feet might blister, and the food is not exactly five-star dining. Provisions have to be lightweight, so you'll be carrying lots of dried ingredients—rice, nuts, dried fruits, freeze-dried coffee, and prepared foods. Backpacking isn't for everyone.

If you're not willing to accept the possibility that things can and do go wrong, there are alternatives: naturalist-led day hikes covering relatively flat terrain, with nights in country inns and meals in elegant dining rooms where the food is even more elegant—apple-pecan pancakes at breakfast, prosciutto-and-

Parmesan sandwiches at lunch, salmon doused with beurre blanc or sorrel sauce and chocolate mousse as an end-of-day reward. Such trips are often (though not exclusively) organized with elderly hikers in mind and often come with a naturalist bent, such as bird-watching or flora identification. The only gear you need for this kind of trip is a camera and sunblock.

Another option is llama trekking, wherein beasts of burden carry most of your camping equipment and food. This lets you cover more terrain than if you carry your own gear. It also makes for campsite meals that, by backpacker standards, would be considered decadent, with fresh meats, poultry, fruits, and vegetables—and wine to wash it down. Pack animals other than llamas, which are particularly well suited to travel in mountainous terrain, are sometimes used.

There's a direct correlation between comfort and cost on the trail; a straightforward, simple, carry-all-your-own-gear six-day trip with the Sierra Club, for example, runs as little as $500, while an inn-to-inn jaunt, complete with van transport to the trailhead and sumptuous meals, is easily triple the price.

CHOOSING THE RIGHT TRIP

Your primary concern ought to be safety, especially for longer, more rigorous trips. Guides should have the proper technical and first-aid gear and be well trained in emergency and safety procedures, including CPR. This may be difficult to determine, because no governing body certifies trail guides or rates guided hiking-tour operators, and the value of the regional groups' efforts to do so is debatable. In some areas, specifically national parks, the number of outfitters may be restricted, and in such cases there is at least some assurance that an outfitter is a responsible one.

So ask questions to determine if the outfitter is reputable and the particular trip is right for your abilities, interests, schedule, and budget. Start with these:

How long has the company been in business? A company that has been around for a few years is more likely to have ironed out all the kinks than one that's just opened its doors for business.

How long has the company been running trips to the destination? A reputable company that's done its research should be able to pull off a new trip without any major glitches, but if you want to go hiking in Alaska, for example, you'll be more assured of a quality experience if you go with an outfitter that has a track record of trips in that specific area.

What are the guides' qualifications? The better the guide, the better the trip. Find out how long the guides have been hiking in the area and how long they have been guiding groups—and ask if they have any other abilities or fields of expertise. Knowledge of local plants, animals, and geological phenomena is a plus. Make sure at least one guide with your group is certified in first aid and can administer CPR.

What size is the group? Trips often set out with as many as 16 hikers. If a group gets much larger, you lose the sense of remoteness and isolation that is one of the sport's great rewards. Group members' age, physical fitness, and hiking experience determine what a group can and can't do. Some trips are organized with families, women, men, or teens in mind—and if you don't fit in, you might not have a good time.

With smaller groups, there's the flexibility to change the itinerary if you want to. In some cases, outfitters encourage suggestions and participation by group members in the trip planning. And if you really want to keep your group small and create your own itinerary, many organizers will arrange custom trips—for a price, of course.

How long is each day's hike, and how strenuous? A 10-mi hike through flat or rolling countryside may be easier than 3 mi in the mountains. Most trip organizers rate their trips, but unlike river rafting or rock climbing, hiking has no standard rating scale to determine a hike's relative difficulty. A trip that one organization considers moderate may be strenuous according to another. To determine whether you can handle a particular trip, inquire about specifics, such as the elevation gain of a mountainous hike, the type of climate you'll be hiking in, or the upkeep of the trails (e.g., is it smooth sailing all the way or will you have to navigate your way through thick brush or over boulders?). And be honest about evaluating your physical fitness level. A conscientious outfitter should be able to tell whether you can handle a hike with a few questions of its own.

What are accommodations like? If you're staying at inns or resorts, find out what the rooms are like and ask about facilities. If you're camping, ask about showers and toilet arrangements. Before you sign up to use the outfitter's tents or sleeping bags, check that they are suited to the location—for example, whether the sleeping bags will keep you warm when it's 20 degrees or whether the tents are built to handle a downpour.

What's the food like? Don't expect anything spectacular, except on llama-trekking journeys or inn-to-inn trips. But some outfitters make more of an effort to bring choice foods along the trail, and some are more virtuous in their preparation of dried foods than others. If you have any dietary restrictions, check whether you can make special requests (well in advance, of course).

What's the cost, and what's included? Typically (and for the trips we list in the back of this book, unless otherwise noted), your trip fee includes guide service, all meals, any transfers after the group has assembled, and accommodations during inn- or lodge-based trips, but not tents, sleeping bags and pads, backpacks, and other camping gear for backpacking trips (sometimes the outfitter can rent you the equipment you need). Most trip organizers provide lists of necessary gear. Meals and motel lodging before the group heads out on the trail and after the walk's conclusion may be included—but often are not.

Ditto for transportation from the nearest airport, which is important only if you're not driving to the assembly point; if transfers are not included (as is usually the case), you may need to rent a car. Airfare into the area is always extra.

How far in advance do I need to book? Usually you'll need to make your plans at least three months in advance, primarily so that outfitters can be sure there are enough participants before making the complex preparations involved in setting up a trip. (Trips may be canceled if not enough people sign up.) On the other hand, you may get lucky and find an open slot just a few days before trip time.

SOURCES

Organizations

American Hiking Society (1422 Fenwick La., Silver Spring, MD 20910, 301/565–6704, www.americanhiking. org) is an advocacy group promoting proper trail management throughout the United States and is also a general clearinghouse on hiking information. **Appalachian Mountain Club** (5 Joy St., Boston, MA 02108, 617/523–0636, www.outdoors.org) is the leading hiking organization in the Northeast. The club maintains backcountry huts and lodges in New Hampshire's White Mountains as well as the Catskills of New York and the Berkshires of Massachusetts. The club is also active in maintaining trails in these areas and offers an extensive program of outings, seminars, and workshops. **National Audubon Society** (700 Broadway, New York, NY 10003, 212/ 979–3000, www.audubon.org) is primarily a naturalist organization. Short outings, typically for bird-watching, are organized through local society chapters; longer trips and international outings are arranged through the national organization. The society is an active book publisher; its magazine, *Audubon,* issued as part of club membership, does an excellent job of covering wildlife-related issues. **Sierra Club** (85 2nd St., 2nd floor, San Francisco, CA 94105, 415/977–5500, www.sierraclub. org) is one of the preeminent advocacy groups in the country promoting responsible environmental and wilderness management. It also offers perhaps the most extensive trip schedule of any organization in the country, although technically the club doesn't organize trips itself; trips are organized by individuals and outfitters under the club's auspices. The club magazine, *Sierra,* issued as a part of club membership, is first-rate in its coverage of environmental issues.

Periodicals

The publication of the American Hiking Society, *American Hiker* (Box 20160, Washington, DC 20041, 703/385–3252), reports on hiking-related issues and hiking destinations. The monthly magazine *Backpacker* (33 E. Minor St., Emmaus, PA 18098, 610/967–8296, www.backpacker.com) is the leading magazine in the country devoted specifically to hiking and backpacking. It's an excellent source of information on trips and equipment, including boots, clothing, and camping gear. Also included is a classified-ad section with organized-trip listings. *National Geographic Adventure* (104 W. 40th St., New York, NY 10018, 212/790–9020, www.nationalgeographic.com) carries on the legacy of its parent company with articles on adventure travel around the world and outstanding photographs. Travel suggestions, gear reviews, and news on outdoor-related exploits are also part of the package, as well as a travel directory of trip outfitters. The longest-running magazine in the country on outdoor and adventure recreation, hiking, and backpacking is the monthly *Outside* (400 Market St., Santa Fe, NM 87501, 505/989–7100, www.outsidemag.com). You'll find personal narratives, capsule reports on recommended trips, product reviews, and articles on environmental issues. The classified-ad section includes extensive listings of trip organizers.

Books

The Complete Walker IV, by Colin Fletcher, gives the last word on the pleasures and techniques of the sport. *Trailside Guide: Hiking and Backpacking, New Edition,* by Karen Berger, covers everything from finding a good backpack to finding a good place to use it.

The Appalachian Mountain Club (*see* Organizations, *above*) publishes, among other books, trail guides for many parts of the Northeast. Backcountry Publications (The Countryman Press, Box 748, Woodstock, VT 05091, 800/245–4151 or 802/457–4826, www.countrymanpress.com) publishes guides to hiking, cycling, and skiing in the eastern United States. Among its best offerings for hikers is the series *"50 Hikes in..."* from Maine to West Virginia. Guidebooks from the Mountaineers (101 S.W. Klickitat Way, Suite 201, Seattle, WA 98134, 800/553–4453 or 206/223–6303, www.mountaineersbooks.org) cover the Northwest, including the Northern Rockies, California, and British Columbia. Books and trail guides from the Sierra Club (*see* Organizations, *above*) focus primarily though not exclusively on areas in the West. Wilderness Press (1200 5th St., Berkeley, CA 94710, 800/443–7227 or 510/558–1666, www.wildernesspress.com), which publishes guides covering California and other parts of the West, stands out for its coverage of the Pacific Crest Trail.

Mountain Biking

By Bill Strickland
Updated by Joe Lindsey

Mountain bikes are time machines. Ride one and you become a kid again. Splash through mud, ride through grass, or jump a rock. It's improvisation and freedom, and boy, can it take you places. You may find yourself reclining on a mountaintop while a lightning storm rages nearby. Or perhaps you'll be lucky enough to be on Washington's Capitol Peak on a clear day that reveals all the state's volcanic ranges in one sweeping view.

You don't need to be an especially good mountain biker to experience any of this. Although its image is that of the gnarly, muddy dude thrashing a way-wicked trail and slinging lingo unintelligible to humans not on an adrenaline spike, mountain biking is for regular people who quickly discover that it's easier than they thought to ride off-road through forests, over deserts, into canyons, and across creeks.

Sure, you need real skill to hack the most technical stuff. Make a mistake in certain sections of the rides we list and you could, well, die. But there are plenty of simple and safe rides for beginners, too.

One reason anyone can mountain bike is that bikes are incredibly user-friendly. They have more gears for easier pedaling, simple shifting, flat handlebars (for an upright sitting position and more stability), and fat knobby tires (for a cushy and super-grippy ride). On the other end of the spectrum are the daredevil machines. If you're fit and you know what you're doing, you can take yourself to the edge of control in settings where your natural instinct is to be as careful as possible. You can lace the rim of a hundred-foot drop-off, bomb down a rock-strewn trail at insane speeds, or catch big air.

The number of operators offering mountain-biking trips is increasing with the popularity of the sport. As with road tours, mountain-bike touring companies provide all sorts of support and expertise. But the biggest benefit to biking with an outfitter may be its knowledge of the terrain. Getting lost on the road can be an inconvenience. Getting lost in the wilderness is plain dangerous. Take a tour and you don't have to worry about your lousy sense of direction or how to read the trail network map.

You also won't have to worry about ancillary concerns: do you have enough food and water to ride through that patch of desert? Will the trail empty out near an inn? How much equipment should you carry? You don't even need to own a mountain bike, since most companies rent good models.

The format of off-road touring resembles that of road touring. Single-track is a narrow trail, usually not more than a foot wide; double-track is twice as wide, fit for two people to ride side-by-side. Double-track is sometimes made by Jeeps. Most vacations are 2- to 10-day trips along preplanned routes. Trails include a variety of descents and ascents, and different types of terrain.

At least two accomplished outdoorsy guides lead each trip. One rides with you while the other drives a support van along the route. In some areas, such as stretches of narrow single-track, the support vehicle can't follow you. In these instances, it will parallel your route on the closest road or drive ahead to wait for you. The vans carry your gear, supply water and snacks, usually house mini–bike shops for trailside repairs, and can even haul a few tired adventurers.

The going can be as tough or easy as you like. There are daylong treks over highly "technical" terrain (difficult to ride because of obstacles in the trail) on which it's not uncommon to walk your bike up and down slopes and over obstacles. And then there are casual jaunts on flat dirt roads. Easier trips usually spend a lot of time off the trail at different attractions.

This diversity means that there's a tour for everyone. You'll find variety even within a single tour. Most companies customize their routes slightly to allow you to ride more or less mileage, or to take different routes—so you can stay on the dirt road if you're unsure about that rocky trail.

There's plenty of range in the price of the trips, too. A five-day trip can range from $600 to more than $1,500. Prices vary greatly due to several factors: accommodations—which can be anything from unimproved campsites in the backcountry (i.e., not a designated campground) to luxurious ski-area condos—food, amount of equipment provided, extra off-bike activities, and demand for the trip.

More than road touring, going on mountain-bike trips seems to create a sense of camaraderie. The challenges are usually greater, or at least more obvious. Riders coach each other through the toughest parts, share advice, and swap war stories.

However, sometimes the group experience seems to work against the lure of the outdoors. Some people find it disconcerting to pick their way through an isolated forest with 10 other people. There are the practical inconveniences, too. Your schedule is tied to the group's. You wake when they do, begin riding when they do, and eat when (and probably what) they do. And when rain turns the trail to soup, don't think you can delay your trip for a day. Put on your foul-weather duds, pal—the group is heading out.

Still, most cyclists say the advantages of commercial off-road touring outweigh the disadvantages—the exception being getting stuck on an inappropriate trip.

If you're a beginner—even an earnest one—don't be rash and sign up for harsh, technical rides, as you may spend most of your time dragging your bike behind you or sightseeing from a van. It won't be, you'll discover, a crowning outdoors experience. Neither is it advisable, if you're a true gnarly dude, to confine yourself to tame dirt roads. The trick is to match your physical ability and off-road experience to the right trip. It's okay to challenge yourself with a tour slightly over your head, or to take it easy on a snoozer. Just be honest with yourself about your ability.

Trip descriptions should give accurate pictures of how tough the riding will be, but don't get fooled by the mileage listings. Off-road miles are tougher than road miles. So don't think that 15 trail mi a day will be a snap compared to that 30-mi-per-day road trip you did once. A general rule for figuring your endurance is that 1 mountain-bike mile equals at least 3 road miles. On tough single-track and technical slickrock, or in steep territory, it can be even harder.

Pay attention to other factors, too. The number of off-bike activities is a measurement of the difficulty of the tour (the more off-trail activities the less strenuous the tour). Weather can cook you or help you and also affects the scenery. Spending a fall weekend on a New England mountainside is more beautiful and more comfortable than a going on a summertime jaunt in the same area.

These days the best commercial rides are found in the Southwest and Rockies, and on the West Coast, where high-altitude ascents lead to overlooks of mind-boggling vistas. Any territory near canyons or mountain peaks is also guaranteed good riding. The East, especially New

England, is loaded with trails, but commercial touring has yet to thoroughly invade the region. West Virginia and North Carolina are also ready to explode as hot spots. Once the touring companies expand into these areas you'll be able to find organized off-road thrills almost anywhere.

Don't kid yourself about your level of comfort when you're choosing a trip. The riding is tough, so don't feel foolish if you want days in the wilderness and nights of pampered comfort. Unlike on a road tour, you're likely to get dirty and all-over tired. Tents and cold showers won't help much.

Mountain-bike touring isn't for everyone. This is because at its worst it can be jarring, difficult, and dirty. At its best, too, it can be jarring, difficult, and dirty.

CHOOSING THE RIGHT TRIP

Everything associated with mountain biking—manufacturers, event organizers, and touring companies—has, in the past decade, transitioned from a niche operation to big-time. There are some growing pains, which we try to help you avoid. To be included in these listings, each touring company has to meet these minimum criteria: offer trips along preplanned, established routes; provide at least two mileage options each day; furnish some type of support (such as motorized route patrols, sag service for tired or injured riders, and luggage transport); supply or assist in arranging lodging and provide at least some meals; require the use of helmets (you never appreciate a skid lid until you need it).

But don't stop with the listings. Make a few phone calls to learn more about the companies you're considering.

Don't be shy about asking these questions. You're about to spend a decent chunk of money. Think of it this way: for the cost of a seven-day tour, you could buy a trick new bike.

How tough is the trip? We offer as many details as we can about the trips listed in the back of this book, but make sure you cover your bases. Describe your road-riding experience and your physical condition. Ask if the riding is technical or buff (smooth), on trails or dirt roads. You may be surprised to find that some of the riding occurs on pavement—necessary to link the off-road routes.

Does mileage vary? The distances probably won't vary widely—off-road companies don't have as much leeway as road operations—but you'll get an idea if you can shorten a ride and stay on your bike, or if you'll be stuck in the van when you're tired.

What are the trail options? Can you find single-track spurs off the dirt road? Will you be stuck on the technical trail, or is there an easy parallel path for a break?

What are the accommodations like? Some trips are able to offer plush rooms even on truly wild excursions. This is because ski lodges and hunting inns are located near many trails. However most offer more rugged accommodations. If you'll be camping (as is common), check such details as rest-room arrangements and the availability of hot showers.

What are the meals like? Some campfire cooks are fit for the finest restaurants. Others serve basic grub. Most companies skip at least one meal—lunch or dinner.

What's the cost and what's included? Prices in these listings are per person, double occupancy, and include gratuities, entrance fees to parks and attractions, and camping fees. Airfare and the cost of renting bikes or camping equipment isn't included in prices we quote, unless we note otherwise. Renting camping equipment (tent and sleeping bag) usually costs between $30 and $55 per trip. Sometimes there are extras. We tell you about as many as we could find, but always ask if there are others: $50 for the optional mule ride down the canyon or $30 for the massage.

What weather can I expect?

Will laundry service be available? It's usually not on off-road tours, but if so, it could save you a suitcase.

What extras are included? Many companies offer T-shirts, sweatshirts, water bottles, or other freebies.

What is the makeup of my touring group? You can find out ages, gender, marital status, home state, and sometimes even off-road cycling experience. This helps you predict the atmosphere of your entire trip. You should also ask about group size.

Is this same tour available for singles (senior citizens, women, and so forth)? We note as many of these as we can, but schedules may change. Some companies offer reduced rates for kids and families.

How extensive is the support? This could be the difference between walking out of the forest with a broken-down bike, or having it repaired on the spot. Some companies may make only one or two runs along a route. Others constantly patrol. Find out how many guides work each trip. The more the better.

What is the rental equipment like? Find out what brand of bike is offered, how many sizes are available, and how old the fleet is. A few companies offer you your choice of suspension or rigid bikes. If you're going on a camping trip, check the quality of the rental equipment. Gear is never more important than on a long mountain-biking trip. Make sure you ask whether helmets are included for free.

Who are the leaders and how are they trained? It may sound nosy, but in the wilderness you need guides who are not only expert cyclists but also skilled outdoors types.

How long has the company been in business? This is especially important in such a newly popular field. You won't necessarily have a problem with an outfitter new to the sport, but an outfitter who has been running off-road trips for several years is probably more prepared to meet challenges. Know that there are no gargantuans in this field—the sport is still growing, and small companies with regional strengths match the free spirit of off-road cycling. The logistics are harder to handle than those of road tours, and the big outfitters aren't completely set up yet to develop a network of mountain-bike tours. And while some of these outfits we list don't have the name recognition of a Butterfield and Robinson, they do offer the same sort of professionalism and attention to detail.

Can the leaders handle minor mechanical repairs? No type of cycling is tougher on equipment than mountain biking. You can count on at least one flat and something else that will need fiddling with. If it's just a quick brake adjustment, I'd expect a freebie. But be reasonable: If you do a biff and pretzel your wheel, cough up a tip for the guide who rebuilds it.

How far in advance do I need to book? Some trips are more popular than others and can fill up as much as a year in advance. So although two to three months is usually far enough in advance to book a trip, you should probably reserve as early as possible. If you find you've waited too long, don't hesitate to put your name on a waiting list, since cancellations may mean you get a spot on a trip even if you call only days in advance.

SOURCES

Organizations

Adventure Cycling Association (Box 8308, Missoula, MT 59807, 406/721–1776, www.adventurecycling.org) sells cycling maps and provides information about off-road touring. It publishes *The Cyclists' Yellow Pages* (including a special mountain-biking supplement) and *Adventure Cyclist* magazine. **American Youth Hostels** (Box 37613, Washington, DC 20013, 202/783–4943, www.hiayh.org) runs off-road tours and provides inexpensive accommodations.

The **International Mountain Bicycling Association** (Box 7378, Boulder, CO 80306, 303/545–9011, www.imba.com) advocates responsible trail use, and helps resolve land-access issues. It publishes *IMBA Trail News.* **The League of American Bicyclists** (190 W. Ostend St., Suite 120, Baltimore, MD 21230, 410/539–3399, www.bikeleague.org), a cycling-enthusiast organization, runs events and provides touring information. It also publishes *Bicycle USA.* Although it's not heavily off-road oriented, it may be of some help. **Rails to Trails Conservancy** (1400 16th St. NW, Suite 300, Washington, DC 20036, 202/797–5400, www.railtrails.org) promotes conversion of abandoned railroad land to cycling trails and provides touring information.

Periodicals

The League of American Bicyclists (*see above*) publishes *Bicycle USA* eight times a year and distributes it to members. Every issue contains at least one touring feature and lots of information on rides and events. *Bicycling* is a how-to magazine, with mountain-bike touring articles throughout the year and a special touring issue (Rodale Press, 33 E. Minor St., Emmaus, PA 18098, 610/967–8093 information; 515/242–0286 subscriptions; www.bicycling.com). *The Cyclists' Yellow Pages,* an annual publication distributed to Adventure Cycling members (*see above*), lists sources of off-road touring information and maps. *Dirt Rag* lists off-road rides and events in New England, on the East Coast, in the Midwest, and in the Southeast (5732 3rd St., Verona, PA 15147, 412/795–7495, www.dirtragmag.com). *Mountain Bike,* the sister magazine of *Bicycling,* has a special off-road touring issue each year and mountain-bike-touring articles throughout the year (Rodale Press, 33 E. Minor St., Emmaus, PA 18098, 610/967–5171 information; 515/242–0291 subscriptions; www.mountainbike.com). *California Cyclist* lists off-road rides and events in this region (490 2nd St. Suite 304, San Francisco, CA 94107, 415/546–7291). *Northwest Cyclist* chronicles off-road rides and events in the Pacific Northwest (Box 9272, Seattle, WA 98109, 206/286–8566).

Books

Pick up a copy of *500 Great Rail Trails* (Living Planet Press) to discover the U.S. rail-trail system, a series of abandoned rail lines that have been converted to bike trails. The 162-page guide tells you where the trails are and how long they run; it also gives highlights along the route and tells you where to get a map. Some of the best touring books available are those in the *Bicycling the Back Roads* series: *Northwest Oregon, Northwest Washington, Pacific Coast, Southwest Washington* (The Mountaineers Books). Each book has more than 200 pages compiled by local experts, with detailed route directions, sightseeing tips, and lodging and food recommendations. Another excellent series, *Mountain Bike America: Arizona, New Hampshire, Oregon, Vermont, Colorado et al.* (Menasha Ridge Press), offers 230-page volumes of well-mapped and detailed off-road rides throughout the United States and is written by local experts. The 228-page volumes of a third fine series—*Mountain Bike Adventures: Four Corners Region, Northern Rockies, Washington's North Cascades and Olympics, Washington's South Cascades/Puget Sound* (The Mountaineers Books)—include many mapped routes and good introductory material on mountain biking.

Nature Camps

By Melanie Sponholz
Updated by Marilyn Haddrill

The days of horseback riding along mountain trails or canoeing across lakes surrounded by fragrant pines are not over. You can visit your summer-camp nostalgia in the many nature and conservation camps run by such organizations as the National Audubon Society, National Wildlife Federation, and Yellowstone Institute. You'll get to conduct fieldwork and observe firsthand how plants and wild creatures fit into nature's grand, complex scheme.

Locales are as varied as they are fascinating: Death Valley, New England forests, the Rocky Mountains, and Yellowstone, Yosemite, and Big Bend national parks. It's typical to spend from several days to a week camping out or sharing a cabin, eating campfire cuisine, and turning in early after a full day of outdoor exploration. Do *not* expect to make key chains in the arts-and-crafts tent or shoot targets in archery class. In these camps, you'll spend your days and evenings studying the natural world.

At nature camps you learn by doing fieldwork or through firsthand observation of your subject. You might collect and analyze a water sample collected from a lake to understand oxygen content and how pollutants can devastate life within the delicate ecological system. Or you may learn how geology, botany, animals, birds, insects, and weather patterns interact. A visit to a mist net, where birds are caught and banded for tracking, provides a lesson on migration. Some camps focus on a single subject—how, for example, people fit into the ecosystem, and how actions we take can have a positive (or negative) environmental effect. Others address local concerns about endangered species or explain how to petition a government representative to help a conservation bill get passed.

Expect to spend the entire 9-to-5 day hiking. The hiking tends to be relatively easy: you proceed slowly, observing your surroundings and stopping often as your instructor points out geological formations or the species of a bird overhead. On some trips, you'll cross rough terrain or venture up high altitudes that demand a high level of physical fitness. Some camps provide van or bus transportation; just make sure you know what you're getting into.

Itineraries are usually flexible, in part because you can only learn about what you encounter—wildlife doesn't follow our schedules. You may start out looking for a mole tunnel and spend an hour watching wasps building a nest. You learn to identify plants, to examine the layers of rock in gorges, to observe birds, and to search for animal tracks. If the camp is focused on a particular animal, be prepared to spend some time waiting for your subject to appear.

Camp instructors are naturalists, experts in the subject matter and geographical area of the camp. Many are college professors or National Park Service employees. Groups are small and manageable—between 8 and 20 people—to minimize the impact on the environment.

In addition to doing fieldwork, you may spend time in a classroom or laboratory. A slide show will help you identify bear tracks in the woods; in the lab you may relearn how best to focus a microscope so you can peer at pond-water organisms or the chlorophyll-containing plant cells that perform photosynthesis.

Accommodations at nature camps range from tent sites with no electricity or water to air-conditioned dorm rooms; shared bathrooms are the norm. Dining options include bring-your-own-food-and-camp-stove, basic cafeteria fare, or family-style meals. In some cases, participants who don't mind the extra expense can opt for more private accommodations (such as your own cabin). Also, stays in nearby luxury resorts with full-service restaurants are sometimes available. Because many camp operators are nonprofit organizations and accommodations are often basic, nature camps can be a very affordable vacation. If you're willing to camp and bring your own food, you can find a tent site and a week of instruction for less than $350.

A few camps have programs for children, but most of the trips we list in this book are geared for adults. The slow pace and long periods of observation are not suited for young attention spans. Participants range in age from 18 to 80. Most operators report that more than 50% of participants are between the ages of 35 and 45 and that women outnumber men on the trips. Some college students are usually in each program, especially at camps that offer course credit.

CHOOSING THE RIGHT CAMP

When deciding which nature camp is right for you, ask the following questions.

What are the instructors' qualifications? Remember you are paying mostly for instruction. Without a good teacher, you may as well be camping out and hiking on your own. Most program instructors listed in this chapter are college professors, well-known researchers in a field of nature study, or veteran park guides. Don't hesitate to find out the names of experts who will be leading the camp. Research their qualifications on your own, or ask specific questions about their experience, education, and where they currently might be teaching.

What is the focus of the camp? Some camps address one topic—geology or wildflowers, for example. Others study all of components of a particular ecosystem, such as the plants, animals, and organisms that typically populate grasslands or forests. Some camps offer bicycling, canoeing, diving, or skiing, in addition to hiking, so make sure you find out exactly what's available.

How tough are the hikes? Find out if the terrain will be rough and how far you'll walk each day. Also make sure you check the campsite's elevation and ask whether you'll be taking high-altitude hikes.

What's the food like? Partial meal plans or no meal plan at all are common. At camps that offer meals, the food is usually standard hot and cold cafeteria fare or basics like macaroni-and-cheese and hamburgers served family style in a dining hall. A few camps provide meals in a hotel restaurant or offer more of a selection at the cafeteria; their prices are proportionately higher. Vegetarian diets can usually be accommodated; ask whether they fulfill other special needs. At camps without meal plans, kitchen facilities are sometimes available. Find out if these include cooking and eating utensils, storage space, and refrigerator space. Also ask about the availability of nearby grocery stores and restaurants.

What are the accommodations like? Types of accommodations included in the cost of nature camps vary greatly, so make sure you find out exactly what you're getting. Private rooms are rarely available; shared rooms may be occupied by more than two people. Rustic cabins may have no electricity or running water. If a tent site is provided, find out if you are responsible for your own camping equipment. Often you must bring your own sleeping bag or linens and your own towels. The bathroom setup also varies. If the bathroom is shared, find out how many people will be using the same facility. Hot showers, in fact any showers at all, are not a given, especially at park campgrounds, so make sure you find out what kinds of facilities are nearby.

What about transportation costs? Instruction and any transportation costs to sites you don't access through hiking are always included in the camp price. However, you'll have to pay for transportation to and from the camp itself.

Is laundry service available? Probably not, but check anyway to see if you can avoid bringing an extra suitcase of clothes.

How long has the company been in business? The longer the operator has been in business, the more smoothly the camp is likely to run. Established camps also are more likely to have long-term associations with experienced instructors.

How far in advance do I need to book? Most groups ask that people reserve three or more months in advance. You may, however, want to book earlier to make sure you don't miss the boat on popular tours. Signing up early for less popular trips can help ensure that they actually run.

SOURCES
Organizations
The **Nature Conservancy** (4245 N. Fairfax Dr., Suite 100, Arlington, VA 22203, 800/628–6860 or 703/841–5300, www.nature.org.), a general conservation and land-trust organization, runs travel programs for its members; these are listed in its quarterly magazine, *Nature Conservancy*. A subscription is included in the $50 membership fee charged to new enrollees.

Basic membership in a national organization ranges in cost from $15 to $50 and includes a subscription to the organization's magazine. You can also elect to donate additional money to a group beyond the membership cost, either annually or on a one-time basis. The following are top, well-respected organizations: **National Audubon Society** (700 Broadway, New York, NY 10003, 800/274–4201 or 212/979–3117), **National Wildlife Federation** (8925 Leesburg Pike, Vienna, VA 22184, 800/588–1650 or 703/790–4306), **Sierra Club** (85 2nd St., 2nd floor, San Francisco, CA 94105, 415/977–5500), **Yellowstone Association** (Box 117, Yellowstone National Park, WY 82190, 307/344–2289), **Yosemite Association** (Box 230, El Portal, CA 95318, 209/379–2646).

Nordic Skiing

By Rosemary Freskos and Jonathan Weisel
Updated by Gregory Benchwick

Picture a skier in skintight, pink-striped leggings racing past you on short high-tech skating skis. Up ahead, an instructor in black stretch pants, a nylon windbreaker, and dark goggles digs her metal-edged skis into the snow, completing a near-perfect telemark turn. Behind her, another skier, dressed in wool knickers and a fisherman's sweater, glides along on machine-set tracks, basking in the sunshine and breathing deep the dry, cold air.

Scenes like this one, which you'll see at Nordic ski areas across the country, say volumes about how the sport has grown in the past 50 years. Because there are so many ways to enjoy it, Nordic skiing appeals to all sorts. First, you learn about nature while you're on the trails (or off them, if you're skiing uncharted backcountry). You also see animals, and come to know what the flow of clouds may mean for weather the next day. Eventually you can guess the temperature based on the sound of your skis gently rubbing on the snow (rule of thumb: the higher-pitched the squeak, the colder it is). And best, it's one of the top sports for low-impact cardiovascular exercise.

Because there's still some confusion about the nomenclature of skiing, the Cross Country Ski Areas Association, a national organization representing cross-country ski operators and suppliers, has come up with some standard definitions. Nordic skiing is an all-inclusive term comprising every kind of skiing other than alpine— track, skating, backcountry, and telemarking are all considered part of the Nordic family. Skis are lighter than their alpine cousins, and all come with free-heeled bindings; your toe is attached to the ski and your heel is allowed to move smoothly up and down. The term "cross-country" is used more exclusively and refers to skiing on machine-groomed surfaces—both tracks and yard-wide compacted skating lanes. Track skiing involves an up-and-down parallel movement of the skis, while skating, as the name implies, takes place on an open surface, where the skier is allowed to open up his or her skis and "skate" across the snow. Most people use cross-country and Nordic interchangeably. The term "ski touring" connotes any type of off-track skiing, from fooling around on skis at a local golf course to trekking in the Tetons. Ski touring is often called backcountry skiing.

A cross-country trip is usually cheaper than a downhill-ski vacation. You can pay as little as $10 for a daily trail pass instead of the $30–$60 for a lift ticket, and rentals run about $15 as opposed to $25 for alpine skis. You can find many out-of-the-way lodges and inns with cross-country networks, most of which are relatively inexpensive—in contrast, in downhill-ski areas the price of accommodations tends to be inflated.

It's best to learn at a cross-country ski resort, where the trails are machine-groomed with tracks. That means the snow is compacted into a consistent surface and two parallel grooves, which are cut into the snow so your skis can't go anywhere but forward. Tracked trails allow anyone to experience the thrill of speed with confident control at any pace, and the trail systems are so well marked and signed, it takes both talent and effort to get lost.

But there's a lot more to cross-country skiing than machine-groomed tracks. You can scuttle through the backcountry on virgin snow on wider, more stable skis; speed down hard-packed skating lanes using short skis much as you would on ice skates; or don heavier, metal-edged skis to descend lift-served slopes, lunging forward on one knee in a telemark position.

To give you a sense of the variety of ski experiences available we list—in the back of this book—several types of cross-country ski vacations. We tell you about entire areas devoted to the sport, such as Jackson, New Hampshire, and Royal Gorge, California, where there are several connected trail systems; we cover individual hotels and ranches with their very own trail networks; and we add a few organized guided trips by outfitters who will take you from lodge to lodge or hut to hut.

Keep in mind that cross-country ski areas are wildly diverse in size and emphasis. If you choose a large area, you have a better choice of accommodations and your trail pass gives you access to a wide network with all kinds of trails. Individual hotels, lodges, and ranches, on the other hand, may have smaller trail networks—but with more personality. Some accept only a dozen overnight guests; others have more than 60 lodgers and hundreds of day skiers. Many include trail fees in multiday packages, which come with a hefty, though worthwhile, price tag, while the day visitor pays $10–$15 for a few hours of skiing. Guided trips with outfitters make it easy: you pay one price and they take care of just about everything, except for pulling you over those last 2 km, which are indubitably uphill. Guide companies generally emphasize service rather than challenging terrain, and they usually offer a combination of track and touring, or even stick just to groomed trails.

Note: In most cases, cross-country skiers measure distance in kilometers (km) rather than miles. To convert kilometers into miles, divide by 1.6.

CHOOSING THE RIGHT EXPERIENCE

Cross-country ski areas have a justified reputation for hospitality, comfort, and culinary excellence; guided tours can be either plush or primitive. When you're researching the ideal site or tour, ask the following questions.

How long has the resort or hotel been operating as a cross-country destination? How long has the guide service been in business? Experience gives any business the knowledge it needs to work out problems with its operation and to meet the needs of all its customers. Also, a long history and proven record will ensure your safety while traveling with a guide in the backcountry.

Are the trails groomed or ungroomed? If you are going on a guided tour, the answer to this question will tell you a lot about the trip. You won't find groomed trails leading to a backcountry hut.

How many kilometers of machine-groomed track are there? Are the tracks single or double and is there a skating lane? Obviously, more track means more skiing terrain to keep you busy. Some individual hotels might have only up to 20 km of groomed track, which is probably enough for a beginner, but more advanced skiers will be happier at a place with 50 km or more. Single-track trails accommodate only one skier going in one direction, which makes them ideal if you're looking for solitude. Double tracks are set so that skiers can travel in both directions. Skiers who want to skate will need a skating lane, a wide, flat trail of packed snow.

Are all the trails groomed or are there backcountry trails as well? If you're a backcountry skier who is visiting a resort or hotel, make sure that there are plenty of marked, ungroomed trails where you can get into the wilderness you love. Only venture into the backcountry if you're familiar with wilderness survival and avalanche safety, however. Taking a guided tour into the backcountry is a lot safer than going it alone.

Is the system connected to other systems, and if it is, does your trail pass cover the connected systems? Some inns and hotels have trail networks that connect with other networks where you are allowed to ski using the same trail pass. This means you get more skiing area for your dollar.

What's the cost and what's included? Costs quoted for packages and guided tours are generally per person and include double-occupancy accommodations, meals (but not alcoholic beverages), and trail fees, unless stated otherwise. Guided trips with outfitters also include the services of a guide, who often gives the group instruction.

Many cross-country ski areas and even individual inns and ranches supply a limited number of group lessons as well as some short guided tours and clinics gratis. Paying extra for lessons and tours can add substantially to the cost of your trip. In all cases, you have to pay extra for private lessons and longer guided tours. Rental equipment is not included in the prices we quote unless stated otherwise.

Keep in mind that the multiple-day packages that we list are not your only option. At some resorts you can simply buy a daily trail pass (we list the price of this when it's available). At others, the trails are open only to overnight visitors, but you can pay for accommodations and a trail pass, without the meals, lessons, and guide that are included in the package.

What are the accommodations like? Hotel rooms vary tremendously, and guided tours may lead you to primitive huts or comfortable country inns. Backcountry treks may also mention staying in a yurt—a round, semipermanent structure stronger than a tent and similar to a hut.

What are the meals like? You could be dining in four-star restaurants or eating beans around a woodstove. A trip into the backcountry will likely entail some bean eating, even with the poshest of guide services. Resorts tend to have excellent restaurants.

Are instructors or guides certified and experienced? Certification by Professional Ski Instructors of America (PSIA) ensures that instructors have the necessary skiing and communication skills required to teach effectively. If a guide is going to lead you into the backcountry, make sure that guide has been there before. Also see that at least one guide has first-aid and CPR training.

What kind of equipment is available? Does the rental shop have waxable skis? What type of binding systems are on the rental skis? Lots of skiers bring their own skis, but if you're renting, you want to be sure the resort has the kind of skis you need. If you want to practice skating and it stocks only touring skis, you'll be out of luck. Many ski shops offer only waxless skis, so if you're an advanced skier who prefers to choose a wax to optimize performance in certain skiing conditions, you'll be out of luck. Also, if you bring your own boots but don't want to carry your own skis, you should be sure that your boots will fit on the rental-ski bindings. New skiers might want to ask about the latest innovation, the micro ski, which is only three-quarters the length of older models and makes turning and learning a breeze on packed snow.

What is base elevation? What is the highest point on your trip likely to be? People who don't do well at high elevations should not pick ski areas in the mountains, and if you have limited time, you may want to avoid areas with high altitudes, where it's important to acclimatize. When traveling from sea level to an elevation of 6,000 ft or higher, avoid strenuous exertion the first few days. Remember that alcoholic beverages affect you twice as fast at higher elevations, and headaches are often a symptom of oxygen depletion and dehydration.

What kids' programs and facilities are available? Many of the adults out on the trails have children under 18. When you bring a child skiing you have to be sure that he or she won't be bored. Ask about day care and baby-sitting, a snow-play area, children's rental equipment, narrowly set tracks for smaller skis and legs, and the availability of insulated sleds that you can use to pull your tiny tot along the trails as you ski.

How far in advance do I need to book? Depending on the popularity of the resort and the time of year, book as much as three months in advance.

SOURCES

Organizations

The **Cross Country Ski Areas Association** (259 Bolton Rd., Winchester, NH 03470, 603/239–4341, www.xcski. org) promotes the sport and aims to protect the interests of operators and skiers. It serves as a clearinghouse of information on where to go and how to get started skiing cross-country.

Periodicals

The Cross Country Ski Areas Association (www.xcski. org) has an extensive Web site with informative articles, a useful resort guide, and links to almost anything you can imagine related to cross-country skiing. *Cross Country Skier* (Box 550, Cable, WI 54821, 800/827–0607 or 715/798–5500, www.crosscountryskier.com) covers U.S. (and a few Canadian) ski destinations, technique, equipment, waxing, and touring tips. *Ski Trax Magazine* (317 Adelaide St., Suite 703 W, Toronto, Ontario M5V1P9, 416/977–2100) is a Canadian publication covering both U.S. and Canadian cross-country skiing; it concerns itself with all relevant topics but emphasizes racing. It's published four times per winter.

Books

In *Cross Country Ski Inns, Northeastern U.S. & Quebec* (Robert Reid Associates), Marge Lamy describes 37 hostelries and their trail systems. The book has excellent color photographs. *Gene Kilgore's Ranch Vacations* (John Muir Press) includes a substantial section on ranches with winter operations. Jonathan Wiesel's *Cross Country Ski Vacations* (Avalon Travel Publishing) is an excellent resource for in-depth planning.

River Rafting

By Lee R. Schreiber
Updated by Julian Tonsmeire

Imagine spray that soaks your clothes and stings your face, the roar of rushing water drowning out your screams, and heart-stopping drops from one ledge to another. But there's relatively little to fear: most guides know every nook and cranny of the river they're running and navigate each potentially bone-crushing rapid or drop with plenty of caution. And white-water thrills aside, rafts can take you places that roads and trails cannot.

The United States has some of the most diverse and scenic river highways in the world, from mild to wild, particularly in the mountains of the West. Many people think the Colorado is the finest rafting river in North America, but there are many that are almost its equal. While some rivers are not dammed and are raftable only during spring runoff, there are others, particularly in the Northeast, whose flow is maintained at runnable levels from spring through fall by regular water releases from the dams.

Many reputable outfitters can show you America's rivers on guided trips, which make even the rowdiest of this white water accessible. Today's rafts are designed to smack against waves or rocks and bend almost in two without breaking or flipping over, and only occasionally do they get "wrapped" (around a rock) or "Maytagged" (tossed and turned, as if in a spin cycle). Rafting isn't as high-risk as you may think—the odds of being seriously injured on a commercial trip are about 25,000 to 1, and there is barely one death per million river runners annually.

Your rafting experience depends first of all on the river. Most provide serenity and the opportunity to catch wildlife unaware, to reach areas deep in the wilderness that would otherwise be accessible only by long hikes. Other rivers stand out for their white water. River rats classify white water as Class I (mild, with slow current and small riffles), Class II (beginner, with moderate waves and rapids, few obstructions, and easy maneuvering), Class III (intermediate, with swift current and more obstructions), Class IV (advanced, with powerful waves and numerous obstacles; previous experience recommended), Class V (expert, with complex and difficult rapids with very strong current and many obstructions). Class VI waters are considered unrunnable, entailing probable serious injury. In general, the steeper the river's drop in altitude, the faster the water and the wilder the ride. (When you encounter water too rough to tackle safely, outfitters either portage around the rapid or resort to "lining"— that is, they empty each boat of all but cargo, then attach it to ropes held by crew members, who walk along the shore guiding the craft through the white water while you go around the rapid on foot.)

Outfitters run some terrific Class IV–V water in the East, including West Virginia's New, Gauley, and Cheat rivers, but almost all the runs are day trips. In the West, trips may last a week or two because western rivers are longer, with longer rapids and stretches of flatwater, and bigger wilderness areas.

Expect the craft you ride to vary from outfitter to outfitter and even from trip to trip; you may even switch from one kind of boat to another on the same trip. Some outfitters use *motorized rafts (also called J-Riggs),* which allow you to cover more miles of river in less time. The downside is the intrusion of noise and modern technology into the wilderness. You may raft in a so-called *oar boat,* on which a guide takes the oars and does the work; no previous rafting experience is required, even on rivers with some serious white water. Or you can run the river in a paddle boat, where you and the other passengers wield the oars under the guidance of an experienced paddle captain; here you may need experience. Some outfitters also give you the option of traveling in *inflatable kayaks* (called duckies or orange torpedoes); these usually accommodate one person and require some skill and strenuous paddling. Still other outfitters use *dories*—flat-bottomed, splay-sided wooden rowboats with upturned ends, which can usually hold four passengers plus a guide and may come equipped with backrests and cushioned seats. Dories were used by Major John Wesley Powell, leader of the first expedition to descend the Colorado through the Grand Canyon in 1869.

Beyond that, every outfitter has its own style. Some take care of all the camp chores and discourage guest participation, while others invite it. Every trip has its own pace, though on most you'll spend four or five hours a day on the river and the rest of the time swimming in pools, picnicking, or hiking. Food on raft trips is invariably tasty (though the freshest foods, like Cornish hens or rack of lamb, are eaten in the first 7 to 10 days and the vegetable lasagnas show up toward the end). On multiday trips, particularly down the great western rivers, expect to pay between $100 and $250 per day plus a gratuity if appropriate.

CHOOSING THE RIGHT TRIP

First pick the river you want to run, then ask questions of the outfitters who run it.

Are you affiliated with any regional or national organizations? Most companies are; it lends a certain legitimacy and provides a higher authority in case a problem arises.

Are you licensed by the state? Licensing requirements vary from state to state, but, in general, they keep outfitters and guides alert to safety and environmental rules.

When you pack your MCI Calling Card, it's like packing your loved ones along too.

Your MCI Calling Card is the easy way to stay in touch when you travel. Use it to call to and from over 125 countries. Plus, every time you call, you can earn frequent flier miles. So wherever your travels take you, call home with your MCI Calling Card. It's even easy to get one. Just visit www.mci.com/worldphone or www.mci.com/partners.

EASY TO CALL WORLDWIDE

1 Just enter the WorldPhone® access number of the country you're calling from.

2 Enter or give the operator your MCI Calling Card number.

3 Enter or give the number you're calling.

Argentina	0-800-222-6249
Bermuda ÷	1-800-888-8000
Brazil	0800-890-0012
United States	1-800-888-8000

÷ Limited availability.

EARN FREQUENT FLIER MILES

Find America *with a Compass*

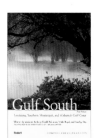

Written by local authors and illustrated throughout
with spectacular color images, the Compass American
Guides reveal the character and culture of more than
40 of America's most fascinating destinations. Perfect
for residents who want to explore their own backyard,
and visitors who want an insider's perspective on
the history, heritage, and all there is to see and do.

Fodor's COMPASS AMERICAN GUIDES

At bookstores everywhere.

What is your safety record, and what are your safety procedures? All rafters should wear life preservers, and commercial outfitters require them (and provide them to all their guests). Helmets are a good idea on Class V and sometimes Class IV water; if you'll be rafting waters with those ratings, ask whether helmets will be provided.

How long has the company been in business? Longevity is often a sign of a company's economic stability. You can generally expect a very high degree of refinement and professionalism from itineraries that have been in use for multiple years.

What's the cost and what's included? Get details about ground transportation, camping and personal gear, meals, and drinks; policies vary widely.

In general, outfitters provide all meals during the trip. However, if the itinerary has you overnighting in a town before your river journey begins or after it ends, you may be on your own for meals. Once the journey starts, most outfitters serve unlimited water, juice, lemonade, or punch on and off the river; soda, beer, or wine is usually available at least off the river.

As for camping gear, many companies provide a tent but charge extra to rent you a sleeping bag and pad (or ask you to make your own arrangements); unless otherwise noted, that's the case on all the trips we list. Personal gear is separate—you may need a wet suit, so ask if it's included.

Shuttle service to and from the put-in point—known as, simply, put-in—is usually included, and it's typically from some central point and not from the airport. Some companies, however, shuttle you to put-in but not from take-out. Don't forget about your car and your luggage; some outfitters transport your luggage from put-in to take-out at no extra cost but charge extra to bring your vehicle.

All prices we quote in the back of the book are adult fares, per person; discounts are usually available for youngsters on trips appropriate for them.

What are your guides' qualifications? Ask how long they have been working with the outfitter and how many years of rafting experience they have. Make sure that they have first-aid certification, if not specialized wilderness first-aid and swift-water rescue training. Knowledge of the history, flora, fauna, and geology of the area is a decided plus.

What's the passenger–guide ratio? The going rate is usually one staffer per three to six passengers.

How many people will there be in your rafting party? The norm is between 20 and 25. If there are too many in your group, you lose a sense of wilderness—and, in some instances, safety could be compromised.

How much white water will there be on the trip? If you are looking for rowdy white water, you don't want to end up on a sedate float trip—or vice versa. If you want to ride in an oar boat or an inflatable kayak, find out how much paddling experience is required. Most outfitters want paddlers to be in good physical condition, and some give a Class V paddler's test, with exercises to evaluate heart, grip, lungs, and mental adaptability; some even give a pre-run oral and written white-water safety exam.

What kind of boats do you use? Find out whether the outfitter uses oar boats, paddle boats, motor-powered rafts, or other crafts. Ask about the maximum boat capacity, and find out how many people will be riding in each boat (some outfitters routinely don't fill boats to capacity). Find out whether the outfitter's boats are self-bailing. Most top companies have gradually replaced their fleets with self-bailing rafts, which are harder to flip than rafts that aren't; a boat full of water is unstable and hard to keep level. If you'd like to paddle part or all of the distance in an inflatable kayak, and you have the experience to do so, ask whether they're available.

What's the food like? Some outfitters stick to home-cooking, while others aim for Continental flair and ethnic accents. Dutch-oven cooking—baking food in a closed pot over an open fire—is fairly commonplace.

What kind of service do you provide? Some outfitters pamper you, some let you help with camp chores, and others insist on it. Decide what you want and find an outfitter that provides it.

What are your days like? Find out how much time you spend on the river, and what you do the rest of the time—whether you'll see wildlife or can go fishing, for example.

What conditions should I expect? Ask if it will be buggy. You don't want to find out later that it's the height of black fly or mosquito season.

How far in advance do I need to book? In most cases, it's between two and six months, but sometimes you must commit yourself even farther ahead, as much as a year in advance. You can always call at the last minute and see if there are cancellations.

SOURCES

Organizations

America Outdoors (Box 1348, Knoxville, TN 37901, 615/524–4814) is an advocacy group of outfitters. **American Rivers** (801 Pennsylvania Ave. SE, Suite 303, Washington, DC 20003, 202/547–6900, www. americanoutdoors.com) is one of the country's leading river conservation organizations. **Friends of the River** (128 J St., 2nd floor, Sacramento, CA 95814, 916/442–3155; Fort Mason Center, Bldg. C, San Francisco, CA 94123, 800/374–8377, www.friendsoftheriver.org) concerns itself with the environment and, among other activities, works on commission with outfitters to arrange rafting trips. The **Idaho Outfitters and Guides Association** (Box 95, Boise, ID 83701, 208/342–1919, www.ioga.com) and the **Oregon Guides and Packers** (Box 10841, Eugene, OR 97440, 503/683–9552, www.OGPA.org) can provide information on outfitters in their areas. The **National Association of Canoe Liveries and Outfitters** (Box 248, Butler, KY 41006, 606/472–2205 or 800/736–2256), which lobbies on behalf of outfitters, can send you lists of outfitters nationwide.

Periodicals

The magazines *Men's Journal* (Box 57055, Boulder, CO 80322, 800/388–2175, www.mensjournal.com) and *Outside* (400 Market St., Santa Fe, NM 87501, 800/678–1131, www.outsidemag.com) regularly cover rafting. *Canoe & Kayak Magazine* (Box 3146, Kirkland, WA 98083, 800/692–2663, www.canoekayak.com), the leading paddle-sports magazine in North America, and the quarterly *Paddler* (Box 775450, Steamboat Springs, CO

80477, 970/879–1450, www.paddlermagazine.com)
cover a broad spectrum of river trips and include product reviews and pieces on paddling skills and techniques.

Books

The Big Drops: Ten Legendary Rapids, by Robert O.
Collins and Roderick Nash, gives a feel for white
water. For ideas about other outfitters, consult *The
Complete Guide to White-water Rafting Tours,* by Rena
K. Margulis, or, perhaps better, the annually updated
Paddle America, by Nick Shears (Starfish Press, 6525
32nd St. NW , Washington, DC 20015), which lists
every outfitter in the country. Also providing good de-
scriptions of the great river runs in the country are
Running the Rivers of North America, by Peter Wood;
*White-water Adventure: Running the Great Wild Rivers
of America,* by Richard Bangs, one of the country's best-
known adventure-travel writers; *White-water Rafting
in Eastern North America* and *White-water Rafting in
Western North America,* by Lloyd D. Armstead; *The
White-water Source Book,* by Richard Penny; *Wild
Rivers of North America,* by Michael Jenkinson; and
Wildwater: Exploring Wilderness Waterways, by Buddy
Mays.

Sailing Schools

By Michael B. McPhee
Updated by Carol Bareuther

Sailing is a wonderfully democratic sport: you don't need exceptional strength, endurance, or wealth to enjoy it, and you don't even need to become an expert. It's also one of the few sports you actually improve at as you get older. And because it takes so many forms—day sailing, offshore cruising, racing—and is affected by the size of the boat, sub-sports have developed for people of all ages and abilities.

There are just over 5 million sailors in the United States today, a number that's increasing by 4% to 5% every year. One reason for this growth is that boats are smaller, lighter, faster, easier to sail, and more maintenance-free than before. The new trend, in fact, is for one-design smaller boats, in the 20- to 30-ft range; these don't break the bank on purchase or maintenance, and they require a minimum of crew. But the main reason, not surprisingly, is money: boats simply cost less, so you don't have to go into debt to buy one. You can get a small boat and everything you need to use it, from a trailer to life jackets, for as little as $3,500. For many, that's no more than the cost of a family vacation.

Sailors are also realizing that, unlike a decade or two ago, it's no longer necessary to own a yacht to sail in some of the world's exotic waters: you can easily fly to Tortola or Fiji and charter a boat, with or without crew. If you bring friends along to split the expense, the trip could end up costing less per person than if you stayed at a hotel.

The catch, of course, is that you can't just sail off alone, without training; sailing requires both knowledge and experience. The good news is that sailing schools are proliferating around the country. In this book we list schools mainly according to the location of their head-quarters; but many schools also offer courses in other regions. You can choose from a range of schools—some cater both to day sailors who want to learn small-boat sailing around a lake or bay to more ambitious sailors eager to try offshore sailing and navigation. And some new sailors enroll in advanced classes with the expectation of chartering a large boat without crew—called bareboat chartering—somewhere in the world.

Sailing has a strange vocabulary, and some of the concepts take getting used to. But, within a week, with good instruction, you can make sense of it all and be on your way. Most sailing school courses range from 1 to 10 days. Plan on three of four days of schooling and sailing to become confident about getting yourself back to the dock. People with mechanical aptitude learn faster, but nearly everyone can pick up the basic skills in less than a week.

If your goal is to learn sailing well enough to charter a boat, it's best to get some sailing experience after beginners' school. You should be comfortable with boat handling, strong winds (over 15 knots), and emergency procedures, and then take at least another five days of advanced instruction and sailing. It's one thing to make a sailboat go where you want it to go; it's another thing entirely to learn how to deal with storms, navigation, currents, and shipping lanes.

Some schools claim they can take beginners and prepare them for chartering in three to five days, but that's a tremendous amount to learn in such a short time. More importantly, sailing is as much experience as it is knowledge—maybe more so—and you cannot expect to learn how to sail in five days and then go out and deal with seriously rough weather. Besides, sailing is supposed to be relaxing—you're only going to go 6 mi or so an hour—so you shouldn't be worried about not having enough experience.

Schools for beginners generally follow three different formats: weeklong courses, two-weekend courses, or courses that last one day or night each week for four or five weeks. Most programs last about 20 hours and offer a combination of three- or four-hour sessions on midweek mornings or afternoons, six- or eight-hour programs on Saturdays or Sundays.

Training is on anything from small 14-ft skiffs and 16-ft catamarans to 30-ft-plus cruising boats equipped with bunks. Some go inland—on lakes and rivers—while others sail on open bodies of water, where tidal currents become a factor. Some stick close to shore, while others take you out into the Great Lakes or open ocean, where learning navigation is a must.

Regardless of the format, expect to spend the first few hours of a basic course in a classroom or on a boat tied to the dock learning the nomenclature, safety procedures, and elementary concepts—for example, how a boat moves against the wind (called points of sail). After that you're actually sailing and putting all that knowledge into practice. If you're learning on a smaller craft, you can usually expect two students per boat while the instructor follows alongside in a powerboat, shouting up to you or addressing the entire fleet of boats with a bullhorn. Larger boats—20 ft or longer—usually carry up to four students and an instructor.

With few exceptions, the day-sailing schools—the ones that teach the basics—offer no food or lodging. When classes end, you're on your own. More advanced students learning how to cruise usually sleep on the boats for up to a week (in extremely tight quarters). Some of these boats stay under sail all night; others anchor in a bay or tie up at docks. Some return to the same port, whereas others sail to a different one each night. But not every moment is spent sailing. There's often time for fishing, sunbathing, and swimming; in the evenings, the student crew sometimes takes dinghies ashore or sits around drinking and telling stories.

Friendships and animosities develop quickly in such close quarters, but learning how to cope with them is part of the training for bareboat chartering. In general, sailing schools are a great way to make new friends, since you're all thrown together in a challenging, confusing situation where everyone's learning. Sometimes you show your vulnerabilities, but you all learn from each other's mistakes as well as your own—that's the beauty of this sport.

Most schools realize that it takes time to remember that port is left and starboard is right, that you pull the tiller to windward in order to fall off to leeward, or that you need to harden the jib sheet (or "trim" the sheet) as you point higher into the wind. Don't worry if you get confused. The names and concepts take time to digest. Very soon, you'll be gliding out across the water agreeing with Rat in *The Wind in the Willows* that "there is nothing, absolutely nothing, half so much worth doing as messin' about in boats."

CHOOSING THE RIGHT SCHOOL

Pay a visit to a school you're considering, if it's nearby, and look at its boats. They should be clean and well maintained. If you see lots of patches on the boats and sails, if the ropes on the sails are frayed and worn, or if there is water sloshing around in the boats, the school probably doesn't take much pride in its fleet or in its program. Once you've narrowed down the choices, ask each school the following questions:

Who are your competitors and what are their weak points? The answer to this may give you some insight into the strengths of the program you're considering. If you're also looking at one of the competing schools, you can ask them to respond to the criticism.

What type of boat does the school use? It makes sense to learn on a boat that's similar to one you hope to buy or rent someday, but ultimately the type of boat you learn on is much less important than the quality of the program. If you're taught well, you'll be able to apply the same principles to virtually any boat (except for catamarans and other craft with more than one hull).

If you're planning to sail small boats, you want to learn on one with a centerboard that can, and should, tip over. (Capsizing should be an important part of any day-sailing program, because you want to learn how to recover—called righting the boat—and continue on your way.) A training boat with an engine allows motoring practice, a valuable part of a modern sailor's education.

If you're learning on a larger, heavier boat, you want one that's responsive, like a J-24, so you can feel every change as the boat responds to the wind and learn how to react quickly and decisively.

Can I continue to take classes until I've mastered the course? Ask about performance (more popular in racing courses) and aptitude guarantees: some schools offer extra lessons without additional cost or let you repeat a portion of the course. Others give a full or partial refund if you're unhappy with the results.

How many hours are spent not just in the boat but also under way, with the sails up? A certain amount of classroom time is necessary so you can learn terminology, safety, and general principles. But you want as much time under way (in motion) as possible—perhaps 70% of the program—because that's when you're learning. The better schools get you in the boats right away, give you basic instruction, and shove you off under close supervision. Ask about the sailing location and how long it takes to get out on the sailing grounds once you cast off. The ideal venue is uncrowded, in protected waters, close to shore or the marina.

If you're planning to go bareboat chartering, you want a learning experience as close to the real thing as possible, so try to sleep on a boat that remains under sail at least a few of the nights. You may have a more fun, relaxed time if you're tied up at a dock every night, but you won't learn as much.

How many students are in each boat, and how much time does each get to steer and work the sails? Expect two students on smaller boats and up to four students with an instructor on boats 20 ft or longer. Divide the hours sailing by the number in your boat to figure out how much time you get to steer or work the sails. Sailing is mostly experience, so make sure the school keeps you busy all the time and has small classes to ensure your constant participation.

Can I be certified on completion of the course? You'll frequently hear the word *certified,* as in, "This course will enable you to become certified." But the truth is, right now there is no single set of standards by which to judge the competency of a sailor other than professional coast guard licensing. However, various organizations are working toward setting those standards, including the American Sailing Association

(ASA) and the United States Sailing Association (also known as U.S. Sailing).

The private, profit-making ASA, based in California, has established two progressive certification programs: a seven-stage Keelboat Sailing Certification Program and a two-stage Small Boat Sailing Program, both of which include beginning to advanced skill training and end with the right to take the ASA certifying exam. ASA schools are concerned with providing a high-quality education, but they're not the final word in sailing schools. In fact, several of the best schools in the country, although very concerned with establishing standards and working hard toward that end, are not members of ASA. Be wary when ASA schools tell you that charter boat operators do not let you bareboat charter their vessels without an ASA certification. This is generally not true. U.S. Sailing is a nonprofit, nongovernmental body that for years set the standards for sailboat racing in the United States, under the authority of the International Sailing Federation (ISAF). Now the outfit is active in recreational sailing as well and has developed a series of certification courses; many are employed by some of the schools we list in this book.

What are the instructors' qualifications? Some of the small-boat sailing schools employ college-age students as teachers. There's nothing inherently wrong with this—but it does say something about the seriousness of the program, and you may want to ask if there are older and more experienced instructors as well.

Some instructors claim a racing background. Don't settle for that as an explanation of experience; responsibilities on a racing boat can be very specialized. The more teaching experience a person has the better. Someone with, say, 10 years of teaching would be great, since poor teachers don't last. It's also a good idea to find someone with significant offshore experience, since offshore sailing requires well-rounded competence.

As for certification, the most universally accepted qualification is a coast guard license, which is common among instructors only in chartering courses. At that level, you should demand it. The ASA also has certification criteria for instructors, as does U.S. Sailing.

What is the school's safety record? Most have stellar records, but don't be afraid to ask. Find out about the last three injuries and their outcomes. If you're day sailing, ask how they plan to retrieve you when your boat tips. Do they have a support boat with an engine? Most schools have a supervisor in a powerboat right in the sailing fleet, ready for anything.

Don't let any school tell you nobody tips over. Schools teaching small-boat and day-sailing courses intentionally capsize the students' boats at the beginning of the course. They test everyone's ability to swim in a life jacket and to recover the boat. You spend the rest of the day drying out. It's a great icebreaker.

What's the cost and what's included? Most daysailing classes provide nothing but instruction; you're on your own for meals and accommodations. Some day-sailing schools, however, let you sleep on boats at no additional charge or offer packages that include room and board. Manuals, notebooks, and certification exams and certificates are usually extra (but not always).

Most live-aboard sailing courses include provisioning (meals and drinks). All day-sailing programs we list in the back of this book do not include food or lodging, unless otherwise noted. For live-aboard programs we tell you whether or not provisioning is included.

Sailing is a sport where learning means doing. Ask about discounts on use of boats, memberships that allow discounted rates on boats, and/or advanced sailing courses or vacation flotillas that let you get in more practice.

SOURCES

Organizations

There are hundreds of reputable programs around the country, particularly for day sailing. The country's two major sailing organizations, the **American Sailing Association** (ASA; 13922 Marquesas Way, Marina del Rey, CA 90292, 310/822–7171, www.american-sailing. com) and the **United States Sailing Association** (Box 209, Newport, RI 02840-0209, 401/849–5200, www. ussailing.com), commonly referred to as U.S. Sailing, list schools by region on their Web sites. ASA has a free two-page member list.

Periodicals

There are numerous sailing periodicals, virtually all of which are worth reading. The biggest difference among them is their target audiences—some are very technical, others are for cruising, and still others are purely for racing.

The monthly *Sail* magazine (98 N. Washington St., 2nd floor, Boston, MA 02114, 617/241–9500, www. sailmag.com) is good on all aspects of sailing, from day sailing to ocean voyages. There's very little for the beginner sailor but lots of sound, practical how-to articles, firsthand tales by fellow sailors, and boat-wanted ads in the back for fantasizing. *Cruising World* (Cruising World Publications, Inc., 5 John Clarke Rd., Newport, RI 02840, 401/845–5100, www. cruisingworld.com) is a monthly magazine written for sailors who cruise on their sailboats but is highly readable for anyone with an elementary understanding of sailing. You'll find stories written from the decks of cruising boats all over the world as well as repair articles, recipes, and humor. *WoodenBoat Magazine* (WoodenBoat Publications Inc., Naskeag Rd. [Box 78], Brooklin, ME 04616, 207/359–4651, www.woodenboat.com) is a very high-quality bi-monthly magazine written specifically for wooden-boat owners and lovers. *Sailing World* (5 John Clarke Rd., Newport, RI 02840, 401/845–5100, www.sailingworld.com) is the authority on performance sailing, with helpful articles on crew organization, tactics, and boat handling. This is a must-read if you're keen on racing. Also check out SailNet online (www.sailnet.com); articles, posted daily, cover such topics as sailing instruction, cruising tips and updates, and racing tactics.

Books

For a good how-to book, try *The Craft of Sail* (Walker), by Jan Adkins. It's a well-written book for beginners, describing how (and why) a boat works; it includes lots of beautiful drawings. *Essential Sailing: A Beginner's*

Guide (Lyons Press) by Roger Marshall is a thorough, fully illustrated handbook with basic instruction for the novice sailor, with photos and drawings throughout. *Sailing: A Woman's Guide* (McGraw-Hill), is by Doris Colgate—whose husband, Steve, started Offshore Sailing School. Colgate's book, a primer for beginning women sailors, provides basic instruction and amusing anecdotes. *Men at Sea* (Random House), by Brandt Aymar, is a collection of the best sea stories of all time. *Royce's Sailing Illustrated,* by H.B. Warren (Fashion Press), is one of a kind. In publication since 1956, it's a comprehensive guide to types of sailboats and rigging, especially dinghies; types of sails; wind direction; tacks and courses; anchors; and reefing. You name it, *Royce's* covers it. *Chapman Piloting Seamanship & Small Boat Handling,* by Elbert S. Maloney, is known as the bible of boating. And, although it's essentially a reference book, it's a fairly easy read. If you're already comfortable in a boat and are more concerned with performance sailing, check out the following books, which are the best on the market: *Advanced Racing Tactics* by Stuart Walker (Norton); *Championship Tactics* by Gary Jobson and Tom Whidden (St. Martin's Press), and *Sailing Smart* by Buddy Melges and Charles Mason (Holt Rinehart Winston). To learn more about wind and the resultant sail trim and sail construction, *Sail Power* by Wallace Ross (Knopf) is indispensable—it covers everything from sail inventory and design to tuning of the rig.

Scuba Diving

By Lisa Skriloff
Updated by Priscilla Burgess

Brilliantly colored creatures swarm around you as you float. You're peering up at the kelp-forest canopy that rests on the ocean surface, watching otters wrap themselves in its fronds to keep from drifting out to sea. Maybe, instead, you're in a freshwater lake that harbors sunfish, catfish, and pike. Or, oddly, perhaps you're in the depths of an artificial reservoir that contains abandoned towns—or a quarry filled with sunken buses, planes, and tractors.

Access to the underwater world is available to just about anyone. Scuba diving doesn't require extraordinary conditioning and strength, and because one of the primary dangers of diving is hypothermia (loss of body heat), a little extra padding doesn't hurt. There are a few essential requirements: you feel comfortable in the water, you don't panic when something unexpected happens, and you're comfortable using breathing apparatus. As for swimming skills, dog-paddling and treading water are about all anyone can do when loaded up with tanks and weight belts.

Any sport enjoyed in the wild is shared with the permanent residents. Some tiny fish are inquisitive and will swim right up to your mask, but most will keep their distance. In popular dive sites, some animals are so accustomed to seeing divers they'll gather round to be fed or petted. Seals, sea lions, dolphins, and porpoises may let you join in their play. As for great white sharks, human beings are not a preferred item on their menu. We're too bony and we lack seals' succulent fat, which is why surfers and swimmers are typically bitten, not eaten. Shark bites are a taste test, often by younger, less experienced hunters. Most sharks immediately realize their mistake and spit out neoprene, fiberglass, and bony legs and arms. Sharks hunt from below their prey, sometimes mistaking humans splashing around at the surface for an injured seal. Divers near the bottom or along walls rarely catch the attention of sharks looking for a meal.

One of the best parts of learning to scuba dive are the stories of experienced divers. Most instructors have endless tales, some perhaps embellished for the listener but wonderful nonetheless. During class breaks, ask your instructor about his or her adventures underwater. Be prepared for shark stories—every diver has some, but if you listen closely you'll soon realize that many of these encounters happened to someone else, far away and a long time ago.

To see if scuba diving suits you—before you go ahead and commit to a full certification course—sign up for a trial dive, known as a "resort dive" (you put on the gear and dive with an instructor). Most dive centers offer resort dives, even places that aren't part of a resort. This doesn't qualify you to dive anywhere else. To do that, you need to take a basic certification course to get a C-card (certification card), which proves you've been trained as a scuba diver. Without a C-card, no reputable dive shop will let you rent equipment or fill an air tank.

With basic certification, you can dive to about 100 ft and explore reefs or weave though chilly kelp forests. Diving on wrecks is also popular, and it gives you a spooky look at history. With advanced training, you can dive in caves or caverns or under ice. Scientific dive training teaches you to capture specimens for biologists or help underwater archaeologists map sunken ships and collect artifacts.

Think twice about bringing your kids along. The minimum legal age for certification is 10 years old. However, a child's lungs (and common sense) are not fully developed at that age, and many instructors will not train children under 15. There's no upper age limit—healthy 70-year-olds have learned to dive without a hitch.

Dive centers or shops offer certification programs, as does the YMCA, which trains divers at their own facilities or colleges. There are four main groups that certify divers: the National Association of Underwater Instructors (NAUI), Professional Association of Dive Instructors (PADI), Scuba Schools International (SSI), and the YMCA National Scuba Program. Since there is no government oversight on scuba training it's best to go with one of these four established groups. Each has its own program, but all provide certification that's honored worldwide.

Training consists of classroom lectures, confined-water training, and, finally, at least four dives in open water. The lectures cover the use of depth charts, explanation of the equipment, and safety information. Confined-water training (usually in a pool) gives you valuable experience using the gear in a safe environment. All you've learned in class and in the pool is to put to use in the open-water dives, which are closely monitored by instructors and dive masters.

Night and weekend classes, which take place over three to five weeks, are taught in every state and Washington, D.C. All certifying groups accept open-water dives in places other than where you did your classroom and pool work. For example, if you did your course work at the YMCA in Omaha, you can have an NAUI instructor in Hawaii sign off on your checkout dives. Tell your instructor if you plan to split your course. Some dive training centers in vacation spots offer distance learning for the course work so when you arrive at your destination you can do just the confined-water training and open-water dives. The way to schedule a scuba-diving vacation, if you're feeling adventurous and don't mind jumping in with your feet first, is to take a four- or five-day intensive course at the location. Be warned, however, that occasionally even people who love the water sometimes respond to being *under* water differently than they had anticipated. Most importantly, give yourself a little time to adjust to the idea, as well as to your new surroundings.

CHOOSING THE RIGHT COURSE

Scuba diving is a safe sport—as long as you follow the proper procedures—so it's important to make sure that dive centers and instructors are scrupulous in following established standards. The best way to find out is by asking someone who is familiar with the place and the people. You can also go to the Web sites of the certifying groups and check that a center claiming to be PADI certified really is. NAUI lists individuals who have been disqualified or who falsely claim NAUI credentials. SSI will tell you who their superstar dive instructors are. You can call any of these organizations to check the credentials of a dive center or instructor who claims affiliation.

Full-service resorts that include hotel facilities and activities are not typically found in the United States. Ask the dive shop about lodging when you call for information.

Here are some questions to ask when you call about scuba-diving courses.

How many years' experience do the instructors have and in what environments? Instructors should have at least three years' experience training divers. Because information and equipment you'll need for tropical dives are different from that needed to dive in kelp forests, try to find an instructor who's familiar with both warm and cool dive conditions.

What certification does my instructor have? A PADI-certified dive center may have NAUI-, YMCA-, or SSI-trained instructors. If you plan to check credentials, you'll need to know the specific qualifications of the instructor you'll have.

How long has the dive center been in business? Find a center that has been in business for at least five years.

What is the class size? A good class size is no more than six students per instructor assisted by at least one dive master (instructor-in-training). A low student–instructor ratio is preferable and more likely off-season.

What's the cost and what's included? It will cost you between $250 and $1,000 for a basic certification course. Courses sponsored by the YMCA are typically less. Many local colleges offer dive classes that anyone in the community can take. The fees we list for scuba centers include course materials, rental equipment, and, in some cases, the purchase of personal items, such as masks, fins, and snorkels. None include food or lodging. Since most dive centers will ask for a deposit, check their refund policy in case your plans fall through.

How often is the equipment overhauled? The maintenance schedule for equipment should be at least twice a year.

How many hours are spent in the pool and in open-water dives? Practical training with the equipment is key. There should be a minimum of 17 hours in confined water and at least four open-water dives.

What kind of dive sites are used for the open-water checkout dives? Since checkout dives are likely to be at your vacation destination, you'll want to pick a place where you can continue to dive after you've finished your course. Underwater scenery varies greatly. In warm ocean waters closer to the equator you'll see coral reefs and schools of tiny colorful fish; farther north, where it's cooler, you'll see kelp forests, garibaldi, lobster, and cunner (bright orange or blue fish that can grow to 15 inches). Freshwater, such as quarries and lakes, has little aquatic life—so vehicles are sunk to give divers something to explore.

Where and when can I dive? Scuba diving takes place year-round along the coasts and in the South. There's no open-water diving in places with severe winters, so a trip to warmer waters will be necessary to finish your course. Check the NAUI, PADI, SSI, and YMCA Web sites (listed below) for a course either near home or at your intended vacation destination.

What will the diving conditions be like? Besides interesting aquatic life, think about temperature and visibility. If you don't like cold water, pick a place like Hawaii or Florida. Visibility is affected by algae blooms (during the warmer season) or particulate matter, such as silt that washes into the water during unusually dry years. Some places, like Florida, are warm and clear year-round.

What kind of accommodations are available? Few dive courses in the United States are part of a resort. If you'll need a place to stay, ask for lodging recommendations when you sign up.

What is there to do in my free time? If you're doing the five-day resort certification training, don't expect to have the time or energy for anything else.

SOURCES

Organizations

There are four certifying agencies:

National Association of Underwater Instructors (NAUI) 1232 Tech Blvd., Tampa, FL 33619-7832 [Box 89789, Tampa, FL 33689-0413, 800/553–6284 or 813/628–6284, www.naui.org.

Professional Association of Dive Instructors (PADI) 30151 Tomas St., Rancho Santa Margarita, CA 92688-2125, 800/729–7234 or 949/858–7234, www.padi.com.

Scuba Schools International (SSI) 2619 Canton Court, Fort Collins, CO 80525–4498, 970/482–0883, www.ssiusa.com.

YMCA Scuba Program 101 N. Wacker Dr., Chicago, IL 60606, 800/872–9622, www.ymcascuba.org.

The following two organizations are useful for information gathering.

Divers Alert Network (DAN) This international nonprofit agency promotes dive safety and sells low-cost dive insurance. The $29 annual membership fee includes an emergency hot line, medical-question line, emergency evacuation (if you're more than 100 mi from home), a first-aid manual, and a subscription to *Alert Diver* magazine. DAN, The Peter B. Bennett Center, 6 W. Colony Pl., Durham, NC 27705, 800/446–2671, www.diversalertnetwork.org.

Handicapped Scuba Association (HSA) This group certifies dive instructors to teach people with disabilities. It has a list of accessible resorts.

HSA International, 1104 El Prado, San Clemente, CA 92672-4637, 949/498–4540, www.hsascuba.com.

Periodicals

While divers prefer to get their information from fellow divers who have experience with equipment or dive operators, four magazines publish articles and information that will help give beginners a sense of the scuba world. Keep in mind that these magazines, except *Undercurrent,* are supported by their advertisers, so be sure to check information before acting on it.

Rodale's Scuba Diving (33 E. Minor St., Emmaus, PA 18098, 800/666–0016, www.scubadiving.com) covers travel, equipment, and underwater photography, and has information on diving in the United States.

Skin Diver (Primedia, Inc., 745 5th Ave., New York, NY 10151, 800/800–3487, www.skin-diver.com) covers dive sites worldwide, but its main focus is dive travel in the warm waters on either side of the equator.

Sport Diver (World Publications, Inc., 460 N. Orlando Ave., Suite 200, Winter Park, FL 32789, 888/333–7234, www.sportdivermag.com) is the official publication of the PADI diving society. Besides information on travel and equipment, you'll find quirkier items, such as a list of Russian dive terms.

Undercurrent (125 E. Sir Francis Drake Blvd., Suite 200, Larkspur, CA 94939, 800/326–1896, www.undercurrent. org) bills itself as the "Private, Exclusive Guide for Serious Divers" and is considered the *Consumer Reports* of dive magazines—it accepts no advertising and therefore is trusted. It doesn't have test laboratories but publishes reviews—by knowledgeable divers—of products and dive destinations. To subscribe, visit its Web site—it's a controlled-circulation publication, so you won't find it at newsstands.

Books

There are two divers' bibles. *United States Navy Diving Manual, Revision 4, Including March 2001 Change A* is the book upon which all scuba training is based—it's the handbook, in fact, for the Navy SEALS. While it may deal with more advanced diving than you plan to do, it's a fascinating read.

NOAA Diving Manual, 4th Edition is the definitive encyclopedia of diving, although it's geared toward scientists. The contents were written by the government's leading authorities on scientific diving and undersea technology. It's published by the National Oceanic and Atmospheric Administration (NOAA). You can order it from NOAA on-line: www.dive.noaa.gov. (Click on NOAA Dive Manual.) It's available in hardcover, softcover, and as a CD-ROM with search capabilities.

If you want to see what diving is all about before jumping in, get Karen Berger's *Scuba Diving, a Trailside Guide.* Another good book for beginners is *Scuba Diving,* by Dennis K. Graver (Human Kinetics, 1999).

For a guide to the Great Lakes, see Cris Kohl's *The Great Lakes Diving Guide.* Kohl, who works with the University of Chicago, is the acknowledged expert on Great Lakes shipwrecks. *The Underwater Explorer—Secrets of a Blue Universe,* by Annemarie and Danja Kohler (The Lyons Press, 1997), has beautiful photography and information about interacting with marine species and preserving marine ecology. Fish identification books are available for all regions of the world.

The Peterson Field Guides series, published by Houghton Mifflin, have books on freshwater fish found in U.S. lakes and rivers, as well as fish that live along the American coasts.

Pisces Press publishes two good books on marine life. *Watching Fishes,* by James Q. Wilson and Roberta Wilson (1992), is a guide to the lives and behavior of coral reef fishes and invertebrates and has a special chapter on shark misconceptions and facts. *Venomous & Toxic Marine Life of the World,* by Patricia Cunningham and Paul Goetz (1996), is both a field guide and first-aid book, with concise descriptions and color photos of hazardous marine species, as well as each species' description, range, habitat, and hazard to humans, and prevention tips. The first-aid section outlines step-by-step procedures for dealing with unpleasant encounters.

Pisces Press also publishes a good series on dive spots. *Diving & Snorkeling California's Central Coast,* by Darren Douglass (1995), covers dive sites in Southern Monterey, San Luis Obispo, Santa Barbara, and Ventura counties. *Diving & Snorkeling Monterey Peninsula & Northern California,* by Steve Rosenberg (2000), includes Monterey Bay, Carmel Bay, and the Big Sur as well as the Sonoma and Mendocino coasts. *Diving & Snorkeling Southern California & the Channel Islands* is by David Krival (2001. *Diving & Snorkeling Texas,* by Barbara Dunn, Janet Myers, and Stephen Myers (1990), covers inland, coastal, and offshore sites, including oil-rig platforms, shipwrecks, and the ancient coral reefs of the Flower Gardens National Marine Sanctuary, in the Gulf of Mexico. *Diving & Snorkeling Hawaii,* by Casey and Astrid Witte Mahaney (2000), describes the best dive sites in

Hawaii's five dive regions: Oahu, the Big Island, Maui County (Maui, Molokini Crater, Kahoolawe, Lanai, and Molokai), Kauai and Niihau, and the Midway Islands. *Diving & Snorkeling Florida Keys,* by William Harrigan (2001), covers the 200 islands of the Florida Keys and its shallow reefs and spectacular wrecks. *Diving & Snorkeling Puerto Rico* by Steve Simonsen (2000) describes dive and snorkel sites around Culebra and Vieques, the Parguera region, and Desecheo Island. *Diving & Snorkeling Guam & Yap,* by Tim Rock (1999), covers dive sites in Micronesia, and the islands of Guam, Rota, and Yap.

Internet

There are countless scuba sites on-line—regional clubs, general information, magazines, newsletters, dive centers, dive travel, and personal pages created by divers. Be cautious, however, and check all information before acting on it.

The National Oceanic and Atmospheric Administration (NOAA) has a terrific dive site (www.dive.noaa.gov); it's one of the best and most complete resources around. It posts weather and tide information, and charts, and lists current research and activities so you can help preserve the world's oceans.

The following sites are managed by individuals who are not sponsored by any of the dive organizations or magazines. Hard-core divers tend to trust information from fellow divers and enjoy the first-person stories. This is also a place to buy and sell equipment.

Scuba Yellow Pages (www.scubayellowpages.com) has information on equipment, dive centers and operators, travel, training, clubs, dive medicine, equipment reviews, and more. Among divers, this is considered one of the most comprehensive sites around.

Scuba Source (www.scubasource.com) has first-person dive stories and chats, including one for women only. You can get free e-mail with dive domains (@divegirl, @divemedic). There's also a bulletin board for buying and selling equipment or finding dive buddies.

In addition to the equipment and dive site information, www.suite101.com/welcome.cfm/scuba_diving publishes articles written by divers—with the sort of offbeat information that doesn't always make it into the magazines.

Scuba Adventurer (www.scubaadventurer.com) provides detailed information about dive sites and shops in Missouri, Oklahoma, Arkansas, Kansas, and Texas. The information is updated regularly and is one of the few that cover the central United States—not an area known for diving.

While the Great Lakes have little in the way of underwater life, they are rich in wrecks. Sponsored by the University of Chicago, the Web site www.chicagosite.org/uasc details the history and locations of wrecks.

Sea Kayaking

By Rena Zurofsky
Updated by Chris Cunningham

Sea kayaking, one of the country's fastest-growing sports, can be as peaceful or thrilling as you make it. More stable than a white-water kayak, more comfortable than a canoe, a sea kayak is maneuverable enough to enter hidden crevices or to beach on spits of sand. Originally designed by Inuit peoples for hunting and swift travel through icy Arctic waters, kayaks are used today in open oceans, sounds, bays, lakes, and slow-moving rivers.

If you don't mind getting a little wet and you're relatively fit, you can easily learn to kayak. The basic stroke is a surprisingly easy push-pull movement done with a double-bladed paddle; most people pick it up immediately. And besides the kayak itself, you don't need much in the way of gear to go sea kayaking. Kayaks come in both single and tandem models and are made from many materials, including but not limited to sealskin (the original kayaks), wood, canvas, Kevlar, fiberglass, and plastic. Some designs are wide and very stable; others are narrow, speedy, and often quite tippy. There are also collapsible, or folding, kayaks, which can be dismantled and packed into a large duffel bag and stored in a closet or taken aboard an airplane. There are open-top kayaks, which don't have the typical cockpit that encloses your lower body. These don't offer as much protection from the elements but are easy to reboard from the water, making them ideal for warm-water coasts—especially if you're paddling out to go snorkeling or swim around.

What kind of kayak do most people use? Standard recreational kayaks generally have a fairly roomy cockpit; you sit with your legs comfortably stretched in front of you and your feet braced on adjustable pedals, which work the rudder of your boat. A spray skirt, made of neoprene, waterproof fabric, or a combination of the two, fits around your torso and stretches around the rim of the cockpit (known as the coaming). It can feel a bit claustrophobic, but its function is to keep water out of your cockpit, not to keep you locked in. If you should happen to be knocked over by a wave, you'll have to release the spray skirt from the cockpit and then slide out—just make sure you practice releasing the spray skirt. You may have to pull the grab loop forward to get the deck of the spray skirt to come free of the cockpit coaming. The real test is to do this—no joke—while you're upside down in the water. Practice in chest-deep water with someone standing by as you release the spray skirt and you do a front-flip out of the cockpit. Once you're out of the kayak there are a number of techniques for getting back aboard and for getting the water out of the cockpit. Learning these skills is part of learning to be a competent sea kayaker.

Don't assume, however, that paddling for a day without capsizing has adequately prepared you to take on even modest crossings. There's a lot to learn, and until you can handle your kayak in a variety of conditions and know how to read tides, currents, and nautical charts, you should go with an experienced guide who has the skills and the equipment to manage a group of clients on the water. (Any reputable outfitter can supply such a guide.)

Sea-kayaking trips with an outfitter generally follow the same basic routine: you and 5 to 11 other paddlers meet one or two guides either at the put-in (where you literally put your kayaks in the water) or at some other point from which you are shuttled to the put-in. On the first day you work on basic kayaking techniques. You usually learn both the wet exit (how to get out of a kayak in the event of a capsize) and self-rescue (how to get back in). On succeeding days, paddling is interspersed with hiking, playing in the surf, improving kayaking skills, and eating M&Ms and peanuts. Itineraries are flexible; how far you paddle each day depends on the ability and stamina of the group as a whole. Although many intrepid sea kayakers do major open-water crossings, it's more common to make modest island crossings of up to, say, 5 mi.

Different outfitters prefer different approaches to guiding, but most station one guide near the front of the group and another near the back to act as "sweep" to make sure the slowest paddlers don't fall behind. Guides are often trained biologists, botanists, or geologists; the best guides are extremely knowledgeable about the locations to which they escort you.

Most kayak outings double as camping trips. You'll be shocked at how much gear can be wedged through the watertight hatches in the front and rear of each kayak: clothes, tent, sleeping gear, cooking gear, food, fresh water, first-aid kit, cooking equipment, and more. Still, even fully loaded, a kayak rarely draws more than a few inches of water, and because of the low center of gravity of its cargo, a packed boat is in fact more stable.

The food on sea-kayaking trips varies in quality. On a true expedition, you're expected to carry your share of the provisions in your boat. To keep weight and volume down, pasta, rice, and beans usually prevail, but some outfitters use miniature freezer packs to carry meats, and many fish along the way. All of the outfitters we list make a point of including as many fresh vegetables and fruits as possible. Keep in mind that on longer trips, if there is no resupply point, you are eventually reduced to rations of dried fruits and few vegetables.

Breakfasts usually consist of granolas, pancakes, oatmeal, or hot multigrain cereal, sometimes eggs and bacon. Lunches are often peanut butter, cheeses, salami, local jams, and homemade breads. Dinners are where an inventive guide can really go to town. Typical are Italian or Mexican menus—still tasty thanks to an appetite sharpened by a day's paddle. You might also be served fish chowders, Thai chicken stews, and curried lentils that would be equally savory on shore. Coffee, tea, and cocoa are standard, and wine is often available.

Food is usually prepared over a campfire or a camp stove. Guides tend to do the work unless chore sharing is required or you offer to help.

Sea kayaking is relatively inexpensive—from $100 to $200 per person per day, depending on whether the trip includes special transportation, such as an air charter. Costs are low because camping is the norm and food supplies are bought in bulk.

CHOOSING THE RIGHT TRIP

When choosing an outfitter, your primary concern should be safety. An outfitter should be equipped with both the proper technical and first-aid gear and should know what to do with them. Question every outfitter carefully so you know what you're getting into.

How long has the company been in business? A couple of years of experience gives an outfitter time to work out problems with its operation and itineraries. All of the outfitters we list in this book have been in business for at least seven years, although many have been leading trips for a decade or more.

How long have the guides been leading trips? The outfitters we list all use guides that have at least seven years of kayaking experience, although not necessarily in a particular location. It's best to have a guide who knows an area really well.

What kind of training do the guides have? Look for outfitters whose guides have successfully completed a guiding course, such as those offered by Outward Bound, National Outdoor Leadership School, and Maine Island Kayak Company, or who have been certified by either the American Canoe Association or the British Canoe Union.

In the United States no certification is required to become an outfitter of guided tours, but training credentials are your assurance that guides and the company they work for have what's needed to take good care of their clients. (There are exceptions: the state of Maine requires that all outfitters be Registered Maine Guides, a license that involves considerable wilderness training and the ability to make fish chowder.)

What is the participant–guide ratio? The recommended maximum is 5:1, although some reputable outfits push to 6:1 or even 8:1 on protected waters—where wind and waves are not likely to make paddling difficult.

How difficult, challenging, and scary is the trip? Keep in mind that if you're interested in a trip but are concerned that it's too advanced for you, most outfitters will give you extra instruction (at a price) before you set out. Be honest with yourself and with the guides about your abilities. Wanting to learn how to handle surf is not the same as knowing how. At best, a novice paddling beyond his or her abilities curtails everyone else's enjoyment; at worst, he or she endangers himself and his paddling companions. Try to take on new challenges with each successive trip, but make sure you evaluate how much you can handle at once—big waves *and* strong currents?

Is seasickness an issue? If you get seasick, some trips just won't be any fun, and you may be unable to keep pace with the group. Small wind waves usually aren't a problem, but bigger ocean rollers might set your stomach off. Watch for Hawaii's giant swells.

What will the weather be? Can you tolerate heat, cold, or dampness? Nothing ruins a trip faster than pervasive discomfort.

What are the accommodations like? Usually you're in tents, but sometimes you sleep in huts or lean-tos or under the open skies. If tents are provided, ask how many people each sleeps.

What's the food like? Some guides are terrific cooks; others don't care about food. Ask for a sample menu.

What kind of boats will you be using? You'll often hear guides talking about "wearing the boat." That means that the kayak becomes an extension of its paddler, a state that makes the paddling experience not only more comfortable but also much more fun. Ask whether the outfitter stocks a variety of boats, so you can experiment until you find the kayak that best fits your weight, strength, ability, and paddling style. This is especially important for women, who are generally smaller and have less upper-body strength than men. If you don't have the strength to paddle a "full-size" sea kayak in challenging conditions, you may find yourself at the mercy of the wind and waves.

What's the cost and what's included? The trips we list start at the point of put-in and include transportation back to that point. Transportation from and to the local airport is not included, although some outfitters provide it at a nominal fee. The trip fee also usually covers meals from lunch the first day to lunch the last. Unless otherwise stated, outfitters on these trips provide all kayaking gear (boats, spray skirts, personal flotation devices, wet suits, neoprene booties if necessary, and paddles), plus tents, cookware, and first-aid equipment, but not sleeping bags and pads.

How far in advance do I need to sign up? For trips offered regularly, 30 days in advance might do. For trips offered infrequently or in faraway places, signing up anywhere from six months to a year in advance is not outrageous. Check for cancellations, too, in case you want to join a trip on short notice.

SOURCES
Organizations
There are many regional kayaking clubs, and most of them actively schedule trips throughout the United States. The best way to find out about outfitters that operate in the areas you wish to visit is to contact the **Trade Association of Paddlesports** (Box 84, Sedro Woolley, WA 98284, 800/755–5228). For listings of kayak clubs check *Sea Kayaker* magazine (www.seakayakermag. com) or *Canoe & Kayak* (www.canoekayak.com).

Periodicals
The bimonthly *Sea Kayaker* magazine (Box 17029, Seattle, WA 98107, 206/789–9536) is devoted exclusively to sea kayaking and offers an in-depth look at equipment, technique, and coastal and inland destinations and journeys. A monthly magazine, *Canoe &*

Kayak (10526 N.E. 68th St., Kirkland, WA 98033, 800/678–5432 or 425/827–6363), includes articles on canoeing and kayaking techniques, destinations, and resources. Bimonthly *Paddler* (Box 775450, Steamboat Springs, CO 80477, 970/879–1450) covers canoeing, kayaking, and rafting; it contains a calendar of events and equipment reviews.

Books

Fully illustrated, *The Complete Sea Kayak Touring,* by Jonathan Hanson, covers basic and advanced techniques and tells you what to wear and how to travel to your put-ins. You'll learn about safety and how to recognize sea conditions in *The Complete Book of Sea Kayaking,* by Derek Hutchinson. *Sea Kayaking: A Manual for Long-Distance Touring,* by John Dowd, covers equipment, techniques, survival skills, and expedition planning. You'll find maps and descriptions of trips along the Northeast Seaboard in *Sea Kayaking Along the New England Coast,* by Tamsin Venn. Its Hawaiian counterpart is *Paddling Hawaii,* by Audrey Sutherland. For the West Coast, check out Joel Rogers' *The Hidden Coast—Kayak Explorations from Alaska to Mexico.*

Ski Schools

By Rosemary Freskos
Updated by Greg Benchwick

Whether you're an expert parallel skier or an adventurous beginner, a ski-school vacation can be life-enhancing. It's *not* the same as going to a resort and taking one or two hour-long lessons. What we're talking about here is intensive skiing—up to six hours daily, with an instructor watching you, drilling you, and pushing you to do your best. Not only do you learn how to ski better, you also learn that if you try harder, you can always improve your skills—on *and* off the slopes.

Nearly every ski resort in the United States has a ski school, but they are not all the same. Some small operations at small resorts offer only short group lessons and private lessons; others have 1,000 instructors teaching programs for every level.

The better (and usually bigger) ski schools hire only the most professional teachers, usually those who are certified by the Professional Ski Instructors of America (PSIA). To get certified, a skier must first take a ski-school instructor-training course and become an instructor. Then he or she can take a PSIA exam. Instructors commonly pass PSIA Levels I and II within two years; passing Level III is a rare achievement that takes from five to eight years. (Most instructors teach for only four years before moving on to other professions.)

There are different methods of teaching people how to ski, but PSIA-certified instructors are trained in the organization's American Teaching System (ATS), which aims to make learning to ski as easy as possible. Following the ATS manual, instructors teach both novices and experts by breaking down the act of skiing into basic movement components: pressure control, edging, rotary, and balancing movements. The ATS allows an instructor to adapt his or her lessons to the particular terrain and to the students' level of skiing ability.

Although the ATS is most popular in the United States, some ski schools also use the Austrian, French, and Swiss teaching methods. With these methods you still need to learn the basic wedge turn, but you learn a different style of skiing. The Austrian style, for example, is more rigid than the American—it emphasizes a stable upper body and strong counter rotation, with legs held together. Alternatively, in the French style you rotate your body and lean into the turns. Some resorts have their own teaching methods, usually variations on the ATS, and some are now using the Perfect Turn method, which was developed by Maine's Sunday River resort (it uses the shape of today's parabolic, or "shaped," skis, combined with a weight transfer, to make easy turns; skiing perfectly, unfortunately, still takes awhile).

No matter which method is used, the quality of teaching at any school is greatly affected by the ski-school director, who motivates instructors and adapts the teaching system to best suit the area's terrain and clientele.

Once you're with an instructor what can you expect? If you've never skied before, expect to spend your first hour learning how to balance, walk around, and climb by side-stepping. Then you learn to slide down a very gentle incline, turn, and, hopefully, stop. The most important lesson is the one on how to fall and how to get up. By the second lesson you should feel secure enough to feel the thrill of sliding while still in control. You'll be making linked wedge turns and steering around obstacles. Those are the basics. Some skiers stay there for years; others get their skis together and make decent parallel turns in three or four days.

Age is no excuse to avoid skiing, but physical condition is. It's best to have all your parts working up to optimum level before tackling the slopes; this lessens the chance of pulled muscles and broken limbs. But even if you're in good shape, don't overdo it. Four to six hours of skiing is only for those in top condition; two to three hours of steady skiing is usually enough for the average person. If possible, avoid beginning your lessons on a weekend, since midweek classes are usually smaller and the slopes are less crowded. It's also less expensive to ski during the week.

Safety is a primary concern of ski areas as well as most skiers. The National Ski Patrol, a well-trained organization of volunteers and paid members, is an important part of every ski area's staff. They help skiers in trouble and try to prevent accidents and promote safe skiing.

CHOOSING THE RIGHT SCHOOL

Many people plan their vacation and then ask about the ski school, but if you're serious about going to ski school you should ask questions about the programs rather than about the resort. Start with these:

How long has the ski school been in business? The more experience the school has, the more smoothly your lessons are likely to go. Generally speaking, any large ski area is going to have excellent programs, while smaller, independent programs may run less smoothly. Make sure these small programs have at least five years of experience.

Who are the instructors and what are their qualifications? At big resorts you are almost guaranteed good instructors. At smaller resorts and private schools you may be choosing from a grab bag. The best instructors, in the end, are the ones with whom you are the most comfortable. If after your first day you don't like your instructor and feel that his or her teaching style doesn't fit, then ask for a new one.

All ski schools will have some PSIA-certified instructors. Having this certification will ensure that your instructor has received instruction in modern ski pedagogy and that he or she is a good skier; however, there are instructors who are not certified who are just as good. Make sure when you begin your lessons to tell your instructor how you learn best. A good instructor will customize his or her class to fit your personal learning style.

How large are the classes, and if I'm the only one signed up for a group lesson will I still get the group rate? The maximum number of skiers for a good class is 10, but it's better to have just six. At most schools you still pay the group rate if you're the only one who has signed up for a group class.

Do you use video for student analysis? Progressive schools film you while you're skiing and use the tape to show you what you're doing wrong (or right). Some even give you the tape at the end of the course. Video analysis can be an invaluable tool for a visual learner and almost all schools now offer it, but sometimes at an extra cost.

What's the cost and what's included? Pricing for ski-school programs varies in a big way. Some schools supply only lessons; others include lodging, meals, lift tickets, and rentals. Unless otherwise stated, the prices we list in this book include your lessons only; when lodging is included, prices are per person, double occupancy. Meals cost extra, except at some all-inclusive programs.

What are the accommodations like? Ski areas have hotels, inns, condos, and, sometimes, bed-and-breakfasts. If you're buying a package, ask for specifics about your room. If you need to book your own accommodations, make sure you know all your options.

What is the food like? Find out what kind of restaurants are on the mountain and if there is a grocery store nearby. In general, you pay for all of your meals. Food at ski resorts tends to be somewhat institutional and very pricey. Big resorts will have one or two excellent on-mountain restaurants.

How far in advance do I need to book? Special programs, such as seminars taught by pro-racers, fill up quickly, so you may need to reserve a spot a few months in advance; other programs will take you on arrival at the resort.

SOURCES

Organizations

Most large cities have local ski clubs and councils that sponsor trips and outings; check the telephone directory or the bulletin boards at local ski shops. State and regional associations publish brochures promoting ski tourism. Among the biggest of these groups are the **California Ski Industry Association** (74 New Montgomery St., San Francisco, CA 94105, 415/265–7201, www.skicalifornia.com), **Colorado Ski Country/USA** (1507 Blake St., Denver, CO 80202, 303/837–0793, www.coloradoski.com), **Ski Utah** (150 W. 500 S, Salt Lake City, UT 84101, 801/534–1779, www.skiutah.com), and **Vermont Ski Areas Association** (26 State St. [Box 368, Montpelier, VT 05601, 802/223–2439, www.skivermont.com).

If you're 50 or older you might consider joining the **Over the Hill Gang** (1820 W. Colorado Ave., Colorado Springs, CO 80904, 719/389–0022, www.othgi.com), a national organization with local chapters that sponsor ski trips and other year-round outdoor activities for members.

Periodicals

SKI Magazine (929 Pearl St., Suite 200, Boulder, CO 80302, 800/678–0817, www.skimag.com), which has articles on all aspects of the sport, is published eight times a year. *Skiing* (929 Pearl St., Suite 200, Boulder, CO 80322, 800/825–5552, www.skiingmag.com), published seven times annually, also has articles focusing on all aspects of the sport. *Freeze* (Box 51444, Boulder, CO 80323, 800/421–8806, www.freezeonline.com), published six times a year, focuses on new-school skiing (big-mountain skiing in steep, extreme conditions). *Freeskier* (1630A 30th St. Post Mailing Box [PMB]272, Boulder, CO 80301, 720/563–0393, www.freeskier. com), which comes out six times a year, also focuses on the new school—so go big or go home (ski hard or stay in the lodge). *Skier News* (Box 77327, West Trenton, NJ 08628-6327, www.skiernews.com) is a hard-news–oriented paper published four times a year.

Books

Handbook of Skiing (Borzoi/Alfred A. Knopf), by British writer Karl Gamma, is a well-illustrated volume covering all aspects of learning to ski. It is especially good for beginners. *Inner Skiing* (Bantam), by Timothy Gallwey and Bob Kriegel, focuses on the psychological aspects of the sport. *SKI Magazine's Managing the Mountain* (Fireside/Simon & Schuster), by Seth Masia, covers terrain-specific problems and tactics for skiers of all levels. *Breakthrough on Skis* (Vintage), by renowned skier-mountaineer Lito Tejada-Flores, is subtitled "How to Get Out of the Intermediate Rut," and Tejada-Flores utilizes some unorthodox methods, as well as clever psychology, to enable middle-level skiers to accomplish that goal.

Surfing Schools

By Rob Aikins

You're sitting on a surfboard in the water, bobbing up and down to the rhythms of the ocean. A sea breeze brushes across your face as you scan the horizon for waves. Suddenly a bump appears on the horizon. It starts to rise. It becomes a full-fledged wave. You turn toward the beach and paddle furiously. As the wave catches up to you, your board picks up speed and starts to move. Jumping swiftly to your feet, you stand up and start riding.

Suddenly the lip of the wave starts to list—over your head. You duck inside its translucent green chamber, skimming the water. Parts of the wave crash behind you, and a rush of air blows you out of the chamber and onto the shoulder of the wave. You grin, exhausted and exhilarated.

This is called a tube, or barrel, ride—and among surfers it's the ultimate maneuver. Nonsurfing observers would probably be more thrilled watching a surfer wipe out. But, for a surfer, a barrel ride can be a truly spiritual moment. It's the kind of experience that makes you consider trading in your desk job for a life in pursuit of endless summers and perfect waves.

Before you can make that barrel-ride fantasy a reality you'll have to pay some dues. Although instruction can help you learn more quickly, the only way to really learn to surf is to paddle out to the breaking waves and try to catch them. It can be a long process. In the old days, instructors weren't readily available. Back then the most common method of learning to surf was to paddle out in big waves and take repeated beatings as you slowly progressed. This method mostly resulted in public humiliation for the practitioner and a few laughs from other surfers as they watched. It was no wonder that many people who tried surfing didn't stick with it. Fortunately, there are now plenty of surf schools to choose from, and the methods of instruction are far more beginner friendly than in the past. A good surf school will encourage you to push your limits while providing you with instant feedback to make your experience more pleasurable.

What you can expect from a qualified surf school? A foundation in all the pertinent aspects of the sport, but *not* skill. You will start out on the beach learning basic terminology, wave knowledge, and technique. After some practice jumping from a prone to a standing position you'll probably enter the water to acquaint yourself with the feel of the ocean and the dynamics of paddling and balancing on a board in the white water. Once you are comfortable, it's time to start catching waves. Usually your instructor will help push you into the wave; he or she may even stand alongside you to steady you so you can experience the feel of standing on a surfboard—if only for a moment. Some schools promise you'll be standing and riding a wave your first day. Most instructors recommend that you take at least four consecutive lessons before you start venturing out on your own (but you'll still be a long way from that barrel ride).

Acquiring wave knowledge and wave judgment are crucial to the craft of surfing. Before you paddle out, whether it's your first or hundredth time, spend some time on the beach watching the waves. Notice where they break and where other surfers are surfing. If you're really new, you may want to avoid large packs of surfers, at least until you're more comfortable being in the water. By watching the waves and the other surfers you can learn a lot—even the wipeouts teach you something.

Wipeouts are not anything to be afraid of (not at a beginner level, anyway). In fact, sometimes they can even be fun. You just take a deep breath, then push your board away from you and let yourself fall. When you come up, do so with your hands covering your head—in case your board is nearby, you don't want to get thunked. After you surface, grab your board and head back out. Just remember that wiping out is part of the sport—everyone, even pros, falls.

It helps to know something about board design when you surf. Basically, a board rides a wave by planing along the water's surface. In general, the longer and wider a board is, the more stability it has and the easier it is to paddle. If you're a beginner, get a board at least a foot taller than you are, and at least 19 inches wide at its widest point. A board that's too thin will make it difficult for you to paddle. If a board's too long, it's tough to maneuver it through the water. Most schools use soft foam boards that are less likely to inflict damage if you smash into them. These boards are good for learning but aren't as responsive in the surf—once you get to a point where you are starting to progress.

So why should you try surfing, and what kind of crazy person wants to venture into the ocean and ride, of all things, *waves*? If you're an intrepid soul and you don't mind being tossed around under and above water, chances are the surf won't scare you off. Keep in mind that surfing is more popular than you think—trends prove that the Hollywood version of the surfer "dude" is, absolutely, an anachronism. Boards are lighter and more maneuverable for beginners, and instruction has grown more competent. Because of this there are a lot more adults—and particularly women—braving the waves. After all, when the sport started, in Hawaii, men and women of all ages surfed the tropical waves together.

CHOOSING THE RIGHT SCHOOL

Learning to surf without instruction can make your experience much less productive; it's also inherently dangerous. The following questions will help you choose a surf camp.

How long have you been teaching and what certifications do you have? There is no official certification to become a surf instructor, but your instructor should have a few years of experience teaching and definitely a CPR and first-aid card. You should also try to find an instructor with whom you have a rapport—someone who will encourage you to find your personal limits but not exceed them.

How many students are there per class, and how many instructors per student? This figure can give you a good idea how much supervision and instruction you'll get. The more personalized the attention, the more likely you are to progress swiftly. A school with no more than a 1:3 instructor–student ratio will ensure that you enough personal attention.

What's the cost and what's included? All the schools we list in this book provide you with the equipment necessary to get you surfing: a suitable board, a leash, and a wet suit (if necessary). Find out whether they use soft foam boards or hard fiberglass boards. Most schools use at least some, if not all, soft boards, as these are better for beginners (they are less likely to hurt you when you wipe out).

What is the average age of campers? Most camps offer separate programs for adults and children. For children's programs the minimum age depends more on the camper's social and athletic abilities than anything. Most schools accept students 10 and up.

What are the accommodations like? At most surf camps you'll either be sleeping in campgrounds near the water or dormitory-style. If you're not comfortable in those surroundings, most schools will recommend better places to stay in the area.

What's the food like? Most schools serve fresh food with an emphasis on healthy cooking. If the classes are small, the instructors may personalize the menu according to campers' preferences. If you have any special dietary needs, let them know ahead of time.

What is a typical day of instruction like? The basics of surfing and the curriculum will be similar anywhere you go, but most schools have different ways of dividing up the day. Some let you surf all day or until you get tired. At others you surf in the morning and go sightseeing or indulge in other adventures in the afternoon. All schools, however, coach you in basic ocean knowledge and understanding waves. Take as a given you'll be tired but relaxed by nightfall.

When do surf camps take place and how far in advance do I need to book? Most camps limit enrollment to give students proper supervision—so classes can fill up. Book as far in advance as possible; some camps require up to a two-month advance notice. Most schools run surf camps during the summer and give lessons year-round or during the winter only (including private, corporate, and group lessons).

SOURCES
Organizations

Surfers by nature are not inclined to join groups. Most surfers' organizations are small clubs based around a particular surf break. The major exception is the 35,000-strong **Surfrider Foundation** (Surfrider U.S.A., Box 6010, San Clemente, CA 92674-6010, 949/492–8170, www.surfrider.org). This international environmental organization works to educate the public about the importance of our oceans to the health of the planet and also as an advocate working for the protection of and access to marine and coastal environments.

Periodicals

In addition to *Surfer Magazine* (www.surfermag.com) and *Surfing Magazine* (www.surfingthemag.com), the two leading surf publications, there are now surf magazines dedicated to various niches in the sport. *SG Magazine* (www.sgmag.com), a sister publication to *Surfing Magazine,* was launched in 2002; it covers all aspects of the rapidly growing women's board sports culture, including surfing, skateboarding, and snowboarding. *Longboard Magazine* (www.longboardmag.com) is dedicated to those surfers who prefer to ride more traditionally designed surfboards known as longboards. Another newcomer, *Transworld Surf* (www.twsurf.com), is geared toward a younger, teenage crowd. All surfing magazines are heavy on photographs and all run features on hot surfers and cool surfing spots, new maneuvers, contest results, and political surfing issues, and do something about surfing culture and the history of surfing.

Books

Surfer's Start-Up: A Beginner's Guide to Surfing (Tracks Publishing), by Doug Werner, is an easy-to-read book that covers equipment and technique. It also captures the spirit of surfing and tells you how to survive localism (surfing's rigid pecking order) during the first year.

Tennis Camps

By Susan Farewell
Updated by Brad Weiss

Whether you've just taken up the sport or you're a top seed at your club, time at a tennis camp can do wonders for your game. There are dozens of options—some camps are held at college campuses or ski resorts in summer, and some are posh and in glamorous locations. A few were built just for teaching tennis, and a handful are under the auspices of some tennis great and/or run by pros who have built their reputation by teaching.

Some camps will give you a weeklong, six-hour-a-day tennis-a-thon, while others offer a vacation with tennis as the primary—but not the only—activity.

Most camps aim to refine and improve your existing style of play. Others—they're rare—have you relearn the game their way. There is a host of teaching styles, and each camp has its own repertoire of drills.

No matter where you go, you should be beyond beginner level, and you need to be in good condition. After all, you're just cheating yourself if you can't keep up with the drills.

Five- to seven-day tennis-camp programs usually involve working over all aspects of the game, from serves, strokes, and net shots to strategy for both singles and doubles play. Nearly all begin by evaluating your ability and grouping you with others at your level. Depending upon the camp, you either move from pro to pro during the day or stay with one pro for the duration. At some point during your stay, the staff videotapes you and analyzes your game during the playback. (Sometimes you get to keep the tape.) Most tennis camps have ball machines; sometimes you use them under the instructor's eye, and sometimes they're for extracurricular practice. Instructors might be former pros, new-to-the-tour pros, people who've developed some particular method, or, occasionally, a superstar teacher—someone who achieved fame and fortune for his or her teaching abilities and methods alone. You will sometimes see it mentioned that a camp's instructors are members of the United States Professional Tennis Association (USPTA), and while this does signal their status as professional tennis players, it isn't an endorsement of them as teacher.

A big selling point at many schools is the number of hours you're on the courts each day and the ratio of students to instructors. Generally speaking, the more hours on the court and the fewer students per instructor, the better. But five hours on the court at a program with a 6:1 ratio may be no more rewarding than three hours in a program with twice the number of instructors.

Off court, most tennis camps fall somewhere on the comfort spectrum between courtside boot camps and exclusive private clubs. Accommodations vary dramatically, sometimes even within the same camp. At tennis camps on college campuses, you usually sleep in no-frills dormitories, where you share a room with at least one fellow camper and use a bathroom that's down the hall. When the camp is held at a resort, you may wind up in anything from your standard hotel room with two double beds to a luxurious suite with a fireplace, patio, and amenities galore. Most resort camps offer a tuition-and-lodging package; if you don't like the basic quarters it includes, you can usually pay extra for an upgrade. When the camp is on a college campus, you eat institutional cafeteria fare; when you're at a fancy resort, menus are fancy, too. Resort programs usually include access to other recreational facilities as part of the package. Several also have luxury spas to cater to their high-end clientele.

Nearly all camps also offer weekend programs. These have increased in popularity over the past few years, especially at camps within a few hours' drive of major cities. The schedule of activities tends to be the same as those in the five- to seven-day programs.

Although tennis camps can cost anywhere from less than $500 to more than $2,000 for five to seven days, most run between $700 and $1,200. The cost for week-end courses is generally half that of the five- to seven-day courses.

CHOOSING THE RIGHT CAMP

What are the accommodations like? They could be anything from spartan dorm to posh resort hotel. Know what you're getting into.

What is the food like? A camp's cuisine takes its cue from the setting: you eat institutional fare on college campuses and feast on more ambitious dishes at luxury resorts. Whatever the case, also find out what your options are if you feel like a change of pace.

What's the cost and what's included? Unless otherwise noted, the prices we list in the back of this book are per person and include lodging, based on double occupancy, and meals.

What are the teachers' credentials? Even at a camp run by a well-known player or teacher, you spend lots of time with other instructors; find out who they are, and ask about their playing and teaching experience. They should be USPTA certified.

How long has the camp been run? If the program is new, be particularly careful to find out about the people in charge and their plans for the camp. The program should be well conceived and well organized. It should, at minimum, offer daily strategy and technique improvement sessions—some schools even provide detailed video analysis of your game after drills or match play.

What's the ratio of students to instructors? The program should not have more than five players per instructor. The top programs may go as low as a 3:1 student–instructor ratio.

And how many hours each day do you spend on the court with your instructors? Programs generally range between three and six hours of court time with instructors per day. This is a good indicator of how rigorous the program will be. If your primary interest is in improving your game, make sure you get at least five hours of instruction per day.

What's the ratio of students to courts? Even with a good student–instructor ratio, too few courts means lots of time spent waiting around for your turn. The ideal ratio would be two players to each court, but don't count on seeing that too often; 4:1 should be fine, since not every student will be on the court at all times.

How physically demanding is it? Find out what drills are involved and how many hours a day you spend doing strenuous physical activity. Then decide whether you want to commit yourself to that level of work.

Are courts covered in case of rain? You don't want to risk losing tennis time to inclement weather.

What are the court surfaces? Trying out all the different surfaces is important, but you may want to hone your skills on the surface you play on at home.

Is there unlimited access to tennis facilities during free time? You want to be able to try out your new moves while the lessons are fresh.

Are courts lighted for night play? This extends the amount of time available for extracurricular play.

You'll also appreciate lighted courts if you're there when the weather is hot.

What's the clientele? Some camps attract mostly singles, while others are more popular with couples and groups of friends traveling together, or people of a similar age. The more expensive the program, the older the crowd. Unless otherwise noted, all of the camps we list attract a varied group from their twenties to sixties.

How social is the program? Some programs have a lot of planned, off-court socializing, and some don't. If you want to play all day and party into the night, don't choose a program whose campers regularly turn in early.

How far in advance do I need to sign up for camp? Few camps have a strict deadline, but all recommend reserving as early as possible. This is especially true for traditional holiday or vacation times and for camps held only seasonally. Still, if they've got the room, they'll sign you up at the last minute.

Is laundry service available? The answer to this determines how many complete tennis outfits you need to pack.

SOURCES
Organizations
United States Tennis Association (Membership Department, 70 W. Red Oak La., White Plains, NY 10604, 914/696–7000) is a nonprofit organization established in 1881. Membership benefits include USTA league and tournament programs; discounts on apparel, publications, videos, and travel packages; and annual

subscriptions to the monthly newsletter "Tennis USTA" and *Tennis Magazine.*

Periodicals

Tennis (810 7th Ave., 4th floor, New York, NY 06611-0395, 212/636–2700, www.tennis.com) is a monthly magazine with how-to tips, features on professional players, tennis resort information, and fitness tips. *Tennis Week* (15 Elm Pl., Rye, NY 10580, 914/967–4890, www.tennisweek.com) has professional tennis news, racquet roundups, book reviews, and how-to information. *Tennis Magazine* (available through the USTA; *see above*) prints a comprehensive list of tennis camps and clinics every year in its February issue.

Books

There are lots of instructional books available. A current favorite is *Winning Ugly,* by Brad Gilbert (with Steve Jamison), which details Gilbert's technique for outsmarting an otherwise superior opponent. A great read is W. Timothy Gallwey's *The Inner Game of Tennis* (Bantam Books).

Wilderness and Survival Schools

By Andrea E. Lehman

Consider living in the wilderness with little gear or food, using skills you've just been taught and your wits, along with those of your fellow adventurers, to survive. Sound daunting? Exhilarating? Life-changing? A wilderness-skills or survival school can be all of these—most programs teach skills but also try to foster personal development. It's no cakewalk, but the training will help you feel more confident among natural surroundings.

How elemental do you want to get—do you want to learn to survive in the wilderness with few resources or do you simply want to accrue some good outdoor skills? Survival schools generally teach you to live outdoors with little or even no gear. You may navigate cross-country without tents or sleeping bags, learning to make your own shelter, build a fire, fashion tools, and forage for food and water. Outdoor-skills schools, on the other hand, teach some of these same lessons but generally allow gear—they emphasize learning how to manage in the wilderness so you can *avoid* survival situations.

Either type of program may include a solo—a day or more when you're on your own in the wilderness. It's a time to practice what you've learned, reflect on who you are, and think about where you're going. Key to all programs is some kind of personal growth—strengthening leadership, mentoring, or team-building skills; becoming more attuned to nature; or facing and succeeding at your own personal challenge. Courses take place all over the country, in all kinds of surroundings, and may last anywhere from one week to several months.

Underpinning all these programs is solid, basic instruction in conservation, environmental protection, and safety skills. Most courses teach the rudiments of navigation, food planning and preparation, equipment maintenance, water purification, wilderness first aid, and wilderness safety. Some also teach natural history and local history and culture, especially Native American lore.

It helps to be moderately fit before you go on a trip, but there's really just one requirement: you must be willing to throw yourself into a wilderness situation. You'll have to judge whether you are ready for a hard-core survival experience or not. In most programs, any meals provided are generally simple—designed to fuel the body, not the soul—and you may have only two per day. Whether you travel from place to place or spend a week or more in a single location, you'll be learning every day: fire building, shelter building, navigation with a map and compass, or plant lore, for example. Free time is at a minimum. And since you will be with instructors or other students much of the time (solos notwithstanding), there's little room for privacy.

Though program fees vary with type and location, a typical weeklong course averages about $100 or more per day. You won't get many creature comforts for the price, but you're likely to have an unforgettable experience in a wilderness setting grander than any luxury hotel.

CHOOSING THE RIGHT PROGRAM

There are plenty of questions you should ask the staff at the programs you're considering—and many questions to ask yourself, too.

What's the school's safety record, and how long has the school been in business? Most wilderness-skills schools and survival schools have excellent safety records; avoid any that has a history of accidents. If you find there are many accidents, inquire about the nature of those accidents, why they occurred, and what steps the outfit has taken to improve safety.

What are the leaders' qualifications? At least one instructor in each course should have first-aid training. Wilderness first-aid training, which is slightly different, is an even better qualification. A leader who's an expert on leadership training may not be an expert on winter conditions or on local flora and fauna, history, geology, and ecology. Make sure your instructor is knowledgeable about topics that interest you.

What is the student–teacher ratio? To get the most out of a course, look for a small student–teacher ratio. Smaller groups are better because you'll learn more. In courses that move from point to point, five students per instructor is a good number. For base camp or classroom courses, the number can be higher.

What are food and accommodations like? Some courses allow more creature comforts than others. Think carefully about what you're willing to do without for the duration, and make sure the program doesn't ask more of you. Most schools forbid alcohol and recreational drugs and recommend kicking the caffeine habit before you leave home. Some courses limit your food intake or give you a diet made up largely of grains and legumes. These measures are not intended to starve you but to simulate either a camping experience where you're carrying as little as possible or a survival situation where food is not abundant. Depending on the terrain, weather, insects, and course philosophy, sleeping arrangements vary from staying in wind-tight tents to dozing under the stars without so much as a blanket. Some courses don't allow you to bring a change of clothes, and you may use local plants as toilet paper.

What is the school's focus and approach? Survival-skills courses are generally tougher than outdoor-skills courses, which primarily teach you how to camp responsibly *with* gear. At some schools, students and instructors work out a plan together; at others, the instructors alone know the distances—that safety is so many hours or miles away—to simulate a more realistic survival situation.

But courses vary in more ways than just how much equipment, food, or information you'll have to work with. Some curricula encourage students to become leaders or work together as a team. Others focus on challenging participants to go beyond the familiar and to take personal risks. Still others dwell on spirituality or environmental responsibility. If you want to learn about the geology or biology of an area—or any other subject—ask in advance if it's covered. Some schools expect students to undertake service work, such as maintaining trails. And in many courses, the itinerary may vary from session to session, as weather and participants' fitness levels and skills dictate.

What kind of people participate? Some trips bring people of all ages together, and some are more specific—designed for those under 18, over 30, over 50, families, women, environmental educators, or those going through life changes. If you're interested in a course for a particular group, ask.

Does the school offer a solo? Not all courses include a solo. The solo experience is a period of reflection, abstinence, and consolidation of your newly learned skills. You're settled in one spot and monitored regularly by an instructor. If you don't know how you feel about spending time alone in the wild, talk to a staff member from the school. Many people regard the solo as the best part of the trip.

What's the cost, and what's included? Prices generally include instruction and whatever meals and basic camping equipment (tarps or tents and sleeping bags if you will be using them) are provided for your time in the wilderness. Sometimes outdoor clothing can be rented. Transportation to and from the staging area is not included.

How fit do you have to be to participate? Daily exercise and some aerobic activity a few times a week is excellent training for these trips. If you don't exercise regularly, you can still go on most courses; you'll just have to work harder. Some courses have very strenuous elements, however, so be sure you know what's expected before you sign up.

How far in advance do I need to book? Sign-up ranges from one month to a full year ahead.

SOURCES

Organizations

The nonprofit **Wilderness Education Association** (900 E. 7th St., Bloomington, IN 47405, 800/855–4095) promotes wilderness education. Membership includes subscription to the "WEA Legend" and the "Outdoor Network," quarterly publications.

Periodicals

Compass: The Outward Bound Alumni Newsletter (Rte. 9D , 888/882–6863) a slim, 16-page newsletter published two or three times a year and is distributed free to alumni. It is devoted to alumni news, instructor profiles, updates on land use, course descriptions, and journal entries. *The Journal of Experiential Education* (2305 Canyon Blvd., Suite 100, Boulder, CO 80302, 303/440–8844) is published three times a year by the Association for Experiential Education, whose members are people involved in wilderness and other outdoor programs.

Books

The New Wilderness Handbook, second edition, by Paul Petzoldt (considered the grand old man of wilderness education) with Raye Carleson Ringholz, covers a range of outdoor skills. The *Outward Bound Map & Compass Handbook,* by Glenn Randall, teaches you how to get from here to there and back again. Although it can't substitute for actually taking the course, the *Outward Bound Wilderness First-Aid Handbook,* by Jeff Isaac and Peter Goth, is a good reference guide. *Tom Brown's Field Guide to Wilderness Survival,* Tom Brown's *Field Guide to Nature Observation and Tracking,* and *The Tracker* (an autobiography) are just three of many titles by or about Tom Brown Jr. Not a guidebook but a thoughtful exploration of the area and its people, *The Pine Barrens,* by John McPhee, is definitely worth reading if you're planning to take one of the Tracker's courses.

Windsurfing Schools

By Elizabeth Gehrman

Once you experience that first rush of the wind in your sail—and the first crush of the sail in the water—don't be surprised if you find yourself addicted. Also known as boardsailing and sailboarding, windsurfing was invented in California in 1968 and continues to gain converts as equipment, maneuvers, and teaching methods evolve. Don't worry about being strong enough—more than biceps you need balance and stamina, and even kids can handle size-appropriate sails.

The easiest, quickest, and least frustrating way to pick up skills is through professional lessons at one of the many schools around the country. If you try to teach yourself or learn from a friend, you may get frustrated and lose interest. Though time on the water is ultimately the only way to improve, a professional instructor will get the basics across and have you up and sailing quickly. You'll find windsurfers—and windsurfing instructors—pretty much anywhere you find flat water in the United States, and most seaside vacation resorts offer inclusive learning packages that can provide everything from professional instruction to equipment rental, ground transportation, accommodations, dining, and alternative activities to fill those windless days.

Instructors who have been certified to teach by the U.S. Windsurfing Association or the U.S. Sailing Association follow various methods, but most break down windsurfing into easily understood components learned on a dry-land simulator (a small board mounted on a swiveling platform that simulates the experience of being on water). You'll get a feel for proper stance and learn to uphaul the sail, catch the wind, and perform a self-rescue before ever touching the water. Learning how to tack comes shortly thereafter, then learning how to jibe—turning the sail downwind by walking around the mast on the board's nose end—though of course it all seems a little easier on the relative consistency of dry land. An average of three hours of daily instruction, both on land and water, often includes being videotaped while you test your skills in the surf. This is followed by solo practice for as long as your strength holds out. Class size is often limited to four or five students.

Beginners use large boards, for greater stability, and small sails, which catch less wind and are therefore easier to control. At the intermediate level, windsurfers graduate to smaller boards, which require the ability to do a "water start"— holding the sail upright while stepping onto your board to get going—as opposed to an "uphaul," where you start by standing on the board and hauling the sail up out of the water. Bigger sails also come along at the smaller-board stage; they're more challenging to control and allow the board to go faster. Most serious windsurfers own a variety of sail sizes and boards and choose which to rig depending on the day's wind speed.

Virtually any body of water will do, from inland lakes—ideal for learning because of their warm, flat waters—to open ocean, where swells and chop offer bump-and-jump challenges for experienced sailors. Though windsurfing is generally a very safe sport, it is crucial for beginners, especially, to remember a few safety points. First, stay warm by wearing a wet suit, if necessary, and stay safe by frequently slathering on plenty of waterproof sunscreen. Sunglasses with a sports cord are also a good idea, since the water's glare can be blinding.

Until you really know what you're doing, never sail on a day when there's an offshore breeze, as you can be blown quite far out to sea before you even realize what's happening. You can learn a lot about reading the wind from other windsurfers, who are usually eager to share their knowledge. It's smart to familiarize yourself with the waters you're navigating; if your fin hits an underground pier, you'll regret not having glanced at a chart or talked to one of the beach's "regulars." Know where swimmers are likely to be, and also where you might encounter boat traffic. Don't let yourself get so fatigued you can't swim back to shore if necessary, but prepare for the possibility that you might find yourself stranded by learning the international distress signal—sit on your board and repeatedly wave your arms over your head and back down to your sides. Never sail alone, don't sail above your skill level, and above all, keep your eyes on the "road"—high-speed crashes can be pretty nasty.

Windsurfers agree that the top spots for beginning windsurfers are Cape Hatteras in North Carolina, Miami and the Florida Keys, Aruba, and Hawaii. Not only do windsurfing schools in these locations offer instructional packages and the best wind and surf conditions for learning, they also happen to be lovely vacation destinations.

People who are serious about windsurfing plan their holidays around it and will trek all over the world in search of the perfect breeze. If you happen to be traveling with someone who doesn't share your enthusiasm for projectile boating, it's easy to find destinations that will appeal to you both. A few excellent choices: Maui; Egypt's Red Sea; Lake Garda, Italy; and anywhere in the Caribbean.

The cost of a weeklong trip can vary greatly but in general averages around $700, including lodging and meals (bring your own wet suit unless you don't mind renting a used one). Ground transportation, if needed, is usually part of the package: a bus or van is used to carry gear and shuttle students between the learning site and lodgings, out for meals, and to slack-day activities (if they're included in the package).

CHOOSING THE RIGHT SCHOOL

Operators will sell space as available up to the last minute, but you should try to book at least 60 to 90 days ahead to make sure you get a spot, especially during peak seasons (generally peak is our summer, but it varies slightly, depending on where you're going).

Check www.worldwindsurf.com for a comprehensive overview of windsurfing schools worldwide, listed by area. The site has nearly 1,500 links to other sailboard-related sites and covers the entire United States by region, overseas destinations from exotic Thailand to the sublime Greece, and, for the truly obsessed, places you may not have considered getting soaking in, such as chilly England and Belgium. Devotees monitor wind and weather conditions before deciding whether to schlep out to the beach and which rigs to bring if they do; forecasts for many parts of the country are listed, along with other useful information, on www.iwindsurf.com.

In picking a windsurfing school, it's important to ask the following questions:

How long has the school been in operation? You want an experienced outfit with a good reputation, not a fly-by-night school. There are no industry regulations for windsurfing schools, but those around for at least three years are generally trustworthy.

What is the location like? Beginners do better on flat, calm waters with steady but mild breezes. Warm water, a sandy bottom, and perhaps some nearby shopping and nightlife will add to the experience.

What are the teachers' qualifications? Professionals are certified in a five-day course, during which they are trained to teach all levels of skill. Check to make sure your instructor is certified.

Are land simulators used? Practicing the basics on a simulator cuts down the learning time considerably.

How long are classes, and how much time is spent on land and versus on the water? Beginners usually spend 15 minutes to a half hour of the class time on land getting a feel for the basic skills before getting wet. Two two to three-hour classes should be enough to give you the confidence to go out on your own; the latest equipment is so stable, as one instructor said, "If you can walk on a dock, you can windsurf." Intermediate and advanced students rarely take classes, but when they do, they look for a school that emphasizes in-water instruction.

Is the equipment current? Equipment is frequently modified to make sailing easier and faster, so it's best to learn on the latest gear rather than on old rigging that will just slow you down. If you're traveling with children, make sure the outfitter has up-to-date smaller boards and sails available.

Must I rig and carry the equipment? Some schools rig for you to get you on the water as soon as possible; others want you to learn to rig and have you do it yourself each time—a valuable skill to have once you go out on your own.

What's the cost, and what is included? Prices listed are usually per person, double occupancy, and include lodging, equipment, meals, and airport transfers.

Every program varies, however, so check carefully before booking your trip. Occasionally, personal gear (harness, wet suit, gloves, booties or sailing shoes, and so on) is included in the package. Some schools are moving away from inclusive packages but do provide assistance in booking nearby accommodations, often at discounted rates. If the school you're interested in no longer offers an inclusive package, you'll be on your own for meals and transportation as well.

Is a rental car necessary? Most outfitters transport the gear to the water if needed, but there are schools that require you to have a car to transport the equipment. Obviously, this will add to the expense of your trip. On the other hand, renting a car gives you the flexibility to have a meal on your own or go sightseeing.

Are other activities available on windless days? You don't want to waste your vacation just because there's no wind, so pick a school that provides alternative activities to fill those slack days. Is it near an active town, or is it located in an area that's conducive to participating in other sports, such as hiking and mountain biking.

What's the food like? Expect a huge range in dining options on these trips—from hamburger cookouts to home-cooked buffets to restaurant meals.

What are the accommodations like? Some schools put you up in tents, others in hotels or small inns. When you book, be sure to ask whether laundry service is available and whether breakfast is included in the cost of the room.

SOURCES

Organizations

The United States Windsurfing Association (326 E. Merritt Island Causeway, Suite 300, Merritt Island, FL 32952, 321/453–7765, www.uswindsurfing.org) is a membership organization. Its mission is to promote safety, water access, water quality, member clubs and associations, racing for all levels, and more. Its Web site offers, among other things, a searchable database for events in your area, and a Windsurfing Travel Partners program: a $100 membership fee will not only help you find like-minded individuals but will also get you a 10% discount at many resorts.

Periodicals

New England Windsurfing Journal, published nine times a year, covers sailboarding in the Northeast, with articles on destinations, schools, equipment news, and current events (Buzzwords Publishing [Box 371], Milford, CT 06460, 203/876–2001, www.worldwindsurf.com/newj). *WindSurfing Magazine* profiles equipment, destinations, and occasionally lists schools. It comes out seven times a year (World Publications Inc., 460 N. Orlando Ave., Suite 200, Winter Park, FL 32789, 407/628–4802; 800/879–0480 subscriptions; www.windsurfingmag.com).

Books

Good introductory guides are *Start Windsurfing Right* (United States Sailing Assn.), by Eleanor Boober, and *Windsurfing: Step by Step to Success* (Crowood Publishing), by Rob Reichenfeld.

Resources

ARCHAEOLOGICAL DIGS

Crow Canyon Archaeological Center

www.crowcanyon.org
23390 Rd. K
Cortez, CO 81321
800/422–8975, 970/565–8975

Established in 1983, this outfit runs full-service experiential-education programs domestically and abroad, for many different skill levels, and also for families. Domestically they focus on the Four Corners region (Utah, Colorado, New Mexico, Arizona). Mesa Verde, Colorado, is hugely popular; the region has extensive ruins from many different periods. Campus-based programs involve students for research; other programs explore the Southwest. Native Americans from the region being explored are often involved in research and education.

One-week domestic programs, $800–$1,595, including backcountry archaeology (hiking into remote sites) or advanced ceramic analysis.

Earthwatch

www.earthwatch.org
3 Clocktower Pl., Suite 100
Box 75
Maynard, MA 01754
800/776–0188

Since 1972 Earthwatch has held hundreds of programs worldwide, from underwater excavations to predator observation. Scientists, educators, and volunteers have contributed to research-oriented work with an emphasis on physical and biological sciences and conservation.

Membership fee $35 individual, $55 two people; project fee $1,000–$1,800 for several weeks. Research, travel, and lodging costs, prorated among participants, are specific to each project.

Four Corners School

www.fourcornersschool
Box 1029
Monticello, UT 84535
801/587–2156

Educational adventures in the Colorado Plateau include archaeology, excavation, mapping and surveying sites, drawing and photographing features and artifacts, or quests to see rock art or ruins (no lab work). Training programs for outdoor educators are also offered.

May–Oct.: 4- to 10-day programs, $500–$1,000, including supplies, food, lodging, and transportation.

The New Hampshire State Conservation and Rescue Archaeology Program (SCRAP)

www.mv.com/ipusers/
boisvert
New Hampshire Division of Historical Resources
19 Pillsbury St.
Box 2043
Concord, NH 03302-2043
603/271–3483

This program serves college-age students and adult volunteers. The Summer Prehistoric Archaeology Field School includes work on Native American sites, with an emphasis on research, resource management, and education. Participants learn basic site excavation methods and field laboratory procedures. In addition to the field schools, workshops, lab work, and independent research projects are available.

Late June–early July: three 10-day field-school programs about $90, including housing and meals.

Passport in Time Clearinghouse

www.passportintime.com
Box 31315
Tucson, AZ 85751-1315
800/281–9176, 520/722–2716

The U.S. Forest Service runs 87 volunteer programs, working with archaeologists and historians on heritage projects in national forests—in far-flung destinations. Programs have included restoring a fire lookout in Washington to documenting rock art (by sea kayak) along coastal Alaska to examining the carvings made by Basque sheepherders on aspen trees in California.

Programs from a weekend to a month, no registration fee. Accommodations: rustic cabins, backcountry camping, developed campgrounds, and occasional RV sites. Meals are sometimes available for a fee.

University Research Expeditions Program (UREP)

urep.ucdavis.edu
University of California Davis
One Shields Ave.
Davis, CA 95616
530/757–3529

This is a clearinghouse for University of California research and fieldwork expeditions worldwide. Programs involve small teams of volunteers and scientists; some expeditions focus on archaeology, animal studies, geology, arts and culture, the environment, or conservation. The Web address for the UC Davis program also leads you to information about other UC schools.

Expeditions $1,200–$1,800, including shared lodging and meals, ground transport, gear, equipment, and supplies.

BIRDING

Field Guides

www.fieldguides.com
9433 Bee Caves Rd.
Bldg. 1, Suite 150
Austin, TX 78733
800/728–4953, 512/263–7295

About 20 birding tours take place nationwide. There are 8–14 birders per trip; a second leader gets added with more participants.

5–14 days, $900–$6,500, including transport, lodging, and meals.

Victor Emanuel Nature Tours

www.ventbird.com
2525 Wallingwood Dr.,
Suite #1003
Austin, TX 78746
800/328–8368, 512/328–5221

This outfit organizes about 65 natural history and bird tours nationwide. About 6–16 people are permitted per tour, and two leaders accompany groups of 11 or larger.

Four-day intro tours and 7- to 14-day regular tours, $985–$5,000, including transport, lodging, and meals.

Wings

www.wingsbirds.com
1643 N. Alvernon Way,
Suite 105
Tucson, AZ 85712
520/320–9868, 888/293–6443

There are about 40 bird tours nationwide offered here. Groups include 4–16 participants, and one leader per 8–10 birders. Combo bird-and-butterfly tours are available.

5–21 days, $910–$7,780, including transport, lodging, and some meals (usually breakfast and lunch), depending on participants' flexibility.

CANOEING AND KAYAKING IN FLAT WATER

Canoe Outpost

www.canoeoutpost.com
Canoe Outpost at the Spirit of Suwannee Park
Rte. 1
Box 98A
Live Oak, FL 32060
386/364–4991, 800/428–4147

The Suwannee base of Canoe Outpost is well established and operates an excellent 500-acre full-service campground. They run excellent multiday outings on many sections of the Suwannee River, which flows for almost 200 mi from the Okefenokee swap in Georgia to Florida's Gulf Coast. The 46-mi stretch between Fargo, Georgia, and White Springs, Florida, has the most abundant wildlife and the least traffic; beginners might have trouble with several rocky shoals here. Spring and fall are the best seasons.

Feb.–Dec.: $35 per day, no meals.

Dvorak's Kayak and Rafting Expeditions

www.dvorakexpeditions.
com
17921-B U.S. 285
Nathrop, CO 81236
719/539–6851, 800/824–3795

Family-owned since 1969, Dvorak runs up to 12-day flat-water canoe trips on Colorado and Utah rivers, including the Arkansas, Green, and Colorado. Guide-to-client ratio is usually 10:1 with groups of up to 25. On the popular Classical Music on the Dolores trip you follow the mighty Colorado River from alpine forests through sandstone canyons and past Anasazi ruins while, each night, members of the Los Angeles Philharmonic provide musical accompaniment to your dinner.

Classical Music on the Dolores, June–July: eight days, $1,745. Other trips range from $425 for three days to $1,800 for 12 days on various rivers. Prices include food but not tent or sleeping bag.

Florida Bay Outfitters

www.kayakfloridakeys.com
104050 Overseas Hwy.
Key Largo, FL 33037
305/451–3018

Florida Bay Outfitters offers exceptional adventures on the Everglades' 99-mi Wilderness Waterway. Depending on your itinerary, campsites are either coastal beaches, bay or river ground sites, or chickees (wooden platforms along interior rivers and bays). Expect challenging tides coupled with winds and difficult route finding; this trip can be a very difficult undertaking, so even experienced paddlers should consider using a guide (permits are required if you venture into the Everglades National Park without one).

Nov.–Easter: two- to seven-day trips. The Everglades Coast: seven days, $1,050. Price includes camping equipment and meals.

Laughing Heart Adventures

www.pcweb.net/
laughingheart/adventures
Trinity Outdoor Center
Box 669
Willow Creek, CA 95573
888/271–6235, 530/629–3516

Founded in 1987, this outfitter operates canoe trips on the federally designated Wild and Scenic Rivers—the Eel, Smith, Trinity, Colorado, and Kalamath.

More than 50% of the customers are return business. One reason is because here you'll find some of the most experienced guides on the rivers of North America—all are ACA certified, and many have 10-plus years' under their belt. Popular trips include a six-day expedition on southern Oregon's rowdy Rouge as well as an exceptional seven-day trip on California's Eel River through lush Northcoast forest.

Thanksgiving and Easter: five days, $650, including family-style meals while on the river; tent and sleeping gear not included. Three- to 14-day mainly custom trips (year-round) start at $100 per day. Eel and Kalamath rivers from $300 and $650, respectively, Mar.–Sept.

Maine Path & Paddle Guides

www.canoemaine.com
60 Easter Ave.
Windham, ME 04062
207/892–3121

One of the most popular runs in the Northeast—more than 96 mi on Maine's Allagash Wilderness Waterway—the river alternates between swift, stony patches and long slow-moving pools. Expect terrific food and expert guides on the paddling trips.

May–Sept.: custom two- to seven-day trips starting at $105 per day, including meals and tent camping.

Southwind Kayak Center

www.southwindkayaks.com
17855 Sky Park Cir.
Suite A
Irvine, CA 92714
714/261–0200, 800/768–8494

Courses cater to kayakers and canoeists and include support rafts and catered camping with Western-style food. A trip entitled "Paddling the Green through Red-Rock Country," with good views of red-orange sandstone, is popular among photographers and novice kayakers (but is a bit challenging for canoeists due to large wave trains that can swamp the opened decked boats). This five-day, 70-mi wilderness paddle is navigable year-round, although fall and spring are best.

Year-round: five days, $1,400, including meals and tent camping.

St. Regis Canoe Outfitters

9 Dorsey St.
Saranac Lake, NY 12983
888/775–2925, 518/891–1838

The Saranac Lake area is an excellent destination for the novice and intermediate paddler looking to head out on a multiple-day trip without a guide. Of the numerous outfitters who can supply you with logistical support, St. Regis Canoe Outfitters is among the best. Whether you want to simply rent a canoe or prefer a prepackaged menu and guide, they flex around your needs, with itineraries from two to eight days. Most longer trips take place in the Everglades, in January.

May–Oct.: The North Flow Lodge Weekend, three days, $429, including food and accommodations. Jan.: Everglades Wilderness Waterway, 11 days, $1,495, including camping (tents and sleeping bags provided). In general, trips run two days–two weeks and average $100 per person per day.

Williams and Hall Wilderness Guides and Outfitters

www.williamsandhall.com
Box 358
Ely, MN 55731
218/365–5837, 800/322–5837

Viewed by many as the end-all-be-all of North American flat-water canoeing, the Boundary Waters Canoe Area Wilderness stretches across northeast Minnesota. Only accessible by canoe are 1,175 lakes in 1.1 million acres of forest, and about 2,200 campsites along at least 1,500 mi of canoe routes linked by lakes, rivers, and portages. Very challenging rivers await the advanced paddler; almost all difficult sections can be portaged. Abutting the Boundary Waters Canoe Area Wilderness to the north is Quetico Provincial Park, with pristine acreage that doubles the wilderness available to you; a system of permits on both the U.S. and Canadian sides limits visitors, so you can paddle for days without seeing a soul. Williams and Hall Wilderness Guides and Outfitters is one of the best of a slew of excellent guide and outfitting services;

they'll customize a trip for you or your group.

May–Sept.: $75–$200 per day, including food and camping equipment.

CANOEING AND KAYAKING IN WHITE WATER

Class VI River Runners

www.800classVI.com
Ames Heights Rd.
Box 78
Lansing, WV 2586–0078
800/252–7784, 304/574–0704

Two of the best white-water rivers in North America, the Gauley and the New, flow through West Virginia. Both rivers are extremely popular for white-water rafting. This outfitter offers introductory through advanced courses on the mighty New river; instruction includes all required equipment.

May–Sept.: three days on New River, $570; four days, $760. Price includes lunch; campsites $7 per person.

Dvorak's Kayak and Rafting Expeditions

www.dvorakexpeditions.com
17921-B U.S. 285
Nathrop, CO 81236
800/824–3795, 719/539–6851

Founded in 1969, this company offers up to 12-day white-water canoe, kayak, and inflatable kayak instruction on the Arkansas, Colorado, Dolores, Green, Gunnison, Rio Chama, Rio Grande, and North Platte rivers. Instruction for beginning to advanced paddlers typically takes place on multi-tiday wilderness trips, with raft support and catered camping. The Rio Grande, which winds along the Texas-Mexico border, is a popular trip. Many stretches are docile and perfect for beginners; the Lower Canyons and Regan Canyon will challenge advanced to intermediate paddlers.

Courses begin at $150 per day. Mid-Mar.–late Apr. Rio Grande trip: seven days, $1,045, including all equipment, food, and lodging (camping).

Mohawk Trail

www.zoaroutdoor.com
Box 245
Charlemont, MA 01339
800/532–7483, 413/339–4010

Terrific Class I, II, and III rapids on the Deerfield will challenge kayakers who are looking for easy waters or even a bit of a challenge. The five-day beginners courses are a good bet. The scenic Deerfield flows past an old railroad bridge and a stone mill and has both easy rapids for novices and more turbulent rapids—with big, fast water—for intermediates and above.

Apr.–Oct.: two-day midweek novice course, $230; three-day intermediate course, $340; five-day intensive course, $535; all prices include breakfast and lunch. Lodging $16 per person/night for canvas tent with bunk beds or $12 camping fee.

Mountain Travel Sobek

www.mtsobek.com
6420 Fairmount Ave.
El Cerrito, CA 94530-3606
888/687–6235, 510/527–7710

For a four-star wilderness experience, try Idaho's Salmon River, one of the most sought-after whitewater runs in North America. It includes 200 mi of fabulous white water; the Middle Fork is the most scenic section, and it offers the most white-water punch—there are almost 100 rapids in as many miles ranging from Class II to Class IV. On the exceptional six-day adventures down the Middle Fork, you take inflatable kayaks—the boat of choice for this demanding white water (you'll be fine, even if it's your first time). The river peaks in late May and early June, which means July–September is best for novice and intermediate paddlers. Everything here is high-end: the guides are very experienced, the equipment is excellent, and the meals are very fine.

Six days, $1,690, all-inclusive, with lodging and meals.

Nantahala Outdoor Center

www.noc.com
13077 Hwy. 19W
Bryson City, NC 28713
800/232–7238, 704/488–6737

Founded in 1972 and now employee-owned, Nantahala is considered by many to be the premier paddling school in North America. Groups are limited to 10 students, with two highly experienced and ACA-certified instructors. You can learn on the Chattooga, French Broad, Little Tennessee, Nantahala, Nolichucky, Ocoee, Oconanluftee, and Tuckaseigee rivers. The six-day intensive river kayaking course is excellent: you learn basic strokes and the

Eskimo roll on a lake, then take multiple runs down the Little Tennessee, Nantahala, and Ocoee rivers (site of the kayak slalom events for the 1996 Atlanta Olympic games).

Mar.–Oct.: six-day intensive course, $1,175; two-day weekend courses start at $395; all trips include meal and lodging (in the modern-rustic NOC lodge); sign up one to two months in advance.

New England Outdoor Center (NEOC)

www.neoc.com
10 Pleasant St.
Millers Falls, MA 01349
413/659–3926

Founded in 1982 by legendary paddler and white-water instructor Tom Foster, NEOC—five hours from Boston—is known for its very technical instruction, based on modern Olympic paddling styles. There's a low ACA-certified instructor-to-student ratio. They run kayak courses on the Class III–IV Kennebec and the Class V Penobscot rivers. These are runs for experienced kayakers only and have an instructor-to-student ratio of 3:1 for added safety.

One- to four-day beginner classes start at $129 per day; meals and bunkhouse cost extra.

Northern Waters

www.sacobound.com
Box 120
Errol, NH 03579
603/482–3817

Expect constant white water on the Androscoggin River, as well as small classes in which you learn beginner and intermediate kayaking fundamentals and rescue techniques. Programs are also available if you want to work with open canoes.

May–early Sept.: four days, $325, including free use of campsite (not tents) but not food.

Otter Bar Kayak School

www.otterbar.com
Box 210C
Forks of Salmon, CA 96031
916/462–4772

The Salmon River of California is virtually unknown except to die-hard kayakers. It's one of California's Wild and Scenic rivers, and its three forks have exceptional white water in late spring and early summer (Class

II–Class IV). Otter Bar Kayak School has intermediate and advanced courses as well as a seven-day introductory kayak programs on both the Salmon and Klamath rivers. On the all-inclusive programs you get individualized instruction.

Seven days, $1,890, including food and camping or accommodations in the rustic Otter Bar Lodge.

Riversport School of Paddling

www.shol.com/kayak
213 Yough St.
Box 95
Confluence, PA 15424
814/395–5744

The Youghiogheny is one of the most popular whitewater runs in the mid-Atlantic: the middle stretch provides great beginner terrain, and the rapids of the lower section will challenge even advanced paddlers. Riversport School of Paddling offers courses for open canoes, closed-deck canoes, and many disciplines of kayaking (slalom, freestyle, and squirt boating). Maximum class size is six per instructor.

Mar.–Oct.: three days, $330; four days, $420; five days, $500, including equipment

and three meals a day during summer (after Labor Day lunch only). Campsite available; bring your own equipment.

Sundance Kayak School and Expeditions

www.sundanceriver.com
14894 Galice Rd.
Merlin, OR 97532
503/479–8508

Founded in 1973 on the banks of the Rogue River in southern Oregon, Sundance teaches most on multiday trips down Oregon's Rogue, North Umpqua, Illinois, and Idaho's Salmon rivers. The Wild and Scenic Rogue is a true western classic trip: a nine-day program includes five days of instruction and then a four-day wilderness run down the Rogue (Class II and III white water). Expert instructors teach you both Eskimo rolls and the paddle strokes you need to master.

Mid-May–mid-Sept.: nine days (including five days' lodge-based kayaking instruction and a four-day raft-supported camping trip), $1,920; five-day beginner courses on the Rogue start at $975; all prices include three meals a day. The Sundance Riverhouse offers comfy accommodation for courses operated out of the company's southern Oregon–Rogue River base.

Zoar Outdoor Paddling School

www.zaroutdoor.com
Mohawk Trail
Box 245
Charlemont, MA 01339
800/532–7483, 413/339–4010

This well-established school is directed by the nationally acclaimed paddler and writer Bruce Lessels. The kayak and canoe school is based out on the Deerfield River of Massachusetts and runs up to five-day white-water classes and river trips for all abilities, with ACA instructors who have six-plus years' experience.

Two-day courses start at $230.

CLIMBING AND MOUNTAINEERING

Adirondack Rock and River Guide Service, Inc.

www.rockandriver.com
Box 219
Keene, NY 12942
518/576–2041

Held in the mountains of upstate New York, the Beginning Ice Climbing in the Adirondacks program introduces aspiring ice-climbers to the use of ice tools, ice screws and other protection, crampons, and ropes.

Beginning Ice Climbing in the Adirondacks, Dec.–Mar.: four days, $415, including all gear except double plastic boots, which can be rented. Accommodations (in one of the school's two lodges) and meals cost extra.

Alaska Mountaineering School/Alaska Denali Guiding

www.climbalaska.org
Box 566
Talkeetna, AK 99676
907/733–1016

This 22-day program focuses on an ascent of Alaska's Mt. McKinley (Denali) by the West Buttress route. Although it's the least difficult approach to McKinley, it still involves very high altitude, arctic conditions, crevasses, steep ice slopes, and unpredictable weather. Previous winter climbing experience is required, and a very high fitness level is essential to reach the summit. The school also offers several mountaineering courses for those who want to gain the skills necessary for an eventual Denali summit attempt.

Mt. McKinley (Denali) Ascent, May–June: 22 days, $4,000, including group technical gear and meals.

American Alpine Institute

www.mtnguide.com
1515 12th St.
Bellingham, WA 98225
360/671–1505

This 12-day intensive program in the heart of the North Cascades takes you into alpine terrain that's unmatched in the Lower 48. You'll learn the fundamentals of rock, snow, and ice climbing and how to identify avalanche hazards and other risks. You'll also acquire self-rescue and minimum-impact camping skills. Although climbing experience isn't required, it's helpful to have some backpacking under your belt; know that you'll be responsible for supplying your own food. AAI also organizes expeditions in Canada, Alaska, the Alps, or South America.

Alpine Mountaineering in the North Cascades, late May–Sept.: 12 days, $1,860, including group technical gear.

Colorado Mountain School

www.cmschool.com
Box 1846
Estes Park, CO 80517
888/267–7783, 970/586–5758

This five-day Rock Camp course, held in and around Rocky Mountain National Park, takes you quickly from the basics to multipitch rock climbs, including an ascent of one of the rock spires in the park's high country. Colorado Mountain School, founded in 1982, is the concessioned guide service for the park.

Rock Camp in Rocky Mountain National Park, June–Sept.: five days, $695–$895 (gear rental and dormitory lodging in CMS's Climbers' Lodge extra).

Eastern Mountain Sports Climbing School

www.emsclimb.com
3124 Rte. 44/55
Gardiner, NY 12525
800/310–4504, 845/255–3280

Thanks to its fractured rock, the 'Gunks is one of the outstanding climbing venues in the United States. You'll get a thorough introduction to rock climbing here, just a 90-minute drive north of Manhattan. During the

Basics on the Shawangunks program, you progress from relatively easy rock faces to multipitch routes that call for more difficult moves and more sophisticated techniques. The school also runs ice-climbing and mountaineering programs, as well as other rock-climbing clinics, from its main office in North Conway, New Hampshire, and branches in New York and Connecticut.

Basics on the Shawangunks, Apr.–Nov.: four days, $560–$640, including all gear but no lodging or meals.

Exum Mountain Guides

www.exumguides.com
Box 56
Moose, WY 83012
307/733–2297

As part of its extensive programs in climbing and mountaineering, this outfit can put you atop the 13,770-ft Grand Teton, one of those alluring peaks that all climbers want to scale. The first two days you take the basic and intermediate mountaineering courses to gain skills for the climb. Following that is a two-day ascent of the Grand, including an overnight at a hut on the mountain's 11,620-ft Lower Saddle.

Ascent of the Grand Teton, late June–mid-Sept.: four days, $575–$650, including all gear except climbing shoes. Lodging in rustic cabins; discounts available for other facilities nearby. Cookware is supplied, but bring your own food.

Joshua Tree Rock Climbing School

www.rockclimbingschool.com
Box 29
Joshua Tree, CA 92252-0029
800/890–4745, 760/366–4745

The Rock Seminar, a four-day course in southern California's Joshua Tree National Monument (where the granite is outstanding), covers the basics during the first two days, including terminology, safety systems, knots, and climbing on low-angle faces. Over the next two days you'll progress to intermediate skills, including more sophisticated climbing moves, hardware placements, and anchors.

Rock Seminar at Joshua Tree, Sept.–June: four days, $315, including all gear. Lodging and meals are up to you; campsites in the park are usually available.

Outward Bound West

www.outwardbound.com
910 Jackson St.
Golden, CO 80401
888/882–6863

This 14-day Mountaineering in the Sierra Nevada course, at and above timberline in Sequoia and Kings Canyon National Park, focuses on mountaineering, backcountry travel, and rock climbing, and challenges you to master a variety of skills, among them low-impact travel. Outward Bound offers plenty of other mountaineering and climbing courses throughout the United States.

Mountaineering in the Sierra Nevada, June–Aug.: 14 days, $2,195, including all gear, sleeping bag and pad, backpack, and meals.

Rainier Mountaineering, Inc.

www.rmiguides.com
Box Q
Ashford, WA 98304
888/892–5462, 360/569–2227

Among mountaineering classes and guided climbs of Mt. Rainier—a heavily glaciated, 14,410-ft dormant volcano—is this five-day seminar, which covers glacier travel, snow anchors, route-finding, crevasse rescue, and technical snow and ice climbing, followed by a summit attempt.

Snow and Ice Climbing Seminar and Mt. Rainier Ascent, May–June and Sept.–Oct.: five days, $1,137, including group gear, some personal gear, breakfasts, dinners, and lodging at a bunkhouse in Ashford and in a hut at 10,000-ft Camp Muir on the mountain.

Sierra Mountain Center

www.sierramountaincenter.com
Box 95
Bishop, CA 93515
760/873–8526

An introduction to mountaineering takes place among the craggy peaks of the eastern Sierra, long a hallowed ground for climbers. Skills taught include climbing moves, belaying, knots, crampon and ice axe use, and snow travel, culminating with an ascent of an approximately 13,000-ft peak. Dorm accommodations or camping is available nearby for the first night; after that, you'll backpack in and set up a base camp below the Mills Glacier.

Mountain Camp, June–
Sept.: four days, $500,
including group technical
gear, tents, and meals in the
backcountry.

Southwest Adventures

www.mtnguide.net
Box 3242
Durango, CO 81302
800/642–5389, 970/259–0370

This five-day course takes
place in the San Juan
Mountains of southwestern
Colorado, the state's most
rugged peaks and a spectacular environment in which
to become acquainted with
mountaineering. Skills
taught include belaying,
rappelling, climbing movements, snow travel, self-
arrest with ice axe, and
anchor placement. You'll
then put those skills to the
test with technical ascents
of Snowden and North
Twilight Peaks. Nights are
spent at one of two 10,000-ft
base camps that you'll backpack in to.

Mountaineering in the San
Juans, May–Sept.: five days,
$575, including group
climbing and camping gear,
breakfasts and dinners, and
helmet and harness.

Sylvan Rocks Climbing School & Guide Service

www.sylvanrocks.com
Box 600
Hill City, SD 57745
605/574–2425

Two days of learning
rock-climbing basics in
the Needles area of South
Dakota's Black Hills, followed by a climb of Devils
Tower, that distinctively
shaped plug of rock featured
in the movie *Close Encounters
of the Third Kind*. Most students are beginners, but
many acquire a high level
of climbing skills by the
time the course ends.

Beginning Climbing in the
Black Hills and Devils
Tower, mid-Apr.–mid-Oct.:
three days, $450–$675, including all gear. Lodging
and meals (available near
both sites) cost extra.

Timberline Mountain Guides

www.timberlinemtguides.
com
Box 1167
Bend, OR, 97709
541/312–9242

Rock Camp includes four
days at Oregon's Smith
Rock State Park, with volcanic rock that constitutes

one of the best climbing areas in the United States. The course teaches you basic and intermediate skills—knots, ropes, hardware placements, and climbing moves. Timberline offers other climbing courses and guided climbs on Mt. Hood and elsewhere in the Cascades.

Rock Camp at Smith Rock, May–Sept.: four days, $420, including all gear except climbing shoes. Food and accommodations are available in nearby Redmond and Bend.

CYCLING

Backroads

www.backroads.com
1516 5th St., Suite B122
Berkeley, CA 94710–1740
800/462–2848, 510/527–1555

This is the biggest touring company in the world, with 90-plus trips worldwide. It's famous for its exquisite lunches and fancy accommodations, and it rents Chimayo bikes. The luxurious Pedal the Northeast Kingdom trip is vintage Vermont—10–30 mi daily through exquisite fall color. Cajun and Plantation Country is an easy ride through Mississippi's mossy, ethereal lowlands; you see Civil War sites and plantations. Beginners can cycle to the spine of the Continental Divide, in Montana's Glacier National Park, on the Going-to-the-Sun Road, one of the most scenic cycling climbs in the country—waterfalls, evergreen forests, and alpine meadows.

Pedal the Northeast Kingdom (VT), Sept.–Oct.: six days, $1,998, including five nights' lodging and all meals except one lunch; road-bike rental $120. Cajun and Plantation Country, Sept.–Nov.: six days, $1,898, including five nights' lodging and all meals; road-bike rental $120. Glacier National Park, June–Sept.: six days, inn $1,898, camping $998, including five nights in lodges/inns (one night Glacier Park Lodge) and all meals except one dinner; road-bike rental $109.

Bicycle Adventures

www.bicycleadventures.com
Box 7875
Olympia, WA 98507
800/443–6060, 206/786–0989

Founded in 1984, this outfit specializes in West Coast touring and is staffed by Pacific Northwest natives who know the area well. The Bryce-Zion National

Park trip in Utah explores the eroded landscape of Cedar Breaks and Zion's rock walls—and you'll ride some of the finest roads in the West. This is a rider's trip: distances average 35 mi, often on hilly terrain. California Redwoods takes you 35 mi daily through the secluded Lost Coast and wine country. On the Oregon Coast trip, expect fun, well-paced riding (45 mi daily) on quiet back roads. The Island Hopping in the San Juans variety tour explores islands in the Puget Sound (33 mi daily). On the Big Island of Hawaii, on the Lava Flows and Snorkeling trip, you spend two days below Kilauea Volcano and one day snorkeling at Kona. The going is tough: a hilly 45 mi daily.

Bryce-Zion National Park, May–June and Sept.–Oct.: six days, $1,626, including five nights' lodging and all meals. California Redwoods, June and Sept.: six days, $1,680, including five nights in fine inns and all meals. Oregon Coast, July–Oct.: six days, $1,818, including six nights' lodging and all meals. Island Hopping in the San Juans, May–Sept.: six days, $1,982, including inn lodging and all meals.

Lava Flows and Snorkeling, Sept.–June: eight days, $2,364, including seven nights at inns and all meals (including pig roasts); bicycle rentals for all trips $126–$144.

Bike Vermont

www.bikevermont.com
Box 207
Woodstock, VT 05091
800/257–2226, 802/457–3553

The organizers have run trips in New England since 1977; with 160 weekend and five-day tours in Vermont, they have more trips here than any other company. The Connecticut River valley trip takes you on a ramble along the Connecticut River (Vermont); you visit Dartmouth College and explore a restored Shaker village. If you want to explore the back roads, small towns, and covered bridges of the Saxtons River and Windham Hill area, expect to ride about 26 mi daily over occasionally hilly terrain.

Connecticut River valley, July–Oct.: five days, from $735, including four nights at inns. Saxtons River and Windham Hill, June–Sept.: five days, including four nights at two of Vermont's best inns; road-bike rentals for all trips $80. All trips include breakfast and dinner daily.

Butterfield and Robinson

www.butterfield.com
70 Bond St.
Toronto, Canada M5B 1X3
800/678–1147, 416/864–1354

It's the oldest organized touring company, and it pampers you to the utmost. Mileage junkies: avoid this outfit, as rides tend to be leisurely. Beginner/intermediate riders: try Mississippi's Natchez Trace, an Indian trail that became a central commerce path of the new American West. You pedal two to three hours daily, with stops for mint juleps and history chats; you also visit Civil War sites and tour New Orleans's hottest jazz spots. The multisport Taos–to–Santa Fe trek traverses New Mexico and has elevations up to 9,000 ft, but you get fabulous panoramas and a leisurely raft float.

Mississippi's Natchez Trace, Oct.: five days, $2,795, including four nights in plush Colonial mansions and plantation houses and all meals. Taos–to–Santa Fe trek, Sept.

29: five days, $2,995, including four nights' lodging and all meals.

Michigan Bicycle Touring

www.bikembt.com
3512 Red School Rd.
Kingsley, MI 49649
616/263–5885

In business since 1978, this outfit organizes 18 bike tours in Michigan. The Mackinac Wayfarer takes you through hilly farmland and forest and small towns, including car-free Mackinac Island; expect to ride 23–65 mi daily. The Grand Traverse Wayfarer covers northern Michigan's cherry region, which has scenic lakes and interesting geology. The trip includes lighthouse visits and a side trip to Sleeping Bear Dunes National Lakeshore.

Mackinac Wayfarer, June–Aug.: five days, $1,229, including lodging at luxury inns and all meals except three lunches. Grand Traverse Wayfarer, June–Sept.: six days, $1,050, including B&B lodging and all meals except four lunches; bike rental (hybrid or mountain) for all trips $100.

Timberline Adventures

www.timbertours.com
7975 E. Harvard, Suite #J
Denver, CO 80231
303/759–3804

The big-mileage and high-altitude tours—in the western United States, northern Great Lakes, and Canada—suit aggressive riders. The San Juans Alpiner (Colorado) is for well-trained, fit cyclists only. The Rogue River Rambler includes the Oregon coast and Cascade Range (Rogue River, Gold Beach, and Crater Lake); expect to bike a strenuous 60 mi a day. On Adventure Alaska you bike beneath the Chugach range and across Thompson Pass and go sea kayaking on Prince William Sound; average mileage, 60-plus daily.

San Juans Alpiner (Colorado), Sept. 8–14: seven days, $1,695, including six nights in restored Victorian hotels, national park inns, and mountain lodges, and breakfasts and dinners. Rogue River Rambler, July 13–21: nine days, $2,195, including eight nights in inns and all breakfasts and dinners. Adventure Alaska, July–Aug.: eight days, $2,095, including seven nights' rustic-luxurious lodging and all breakfasts

and dinners; road-bike rental for all trips $100.

Vermont Bicycle Touring (VBT)

www.vbt.com
Box 711
Bristol, VT 05443
800/245–3868, 802/453–4811

Going strong since 1972, VBT runs 27 different tours worldwide. Accommodations rival those of other top-notch companies, but the spreads (and cost) are more economical. VBT will customize routes for casual cyclists or hammers. Purely Acadia is a leisurely tour along Maine's coast, 13–26 mi daily; besides biking Acadia National Park, you take a naturalist cruise in a fjord and go sea kayaking and whale watching. For easy rides along the Atlantic seaside, take the Martha's Vineyard and Nantucket trip. On the North Carolina Coast trip you explore wildlife refuges and the historic landing spot of Bluebeard the Pirate and ride on a 45-ft catamaran.

Purely Acadia, June–Oct.: six days, $1,425, including five nights' inn lodging, most meals and activities, and road- or hybrid-bike and helmet rental. Martha's Vineyard and Nantucket, May–Oct.: six days, from $1,425, including five nights' lodging, five breakfasts, three dinners, most activities, and road- or hybrid-bike and helmet rental. North Carolina Coast, Apr.–Oct.: six days, $1,075, including five nights' lodging, five breakfasts, four lunches, and four dinners and road- or hybrid-bike and helmet rental.

FISHING CAMPS AND FLY-FISHING SCHOOLS

Beaverkill Valley Inn

www.beaverkillvalley.com
Lew Beach, NY 12753
845/439–4844

This 20-room colonial inn on conserved land by the Beaverkill River (where fly-fishing began in America) is two hours northwest of New York City, so it's popular among fishermen who want comforts and easy-access fishing—and those with families. There's a casting pond for trout here; bring your own equipment. Guides cost $150–$300 per day.

Apr.–Sept.: one night double, private bath, meals, and fishing, $350; one night single, shared bath, meals, and fishing, $175.

Bishop Creek Lodge

www.bishopcreekresorts.com
2100 S. Lake Rd.
Bishop, CA 93514
760/873–4484

This cozy rustic lodge has a fully outfitted fly-fishing shop attached. There are no classes or guides, but it's worth coming here for the native golden trout, which are readily accessible from surrounding lakes and streams. If you don't want to bring your own equipment, you can buy fishing equipment on-site.

Apr.–Oct.: two-night minimum stay; cabin, $60–$80 per night (includes Continental breakfast only).

California School of Fly-Fishing

www.flyline.com
Box 8212
Truckee, CA 96162
530/587–7005

This wilderness fishing school and camp runs beginner, intermediate, and advanced classes that cover the basics of casting to playing, landing, and releasing fish. Streams and lakes in the vicinity are stocked with rainbow, brown, brook, and golden trout. The student–instructor ratio is 2:1 to 4:1. The school runs weeklong trips to Yosemite.

May-June: two-day classes, $489, including gear and lunch, no lodging. All-inclusive weeklong trips to Yosemite, the Yucatan, and the Amazon, about $2,200.

Catch Montana

Box 428
Hamilton, MT 59840
800/882–7844

This guide service has mul-tiday trips for serious fly fishermen for catch-and-release trout (you can't eat it); you navigate the lakes and streams on rafts. There's a 1:1 or 2:1 angler–guide ratio—personalized atten-tion is a major benefit of hir-ing a guide service instead of a school, though you'll have to bring your own tackle and gear.

Late Mar.-mid-Oct.: five days, $1,995, meals and lodging included; $1,695 for guided fishing only, for one to two people.

Chris Nischan's Rod & Gun Guide Service

www.rodandgunguide.com
3502 Amanda Ave.
Nashville, TN 37215
615/385–1116

This guide service takes you out on local trout streams in the Smoky Mountains. You can fish for trout, bass, and panfish by floating or wading on lakes, rivers, and streams here, and the angler–guide ratio is a fine 2:1. Instruction covers fly-fishing and spin-casting techniques; beginner and advanced classes are run separately, but anyone who's qualified (including children) can take part in either.

Year-round: four hours, $200 (two anglers); eight hours, $275 (two anglers, in-cluding transportation and lunch). Lodging available nearby.

Clearwater House

www.clearwatertrout.com
Box 90
Cassell, CA 96016
530/335–5500; 415/381–1173 off-season

This lodge, guide service, and outfitter runs a four-day school with four levels of classes, from recreational be-ginner to advanced, for those who want to become fishing guides. Women's-only classes and shorter guide-service-only sessions are also available. You fish for trout on creeks, and there's a 2:1 angler–guide ratio. You can bring tackle and gear or rent them on-site.

May–Nov.: four days, $335 per person per day (includes lodging, three meals, one day guiding).

Colonial Sportsman's Lodge

www.fish-gls.com
Box 167
Shaw St.
Grand Lake Stream, ME 04637
800/250–5064, 207/796–2655

If you want a wilderness camp but don't want to rough it, this is a good bet, especially since the camp teaches people of all skill levels. You can fish for land-locked salmon, smallmouth bass, brook trout, white perch, and crappie from land or boat on nearby streams and lakes. Bring your own equipment.

May–Sept.: five days, $125 housekeeping units in cottages; $425 with meals. Guide available for $150 per full day for two anglers.

Custom Caster

members.mato.com/
bhangler
21207 Thunder La.
Lead, SD 57754
605/584–2217

This guide service organizes fishing trips for trout, pike, bass, crappies, bluegills, and perch. You take canoes or float tubes, or wade on streams. The angler–guide ratio is 2:1; bring or rent tackle and gear.

Year-round: four hours, $120, for one to two anglers, lunch not included; eight hours, $225, for one to two anglers, including lunch. No lodging; campgrounds, RV parks, and motels nearby.

Fly Fishing Outfitters

ccam.coolpod.com/flyfishingoutfitters/index.html
463 Bush St.
San Francisco, CA 94108
415/781–3474

Fishing clinics take place in Lafayette and San Francisco, as well as in rural Putah Creek, the Yuba River System, and Stanislaus River. For a two-day comprehensive fishing instruction courses for salmon and trout on local streams and rivers, you get a 3:1 student–instructor ratio. Rods and reels are provided. The outfit also offers intensive-beginners' multiday fishing trips, including a popular trip through Oregon's Deschutes River canyon, for rainbow trout. It also runs trips to Montana, Idaho (a ladies' trip), Alaska, and Wyoming, and others worldwide.

June–Sept.: two-day course, $250, including lunch, no lodging. Oregon's Deschutes River canyon, June or Sept.: four days, $1,300, including lodging (tents), food, supplies, and guiding.

Gypsy Guide Service/ Boca Grande Fly-Fishing School

www.floridaflyfishing.com
2416 Parson La.
Sarasota, FL 34239
941/923–6095

Owner "Captain" Pete Greenan gives you personal attention at his school: either a 1:1 or a 2:1 student–instructor ratio. He runs novice, intermediate, and advanced classes, with hands-on instruction in a variety of techniques and tactics. The setting is rural and tropical. Some instruction is on dry land, but Pete prefers to take you out on the boat and just fish—for redfish,

snook, tarpon, jack crevalle, cobia, and grouper.

Nov. and Apr.: $450 per day, including lunch, license, and tackle (no lodging).

Kinzua Fly Fishing School

users.penn.com/~skvarka
44 Parkview Ave.
Bradford, PA 16701
814/362–7500

Based on the University of Pittsburgh at Bradford campus, the school offers two- and three-day courses for beginner and intermediate anglers age 12 and older. The student–instructor ratio is 4:1 or 5:1. You learn partly in a classroom; outdoor sessions take place on a stocked trout stream. Bring tackle (flies are provided).

May–June: two days, $250; three days, $350; including campus housing and all meals.

Lake Fork Fisherman's Cove Marina

ets-systems.com/
fishermanscove/
lakeforkguides.htm
2712 N. FM 17
Alba, TX 75410
888/818–3675, 903/765–2943

This guide service offers full-day and half-day packages to fish for bass and crappie from a boat on Lake Fork, a man-made reservoir and the site of record bass catches, including the Texas state record of 18.18 pounds (caught on Jan. 24, 1992). The angler–guide ratio is 1:1 or 2:1. On the all-inclusive big bass fishing vacation on Lake Fork you're out for nine hours at a time, for however many days you want to fish.

Year-round: five-hour half day, $175; nine-hour full day, $275 for guide and fishing (no meals or lodging). Big Bass all-inclusive fishing vacation $250 per day, including nine hours' fishing with guide service, supplies, motel room (based on double occupancy), all meals (there's a steak house on-site), and drinks.

Lewiston Inn

www.theoldlewistoninn.com
Box 688
Lewiston, CA 96052
800/286–4441

This rural inn is popular with people (especially families) who want to fish for rainbow and brook trout on Trinity River, which is behind the inn, and on Lewiston Lake down the road. There's a guide service

for an added charge; guides provide instruction on casting and techniques from shore, drift boat, powerboat, or float tubes, with a maximum 3:1 angler–guide ratio. Bring your own tackle and gear; fly-fishing equipment and accessories are sold on-site.

Year-round: one night, double occupancy, $95 (includes breakfast); full-day guide for one to two anglers, $250–$350, with lunch but no license (rates vary depending on number of people and whether you need gear).

Lodge at Palisades Creek

www.tlapc.com
Lodge at Palisades Creek
3720 Hwy. 26
Irwin, ID 83428
208/483–2222

A multiday package at this elegant, rustic wilderness lodge on the South Fork of the Snake River includes guided fishing (from shore and boat, on rivers) for cutthroat and rainbow and brown trout. There's a 1:1 or 2:1 angler–guide ratio. Bring tackle and gear or purchase them on-site.

Apr.–Dec.: $250–$325 per night for double in log cabin, including three meals daily and open bar, four-day minimum stay; daily guide for one to two anglers $395.

MacKenzie Trail Lodge

mackenzietraillodge.com
27134 N.W. Reeder Rd.
Portland, OR 97231
800/615–3713

This outfit runs all-inclusive fly-in packages to a wilderness lodge-guide service on Tsacha Lake, British Columbia. It's for serious anglers; during the 6- and 10-day trips for trout you fish from motorboats, pontoons, float tubes, canoes, or by wading along lakes and rivers. Bring tackle and gear or purchase them on-site.

Late June–late Aug.: six days, $2,299; 10 days, $3,499; including lodging in log cabin, meals, and transportation.

Montana River Outfitters

www.mt-river-outfitters.com
923 10th Ave. N
Great Falls, MT 59401
800/800–8218, 406/761–1677

Fly-fish on three of the greatest trout-fishing streams in the world, on five- and seven-day drift boat or float trips for cutthroat, rainbow, and brown trout. The angler–guide ratio is 1:1 or 2:1, and children are welcome (charges apply). If you don't bring your own tackle and gear you can rent them here.

Mar.–Oct.: five days on the Missouri River, $1,825 ($1,975 for two people); five days on the Smith River or South Fork, $2,175; six days, $2,475; seven days, $2,775. Prices include lodging in motel/cabin units but no meals (restaurants are nearby).

The Mountain Connection at the Glade Springs Resort

www.gladespringsresort.com
200 Lake Dr.
Daniels, WV 25832
800/634–5233, 302/763–2000

Short sessions at this rural, upscale 4,100-acre resort cover casting, knot-tying, and fly and equipment selection. There's a maximum 3:1 student–instructor ratio; tackle is provided. There are eight lakes on the property, including a stocked trout creek. Better yet, tailor a fishing trip to your interests—there are miles of trout streams nearby, so you can fish from shore or raft on streams and rivers nearby. The property is near the New River gorge, which supposedly has the best bass fishing in the country.

Year-round: Float and Fish Adventure trip, $195 per person on weekends, including two nights' lodging, full breakfast, guided float and fishing on New River, and lunch.

Murray's Fly Shop

www.murraysflyshop.com
Box 156
Edinburg, VA 22824
800/984–4895, 540/984–4212

This fishing outfit in the Shenandoah Valley offers two-day programs for beginner to advanced anglers. You fish for smallmouth bass and trout on nearby creeks and rivers; the student–instructor ratio is 4:1, and tackle is provided.

Mountain Trout school Mar.–Apr: two days, $325; Small Mouth Bass school May–Aug.: two days, $325; all prices include gear only, no license, food, or lodging.

Oasis Springs Lodge

www.oasisflyfishing.com
32400 Hwy. 36
Payne's Creek, CA 96075
800/239–5454, 510/653–7630

The three-day course at this fly-fishing school covers fly casting, fly tying, and catch-and-release techniques— you fish for 2½ days and have a half day of free fishing time. You can fish for brown and rainbow trout from the banks or by wading in creeks; the angler–guide ratio is 4:1. Some equipment is provided, but not flies and tippets; rental tackle is available.

Apr.–Nov.: three days, $430 per person double occupancy (for fly-fishing school); full-day guide only (no school), $320 for one to two anglers; tackle rental $55 per day; lodging and meals included.

Orvis Fly-Fishing School

www.orvis.com
1711 Blue Hills Dr.
Roanoke, VA 24012-8613
888/235–9763, 540/345–4606

This long-established fishing-tackle manufacturer sponsors fly-fishing schools in rural areas of Vermont, New York, Massachusetts, Virginia, Georgia, Wisconsin, Colorado, Idaho, Wyoming, and California. Courses range from 2 to 2½ weekend or weekday days, but virtually all Orvis schools can help you round out a week's vacation by arranging guided or unguided fishing trips for the remainder of your time. The schools provide Orvis equipment and teach all levels of angler—as individuals or in groups with a 4:1 student–instructor ratio—how to hook, land, and release a fish.

Early Apr.–late Aug.: two days, $370, including lunch; 2½ days, $430, including lunch. Special rates on lodging available.

Reno Fly Shop and Truckee River Outfitters

www.renoflyshop.com
294 E. Moana La., No. 14
Reno, NV 89502
775/825–3474

This guide service runs full-day, half-day, and evening trips for trout on boats, or float tubes; you can walk or wade on excursions to lakes, creeks, and streams. There's a 1:1 to 6:1 angler–guide ratio. You can either bring or rent tackle and gear here. Lunch is $10 per person.

Apr.–Oct.: full day, $225; half day, $175; evening, $125; equipment rental: rod and reel, $20 per day; waders and boots, $20 per day. Lodging not included.

Shenandoah Lodge & Outfitters

www.shenandoah-lodge.com
100 Grand View Dr.
Luray, VA 22835
800/866–9958, 540/743–1920

This school, at a rural lodge, runs two- and three-day beginner programs. You can fish for smallmouth bass, carp, and trout on rivers and streams, on drift boats. There's a 4:1 student–instructor ratio.

Apr.–Oct.: one-day guide, $195 (additional anglers $75 each); two-day, $495; three-day, $695; one-day boat trip with two anglers, $325. Lodging and meals included for overnight trips; lunch provided on day trips.

Southern California Bass Fishing Guide

www.swiftsite.com/
socalbassguide
Box 901
San Jacinto, CA 92581-0901
909/925–3885

With 20-plus years of experience, this guide service runs half- and full-day trips for largemouth, striped, and spotted-bay bass, by boat on various lakes in the area. The angler–guide ratio is 2:1 or 3:1.

Year-round: half day, two anglers, $125; full day, two anglers, $200; includes drinks but not food, fishing license, or lodging.

Stream and Brook Fly Fishing School

www.streamandbrook.com
Cortina Inn
Rte. 4
Killington, VT 05751
802/773–3333, 800/451–6108

This school, at a luxury resort in central Vermont, runs a two-day beginner program. Conveniently, there's a stocked trout pond on premises (for casting lessons). Instruction takes place both on and off the water. The school caters to people of all levels. Trips include trout fishing and float fishing (in a raft or canoe, you fish for walleyes, peckoral, and bass).

Early May.–late Oct.: two-day midweek double, $489 per person ($124 nonparticipant), including two nights' lodging, two days' lessons, breakfast, and lunch; prices increase $60 per night during foliage season. Two-day weekend double, $509; $139 nonparticipant.

Tightlines Charters

913 Sunset Beach Rd.
Waterport, NY 14571
800/443–2510

This guide service is geared to anglers of all skill levels. Expect two to six people per trip. There are wilderness and rural locations: you can fish—for trout, salmon, muskies, and walleyes—on Lake Ontario and the St. Lawrence and Niagara rivers.

Mid-Apr.–mid-Sept.: five days, $925 per person with small boat (two-person minimum), $1,200 with large boat (four-person minimum). Price includes equipment only, no food or lodging.

Trinity Canyon Lodge

www.virtualcities.com/ons/ca/n/can9502.htm
27025 Hwy. 299 W
Junction City, CA 96048
530/623–6318, 800/354–9297

This rural lodge in the heart of Shasta-Trinity National Forest, on the banks of the Trinity River, is a diverse year-round fishery for salmon and trout. They run half- and full-day workshops on fly-fishing for trout, steelhead, and salmon; independent guides are available for drift boats and raft fishing. The angler–guide ratio is 2:1; bring tackle and gear.

Year-round: two-night minimum stay; cabin $55–$80 per night; motel $39–$65 per night; RV spot $20 per night; tent $10 per night (no meals). Guide service, half day $250 and full day $325 for one to two anglers.

Wood River Lodge

www.woodriverlodge.com
Box 1369
Dillingham, AK 99576
800/842–5205

Accessible only by air or by a long boat trip, this luxury fishing camp on the Agulowak River is in the bush, in southwest Alaska. If you're serious about fishing, these kinds of trips are often well worth it. Here you can fish for rainbow trout, lake trout, northern pike, Dolly Varden, Arctic char, and all of Alaska's salmon species on rivers, streams, and lakes—from a boat or by wading. The angler–guide ratio is 2:1 or 3:1.

June–Sept.: three days, $4,000 per person; four days, $5,000 per person; seven days, $6,000 per person; including flights, lodging in private cabins and all meals, guides, and gear but no license.

GOLF SCHOOLS

The Academy of Golf Dynamics

www.golfdynamics.com
45 Club Estates Pkwy.
Austin, TX 78738
800/879–2008, 512/261–3300

Three-day schools—personal improvement programs—take place in Colorado and Texas. The class ratio is 3:1, and the emphasis is not just on your skill level but also on your goals and temperament and the way you learn.

Texas: $850–$950, no lodging, daily Continental breakfast and one lunch, choice of on-course instruction or play on golf course after instruction. Colorado: $1,275 double, $1,450 single occupancy; includes lodging, three breakfasts, three lunches, and one round of golf.

Ben Sutton Golf School

www.golfschool.com
809 N. Pebble Beach Blvd.
Sun City Center, FL 33573
800/225–6923, 330/499–5235

In these three-, five-, and seven-day schools you get a class ratio of 5:1. There's a 50-acre learning center here, and the focus is on actual playing situations—you get digital photos of your swing, for example.

Prices from $425 to $1,800, including green fees and cart fees, and breakfast and dinner daily.

Dave Pelz Short Game School

www.pelzgolf.com
1310 R.R. 620 S
Suite B-1
Austin, TX 78734
800/833–7370, 512/263–7668

In the three-day school, with an instructor–student ratio of 4:1, you learn short game and putting in classroom and outdoor sessions. Schools are in California, Colorado, Florida, and Georgia.

Three days, $2,200–$3,585; prices differ per location and time of year. Boca Raton: $2,695 double, $3,230 single occupancy. Reynolds Plantation: $2,690 double, $3,050 single occupancy. Cordillera: from $2,840 double, $3,585 single occupancy. Napa Valley: $2,200, no lodging included. Package prices don't include meals.

David Leadbetter Golf Academy

www.davidleadbetter.com
1410 Masters Blvd.
Championsgate, FL 33896
888/633–5323, 407/787–3330

In the three-day schools, instructor–student ratios range from 1:1 to 4:1. Teaching is classroom oriented, though the schools also include on-course instruction; you focus on various aspects of the game. At the Mini school you spend two days on full swing technique and one day on short game. The Retreat school focuses on all aspects of the game; you get a detailed video and computer analysis, and a 9-hole on-course play on day three, then spend the balance of the day on a practice tee. With the Players school, playing and scoring are emphasized, as well as technique changes; there's a 3-hole play analysis, a 9-hole play with instructor, and then you play 18 holes with the instructor on the final day. They also run a school in Texas.

Three-day Mini school (three-hour sessions), $875, including lunch daily, club fitting, and gift bag. Three-day Retreat school (eight-hour sessions), $2,400.

Three-day Players school (eight-hour sessions), $3,000, including video and computer analysis, take-home video, club fitting, and lunch daily. Academy offers corporate rates for lodging at several area hotels.

Golf Advantage Schools

www.pinehurst.com/golf/advantage.asp
Box 4000
Pinehurst, NC 28374
800/795–4653, 919/295–8128

The four-day school has a ratio of 4:1 to 5:1; you focus on building fundamentals and even get videotape analysis. Besides the schools in North Carolina and Texas, there are schools in South Carolina and Virginia with three-day programs.

Pinehurst, North Carolina: four-day school, $2,250 double, $2,820 single occupancy, including lodging, three meals daily, green fees, and cart (not on No. 2, 7, or 8 course). Barton Creek, Austin, Texas: four-day school, $2,030 double, $2,330 single occupancy, including lodging, three meals daily, and instruction.

Golf Digest Instructional Schools

www.golfdigest.com/instruction/golfschools
7825 E. Redfield Rd.
Suite E
Scottsdale, AZ 85260
800/243–6121, 480/998–7430

Headquartered in Arizona, Golf Digest runs four-day schools across the country, with a maximum 6:1 student–instructor ratio. The outfit tailors its teaching to your particular, unique needs; there are also women's schools. Locations offering four-day schools include Arizona, California, Florida, Georgia, Nevada, South Carolina, Texas, and Virginia. Other programs are in Idaho, Illinois, Massachusetts, New Jersey, and New York.

Four-day school, $1,775 double, $4,395 single occupancy, depending on location and time of year. Price includes lodging and daily breakfast and lunch. Some locations also include a dinner/reception.

Jim Mclean Golf School

www.golfspan.com/instructors/jmclean/jmclean.asp
4400 N.W. 87th Ave.

Miami, FL 33178
800/723–6725, 305/591–6409

The six-day school in Miami and at two locations in LaQuinta, California, is the ultimate package for the better player. The school only accepts men with a 10 or lower handicap and women with 19 or lower handicap. In this program you get more than 40 hours of instruction and a 3:1 student–instructor ratio, including on-course lessons from Jim McLean, one of the top-ranked teachers in the country. There are five rounds of golf (four with your instructor) and a personalized videotape with comments from the instructor. In general the six-day and other schools here focus on your overall game but also offer short-game (from 100 yards in) and power schools (tee shots and long irons).

Six-day school, $6,050 double, $6,725 single occupancy. Price includes lodging, breakfast, and lunch daily. Other packages are also available at various locations in California, Florida, and Michigan.

John Jacobs' Practical Golf Schools

www.jacobsgolf.com
7825 E. Redfield Rd.
Scottsdale, AZ 85260-6977
800/472–5007, 480/991–8587

The emphasis of the four-day school, which has a 5:1 ratio, is on analyzing your swing faults. Instruction is in Alabama, Arizona, California, Colorado, Florida, Illinois, Indiana, Minnesota, Missouri, Nevada, New York, North Carolina, Pennsylvania, Texas, and Wisconsin along with Canada and Mexico. Five-day schools take place at some of these locations.

Four-day schools, $1,195 double, $1,425 single occupancy, including lodging, breakfast, and lunch daily.

Nicklaus/Flick Golf Schools

www.jimflickgolf.com
8070 E. Morgan Trail
Suite 150
Scottsdale, AZ 85258
800/642–5528, 480/991–4653

At the three-day schools there's a maximum 6:1 ratio. The focus is on personalized instruction, including health and fitness. You can opt for a Gold package, in Arizona, Florida, or Nevada, or choose the Platinum program in California, at Pebble Beach Golf Links, the Links at Spanish Bay, Spyglass Hill Golf Course, or Del Monte Golf Course. The Caribbean Cruise Lines, Ltd., operates a seven-day golf cruise called the Nicklaus-Flick Golf Academy at Sea.

Prices from $450 to $7,995. All packages include accommodations and daily breakfast and lunch. Three-day golf schools start at $3,795 double, $3,995 single occupancy for the Gold program and $7,300 double, $7,995 single occupancy for Platinum. Seven-day Nicklaus-Flick Golf Academy at Sea cruise package starts at $3,599 per person; book through www.golfahoy.com or 877/415–5442.

The Phil Ritson–Mel Sole Golf Schools

www.ritson-sole.com
Box 2580
Pawley's Island, SC 29585
800/624–4653, 843/237–4993

In the three-day school, with a maximum teacher–student ratio of 4:1, your individual needs are the focus. They stress comprehensive instruction, but you will also receive a personalized-instructional videotape for your home use. The school teaches all people of all abilities, and also runs courses specifically geared to women and seniors. Programs are in Georgia, Kansas, North Carolina, South Carolina, and Pennsylvania.

Prices from $1,030 to $1,470, depending on single or double occupancy and date of stay. Three-day package at Pawley's Island: three nights' lodging, three breakfasts, and use of practice range. Complimentary green fees based on availability; cart fees extra. Other three-day programs don't include food or lodging; Pawley's Island also runs a five-day school.

Rick Smith Golf Academy

www.ricksmith.com
3962 Wilkinson Rd.
Gaylord MI 49735
800/444–6711, 517/732–6711

The three-day school has an excellent 2:1 ratio and uses video extensively. They offer personalized instruction on full swing and short game. Instruction takes place in Florida, Michigan, and New York.

Three-day school, $1,250–$1,615.

Kitty Hawk Kites

www.kittyhawk.com
Box 1839
Nags Head, NC 27959
800/334–4777, 919/441–4124

Kitty Hawk Kites is the world's foremost hang-gliding school (founded 1974), giving 10,000 to 15,000 bunny-slope lessons a year—up to 30 certified instructors are employed June–September, so they maintain a 5:1 student–instructor ratio. There's all-season gliding (cooler northeasterly winds make the spring and fall ideal), so you can buy a lesson here year-round except Christmas Day. The Wright Brothers came here for a reason.

Outer Banks Chamber of Commerce, 919/441–8144. Year-round (by appointment only): Beginner Pilot Package, three tandems and 20 dune flights, $449; Novice Pilot Package, seven dune lessons, one 2,000-ft tandem aero-tow lesson, and two solo aero-tow flights, $1,249.

Lookout Mountain Flight Park

www.hangglide.com
Rte. 2
Box 215H
Rising Fawn, GA 30738
706/398–3541

This outfit is known for its "wonder winds," or gentle upward drafts, which are caused by warm air rising from Lookout Valley. These winds increase during the fall and spring seasons.

Closest accommodations at the Lookout Inn, 706/820–2000, or call the Chattanooga Chamber of Commerce, 615/756–2121. Closed Wed. Year-round (by appointment only): weekend package, 20 training hill flights, three tandem aero-tow flights, $399.

Mission Soaring

www.hang-gliding.com
1116 Wrigley Way
Milpitas, CA 95035
408/262–1055

Here you'll get extra-light, extra-slow, and extra-easy crafts, and training harnesses specially designed with student comfort in mind. The Hollister training site has bunny slopes that allow straight-into-the-wind launches in different directions; consistently gentle wind conditions; a huge landing area; and enough roadway to allow tandem and solo tow-launch via truck and winch.

Milpitas Chamber of Commerce, 408/262–2613. Lessons by appointment year-round: New Pilot Package (five 5-hour days on the bunny slope); $600. Inquire about tandem flights; prices often vary by altitude or with the number of flights in a package.

Morningside Flight Park

www.flymorningside.com
357 Morningside La.
North Charleston, NH
03603
603/542–4416

Morningside has a 250-ft gently sloping hill and all-terrain vehicles rigged to shuttle pilots and gliders from bottom to top between flights. The 3,800-ft runway is ideal for aero-towing. Slopes face northwest-west-southwest (240–310 degrees). The flight park includes a retail shop, camping area, and swimming pond.

For lodging call Claremont Chamber of Commerce, 603/543–1296. Apr.–Nov. (lessons by appointment only):

Weekend Introductory Package, two days of lessons, $190. Hang-1 Training Program, six days of lessons, $530.

Raven Sky Sports

www.hanggliding.com
Box 101
Whitewater, WI 53190
414/473–8800

Owner Brad Kushner has been flying for 20 years and teaching for 17. His methods include special instruction for people with disabilities, using equipment that permits rolling takeoffs and landings. This method also allows Kushner to train folks up to 300 pounds (200 is typically the cutoff). The 30- to 80-ft bunny slopes here conveniently face different wind directions, so you can catch the wind wherever it's blowing.

Whitewater Chamber of Commerce, 414/473–4005. Whitewater Lakes Recreation Area, 414/473–6427. Mar.–Nov. (lessons by appointment only): five-day package, $350; tandem flight (aero-tow to 3,000 ft), $145; intro package (one hill class and one tandem flight), $225.

Sky Masters School of Hang Gliding

www.users.qwest.net/~skymasters/index.html
37509 N. 7th St.
Phoenix, AZ 85086
623/465–3240

This outfit offers multiple aero-towing and weekend foot-launch packages. Best, you learn hang gliding in a unique environment—by launching off Sheba and Merriam craters, two ancient shield volcanoes on the edge of the painted dessert, near Flagstaff, Arizona.

Greater Phoenix Chamber of Commerce, 602/254–5521. Aero-tow Level 1 instruction package (includes ground school and eight tandem flights to 2,500 ft), $595. Footlaunch Level 1 instruction package (weekend at the Craters, radio supervision), $295.

Wallaby Ranch

www.wallaby.com
1805 Dean Still Rd.
Wallaby Ranch, FL 33837-9357
800/925–5229, 864/424–0070

This outfit, open 365 days a year, offers aero-tow instruction only. You can launch in any direction here. Camping is on the grounds, and shower facilities are available; breakfast and dinner are served daily. A swimming pool, trampoline, and bike trails are on-site, and the ranch is minutes from Disney World, the Fantasy of Flight Museum, and other Orlando theme park attractions.

Kissimmee/Osceola County Chamber of Commerce, 407/847–3174. Lessons year-round, reservations not required. Ten-lesson package, $650.

Wasatch Wings

www.wasatch.com/~wings
10889 South Shady Dell Dr.
Sandy, UT 84094
801/277–1042

It's one of the few places in the country where you can earn a Hang I (beginner) rating in a week or a Hang II (novice) rating in two weeks. The wind conditions make this possible: the morning wind funnels straight up its 300-ft south-facing slope, and the afternoon wind funnels straight up its 1,000-ft north-facing slope, so more experienced students can get two lessons a day. (At most schools you can only take two to four lessons a week.)

Mountain Shadows
Campground, 801/571–4024.
Salt Lake City Chamber of
Commerce, 801/364–3631.
Apr.–Nov. (lessons by ap-
pointment only): Gliding
Course, five lessons and
half-hour tandem, $470.

Windsports Hang Gliding School

www.windsports.com
12623 Gridley St.
Sylmar, CA 91342
818/367–2430

Besides being one of the oldest continuously operated
hang-gliding schools in the
country (founded 1974), this
outfit has a three-story beginner site at Dockweiler
Beach (near L.A. airport),
and run more advanced and
tandem flying at their
mountain site at the base of
Los Angeles's Kagel
Mountain.

Van Nuys Chamber of
Commerce, 818/989–0300.
Closed Mon.; open year-
round by appointment only.
New Pilot Package: five lessons (four hours per day for
five days), $495.

HIKING AND BACKPACKING

Adirondack Mountain Club New York (ADC)

www.adk.org
814 Goggins Rd.
Lake George, NY 12845
800/395–8080, 518/668–4447

Backpack 4 mi into base
camp at the Johns Brook
Lodge, and then spend four
days exploring trails and
peaks in the checkerboard of
public and private land
known as Adirondack Park,
the largest park in the country outside of Alaska. Day
hikes on this High Peaks
Traverse in the Adirondacks
trip range from 6 to 8 mi
and may include a climb of
5,543-ft Mt. Marcy, crown
jewel of the High Peaks.
You can also see other parts
of the Adirondacks with
ADC, as well as Maine,
Utah, Colorado, and
California.

High Peaks Traverse in the
Adirondacks, Aug.: five
days, $312 ($281 for mem-
bers), including bunk-room
accommodations and meals.

Appalachian Mountain Club New Hampshire (AMC)

www.outdoors.org
Box 298
Gorham, NH 03581
603/466–2727

A strenuous but panoramic six-hut traverse—called Hut to Hut in the White Mountains' Presidential Range—winds through a weather-scoured succession of peaks, mostly above the tree line. The AMC's hut system is reminiscent of the old stone huts and auberges found in the Alps. The Club offers an extensive schedule of other hiking and back-packing trips (called "out-door workshops") throughout the White Mountains and Catskills and near the Delaware Water Gap.

Hut to Hut in the White Mountains' Presidential Range, Aug.: eight days, $1,094 ($985 for members), including dormitory-style lodging in huts and meals.

Backroads

www.backroads.com
801 Cedar St.
Berkeley, CA 94710
800/462–2848, 510/527–1555

On the six-day Walking Santa Fe and Taos (New Mexico) trip you explore the scenic and cultural contrasts that define northern New Mexico, with hikes in Bandelier National Monument and the Pecos Wilderness, and guided tours of Santa Fe and Taos. Backroads is one of the largest adventure travel companies in the United States; among its other hiking trips are outings in New England, Georgia, the Rockies, and California.

Walking Santa Fe and Taos, May–June or Sept.–Oct.: six days, $1,998, including lodging in inns and all meals except one dinner.

Country Inns Along the Trail

www.inntoinn.com
Box 59
Montgomery, VT 05470
800/838–3301, 802/326–2072

Six days of hiking, on the Haunted Vermont trip, brings you through history- and legend-rich west-central Vermont, in search of ghosts, haunted houses, and grave-yards. Routes cover 5 to 8 mi daily. A van provides trans-portation to each night's lodging. Country Inns also offers other guided, as well as self-guided, hiking trips in Vermont.

Haunted Vermont, Oct.: six days, $849, including lodging in historic inns and meals.

Glacier Wilderness Guides

www.glacierguides.com
Box 330
West Glacier, MT 59936
800/521–7238, 406/387–5555

Six-day backpacking trips take place amid the glacially sculpted rock walls and parapets, high-alpine basins, and waterfalls and ice caves that are Glacier National Park's glory. Itineraries vary according to current trail conditions and the desires and physical fitness of the group, but daily distances cover 7–9 mi, with moderate elevation gains.

Glacier National Park, June–Sept.: six days, $630, including meals (not tents or other gear).

GORP Travel

www.gorptravel.com
Box 1486
Boulder, CO 80306
877/440–4677, 303/516–1153

This adventure-travel agency runs dozens of hiking trips throughout the United States, including a six-day van-supported trip through Bryce and Zion national parks in southern Utah. Bryce is known for its hoodoos, rock spires sculpted by erosion with a delicate artistry. Zion is rockier, with cliffs rising as much as 3,000 ft above the various forks of the Virgin River.

June and Sept.: six days, $1,795, including lodging and all meals except one dinner.

Mountain Travel-Sobek/Alaska Discovery

www.akdiscovery.com
5310 Glacier Hwy.
Juneau, AK 99801
800/586–1911, 907/780–6226

A rigorous 10-day trip—Hiking and Sea Kayaking in Wrangell–St. Elias National Park—takes you along the fjords of remote Icy Bay, at the foot of the St. Elias Mountains in southeastern Alaska. By sea kayak and on foot, you'll explore an untamed region of immense glaciers, abundant wildlife, and high peaks, crowned by 18,000-ft Mt. St. Elias. Each night's camp is reached by paddling. Alaska Discovery is owned by Mountain Travel-Sobek, one of the biggest international adventure-travel outfitters.

Hiking and Sea Kayaking in Wrangell–St. Elias National Park, July: 10 days, $2,450, including meals, tents, and sea-kayaking gear.

On the Loose Expeditions

www.otloose.com
1035 Carse Rd.
Huntington, VT 05462
800/688–1481, 802/434–7257

For eight days you hike on easy to moderate terrain among the red rock desert landscape of Grand Gulch canyon in southeastern Utah. Thanks to gear-toting llamas, you can eschew carrying a heavy pack and instead focus on the petroglyphs, kivas, and other cultural remnants of the once-vibrant Anasazi who lived in this sometimes mystical region. On the Loose also offers hiking trips in Vermont's Green Mountains.

Grand Gulch Llama Packing, Apr.: eight days, $1,350, including meals and tents.

REI Adventures

www.reiadventures.com
Box 1938
Sumner, WA 98390
800/622–2236, 253/437–1100

During the seven days (35 mi) you backpack in the shadow of Mt. Rainier, you'll encounter dense forests, wildflower-filled meadows, cascading waterfalls, and abundant wildlife. The route loops through a northern section of the park and includes a section of the famed Wonderland Trail, which circumnavigates the peak. REI also runs other hiking and backpacking trips in Alaska, California, and the Rockies.

Backpacking in Mt. Rainier National Park, July–Aug.: seven days, $995, including meals and tents. Sign up three to four months in advance.

Sierra Club Outings

www.sierraclub.org/outings
85 2nd St., 2nd floor
San Francisco, CA 94105
415/977–5522

Backpack in John Muir's Footsteps—on this trip you undertake six days in the Big South Fork National Recreation Area in northern Tennessee, where John Muir visited in 1867. You travel through remote forests, past precipitous gorges, and over the wild Cumberland plateau, for an average of 6 mi per day. This is just one trip from the Sierra Club's extensive slate of hiking and backpacking trips throughout the United States; specific offerings vary from year to year, and precise itineraries are up to each group leader.

Backpacking in John Muir's Footsteps, Sept.: six days, $475, including meals (lodging is camping out; no gear is included).

Sourdough Outfitters

www.sourdoughoutfitters.com
Box 66
Bettles, AK 99726
907/692–5252

Among the backpacking trips offered by Sourdough Outfitters in north-central Alaska's Brooks Range is an eight-day outing in the Arrigetch Peaks. Backpack into base camp in the Arrigetch's primary valley, then day hike into the wild surroundings: austere mountain wilderness; abundant wildlife, including caribou, wolves, and grizzly bears; glacier-fed streams; open tundra; and near-vertical granite peaks that take their name from the Eskimo term for outstretched fingers.

The Brooks Range/Arrigetch Peaks, June–Aug.: eight days, $1,950, including meals and tents.

Timberline Adventures

www.timbertours.com
7975 E. Harvard
Suite J
Denver, CO 80231
800/417–2453, 303/368–4418

On the six-day trip into Grand Canyon's South Rim (Arizona), you hike down into the Grand and Havasu canyons—and going downhill may be more demanding than going up. The three waterfalls in the latter make it the Grand's most spectacular tributary canyon. Though originally a bike-tour specialist, Timberline also runs hiking tours and several hiking-biking combos in the West.

Grand Canyon's South Rim, Apr.–May and Sept.–Oct.: six days, $1,495, including lodging and meals.

Walking the World

www.walkingtheworld.com
Box 1186
Fort Collins, CO 80522-1186
800/340–9255, 970/498–0500

This outfit specializes in hiking trips for people over 50, but it doesn't soft-peddle the itineraries under the assumption that older people are less fit. On a trip through Maine—The Coast for Active Seniors—you hike among the fall foliage in Acadia National Park and near Camden, enjoy a sail on Penobscot Bay, and attend lobster feasts. Other U.S. destinations include the Blue Ridge Mountains of North Carolina, the desert Southwest, and volcanoes in Hawaii.

The Coast for Active Seniors, Sept.–Oct.: eight days, $1,895, including lodging in bed-and-breakfasts and meals except four dinners.

Wild Horizons Expeditions

www.
wildhorizonsexpeditions.
com
Box 7627
Jackson Hole, WY 83002
888/734–4453

A seven-day backpacking trip takes you through the craggy and remote Wind Rivers, Wyoming's most extensive mountain range. Itineraries vary, but groups usually cover 8–9 mi of trail each day. Steep climbs, some off-trail hiking, and rugged terrain earn this trip a strenuous rating. Wild Horizons offers other backpacking trips in Wyoming, as well as southern Utah and Arizona.

The Wind River Range, Aug.: seven days, $1,225, including meals, tents, sleeping bags/pads, and all other backpacking gear.

The World Outdoors

www.theworldoutdoors.com
2840 Wilderness Pl.
Suite F
Boulder, CO 80301
800/488–8483, 303/413–0938

Among the hiking trips it offers in the West, the World Outdoors runs a six-day trip into the heart of Colorado, with hikes averaging 6–10 mi daily (a van carries your gear). Day hikes cover sections of the Colorado Trail and the nearby Holy Cross Wilderness. You overnight in the rustic log cabins of the 10th Mountain Division Hut System.

Hut to Hut in the Holy Cross Wilderness, July–Aug.: six days, $1,295, including lodging and meals.

MOUNTAIN BIKING

Austin-Lehman Adventures

www.backcountrytours.com
Box 81025
Billings, MT 59108-1025
800/575–1540, 406/655–4591

Founded in 1986 as Backcountry Bicycle Tours, this outfit is known for its environmentally conscious touring programs and its exploration of new trails in the Southwest, Rockies, and on the West Coast. Northern Arizona's Red Rock Country, a six-day dirt-road ride, covers three distinct areas of Arizona: the forested southern ridge of the Colorado Plateau, the red rock country of Sedona, and the high forest of Mormon Lake—at a leisurely 5–20 mi per day.

Northern Arizona's Red Rock Country, Apr., May, and Sept.: six days, $2,295, including five nights' lodging (the posh Enchantment Resort in Sedona, mountain-top cabins, and inns) and all meals (highfalutin' fare or southwestern cuisine); mountain-bike rental $129.

Back Country Excursions

www.bikebackcountry.com
Box 365
Limerick, ME 04048
207/625–8189

Excursions are run from the lodge outside Limerick (2½ hours from Boston), in the middle of heavy forest and hills, surrounded by 10,000 acres of a semi-wilderness preserve. On the Land and Sea (Maine) trip you cover, daily, 20–35 mi of single-track and dirt roads that wind up to the foothills (no murderous climbs), around lakes and forest. Fit beginners will learn lots about mountain biking on the varied trails; advanced riders can bang away.

Land and Sea, May and Sept.: two days, camping $140, yurt $160 (a circular Quonset hut–style tent), private room $180, not including dinners. Mountain-bike rental $30 per day.

Craftsbury Mountain Biking Center

www.craftsbury.com
Box 31
Craftsbury Common, VT 05827
800/729–7751, 802/586–7767

You show up, tell the guides what kind of riding you'd

like to do, and they take you out on the best stuff they know. You need at least four people to set up a stay here, unless you piggyback with other stragglers. Lodging options include bed-and-breakfast rooms, suites with private baths, and cottages with kitchenettes. The food—the group decides how many meals a day are provided—is homemade.

Any duration, all season (May–Oct.), guides $200 full day first person, $15 each additional person. Prices don't include lodging or meals. Mountain-bike rental $25 per day or $35 for two days.

Elk River Touring Center

www.ertc.com
Hwy. 219
Slatyfork, WV 26291
304/572–3771

The center is a former sheep farm in an area of West Virginia (heaven for hard-core riders) that's poised to become the next hot mountain-bike destination. It has mountain single-track without altitude problems, technical challenges as good as any of the rocky trails farther north in the east, and in-credible valley vistas. The Twin Peaks trip is full of muddy and treacherous trails, heading into the vast Monongahela National Forest. Days are long, and much of the ride is not supported. Beginners and intermediate riders: opt for the primarily self-guided trip along West Virginia's Greenbriar River; if you get tired, you can take the shuttle back to the touring center.

Twin Peaks, July 14–19: four days, $499, including B&B and inn lodging and breakfasts and dinners. Greenbriar River, May–Oct.: four days, $329, including inn lodging and dinners and breakfasts (lunch is do-it-yourself, in towns you ride through).

Escape Adventures

www.escapeadventures.com
8221 W. Charleston, No. 101
Las Vegas, NV 89117
800/596–2953, 702/596–2953

Founded in 1992, Escape runs tours nationwide but specializes in Colorado and the desert Southwest. Single-track purists: check out the remote Grand Staircase–Escalante National Monument (UT), the desert Southwest's most stunning country; expect to ride 18 mi daily on primitive trails (technical and bumpy). Rated one of the 50 best trips in America by *Bicycling* magazine, the five-day Tahoe Singletrack takes in the Tahoe Rim Trail and the legendary Flume trail. It's hard, high-altitude riding, but worth it. The six-day Cascade Lakes Singletrack trip explores the newly discovered single-track of the Deschutes National Forest in Oregon's dramatic Cascade Range. You ride Mt. Bachelor and the Three Sisters volcanoes, with incredible views of waterfalls and mountain-fed lakes, covering 17 mi of great single-track daily.

Grand Staircase–Escalante Singletrack, June, Aug., and Sept.: six days, $995, including five nights' lodging and all meals. Tahoe Singletrack, two all-inns trips July–Aug., one camp/inns trip July 7–12: five days, $1,620; $1,095 camp/inns, includes lodging and meals. Cascade Lakes Singletrack, July and Sept. six days, $1,095, including lodging (camping) and meals. Bike rental $108–$250 per week for all trips.

Kaibab Mountain Bike Tours

www.kaibabtours.com
Box 339
Moab, UT 84532
800/451–1133, 801/259–7423

Established in 1987 to provide trips in southern Utah and the Colorado Plateau, this camping-oriented outfitter offers mainly dirt-road or rocky-surface trips (but single-track is available). The North Rim of Grand Canyon trip begins in Arizona's Kaibab National Forest and then follows the Grand Canyon's North Rim (unsullied pine forest) via a network of crisscrossing dirt roads and the single-track of the Arizona Trail. Daily you cover 20–25 mi of tough single-track (with dirt-road options). Riding is rough through the Maze in Canyonlands National Park: you pedal 27 mi daily and test your skills on the slickrock, a bed of rumpled sandstone rock that provides a veritable roller-coaster thrill ride.

North Rim of Grand Canyon, May–Oct.: four days, $750; five days, $875, including camping, meals, shuttle from St. George; mountain-bike rental $125–$250 per week. The Maze,

Apr.–May and Sept.–Oct.: five days, $995, including meals and return flight to Moab (bring or rent camping equipment); mountain-bike rental $35–$50 per day.

Michigan Bicycle Touring

www.bikembt.com
3512 Red School Rd.
Kingsley, MI 49649
616/263–5885

Michigan's upper peninsula may be the wildest and most undeveloped area in the Midwest. The five-day Porcupine Mountain Bike and Hike tour explores Michigan's wild lands; intermediate cyclists can ride both double- and single-track that twists through thick woods or winds down to Lake Superior. The area has nearly 100 waterfalls, miles of shoreline, and thousands of small lakes. Several nature hikes are included in the trip price.

Porcupine Mountain Bike and Hike, July–Aug.: five days, $965, including lodging (three nights Black River Lodge, two at the base of the Porcupine Mountains in Silver City) and meals. Shuttle from Marquette $25. Mountain-bike rental $95.

Rim Tours

www.rimtours.com
94 W. 1st North
Moab, UT 84532
800/626–7335, 801/259–5223

This was the first mountain-bike touring company in Moab, Utah, the sport's original vacation destination, and the company lives up to its reputation for doing classic rides exceptionally well. Views from the 100-mi White Rim Trail (Utah) dazzle. The trail follows the Green and Colorado rivers from high atop Canyonlands National Park. The riding is rolling, with technical bits; you ride 20–30 mi daily and also take hikes into the canyons. On the Colorado Singletrack trip, you get the tech stuff, the buff stuff, screaming descents, big-altitude gaspers. Everyone from novices to die-hard dirtheads can hack it, but expect to ride 20–30 mi daily and to suck big wind if you're a flatlander (the altitude will get you).

The White Rim, Apr.–May and Sept.–Oct.: four days, $650; three days, $550; includes all camping and meals. Colorado Singletrack, July–Sept.: five days, $825, including four nights in inns/ski resorts, and all meals. Mountain-bike rental for all trips $35 per day.

Western Spirit Cycling

www.westernspirit.com
Box 411
Moab, UT 84532
800/845–2453

This outfitter has a knack for finding rarely used single-track and interesting new routes. Established in 1989, Western Spirit runs 10 tours in Utah, Colorado, and Idaho (think "Civilized tours in un-civilized terrain"). On the popular Backcountry Hot Springs trip (Idaho) you punctuate your 12-mi-daily rides with nightly soaks. There's some single-track and climbing, notably an 8-mi grind on the third day; athletic beginners will be fine. The Sawtooth Singletrack expedition (Idaho) explores the Stanley Basin, sandwiched between two wilderness areas—it's a stash of the best remote single-track in America.

Backcountry Hot Springs, July–Aug.: five days, $895. Sawtooth Singletrack, July–Aug.: five days, $875. All trips include four nights' lodging (usually camping) and all meals. Mountain-bike rental, $35 per day.

NATURE CAMPS

Cornell's Adult University

www.cau.cornell.edu
626 Thurston Ave.
Ithaca, NY 14850
607/255–6260

The draw here is the instructors—all are current or retired professors from Cornell. Each summer there are 40-plus expert-taught classes, including five- to seven-day ecology workshops. Lectures and lab work are combined with hiking, bird walks, and field trips; there's a maximum of 15 students per class. A youth program serves children ages 3–16. Programs are taught in up-state New York, New Jersey, and other U.S. and international locations.

Tuition: $960 per week adults, $366–$526 children, including room and board (second child at 50% dis-count).

National Audubon Society

www.audubon.com
Ecology Camps & Workshops
613 Riversville Rd.
Greenwich, CT 06831
806/428–3826, 203/869–2017

These 6- to 11-day adult summer camps combine political activism with wilderness exploration. Expect approximately 40 students and 8 instructors (professors or naturalists) per camp. Camps are run at locales nationwide. The focus is on geology, marine life, birds, mammals, plants, insects, and weather.

Tuition: $380–$995. Room and board usually included (depending on the program).

National Wildlife Federation

www.nwf.org
Family Summits Office
11100 Wildlife Center Dr.
Reston, VA 20190
800/606–9563

The single program here emphasizes conservation in a different locale (a resort) each year. Conservation education may include such areas as declining wild wolf populations and methods of advocating preservation. Adult classes and field trips are led by expert naturalists. Daytime youth programs are available for kids ages three and up, including teen service projects. Camps are open to everyone and are very kid-friendly; family evening activities including dances and slide shows.

Tuition: $400 adults (with $15 annual membership), $200 children; room and board extra.

Sierra Club Outings

www.outings.sierraclub.org/
national
85 2nd St., 2nd floor
San Francisco, CA 94105
415/977–5522

Founded in 1901, the Sierra Club offers more than 330 domestic and international excursions in hiking, backpacking, biking, and kayaking. They focus on wilderness conservation and environmental issues, such as conflicts between native and non-native species. In service-oriented trips, you'll participate in trail-building, revegetation, or reconstruction of historic sites; trips are aimed at giving you an unforgettable outdoor experience. There are some family-oriented programs, and most programs are open to children passing physical fitness and experience requirements.

Tuition/fees: $350–$1,000, including meals and accommodations (tents, campgrounds, rustic cabins, lodges).

The Yellowstone Institute

www.yellowstoneassociation.org
Box 117
Yellowstone National Park, WY 82190
307/344–2294

This nonprofit organization, established in 1976, has 165 mainly adult-oriented, expert-led programs. Fieldwork is emphasized: topics include geysers, wildlife watching, wildflowers, and history. There are 15–20 participants per class (in Yellowstone National Park). Sixteen cabins are available (no plumbing, each sleeps one to three), and there are facilities in a new bathhouse and the main building.

Most programs cost $180 and last three days. Other programs vary in cost and length, ranging from $55 to $835 (extra $30 nightly charged for cabin stay).

Yosemite Association Field Seminars

www.yosemite.org
Box 230
El Portal, CA 95318
209/379–2646

Founded in 1924, the Yosemite Association runs five-day environmental education programs—typically field trips with group leaders (naturalists or other experts). You can usually expect between 8 and 20 participants, ages 18 and up. Activities include plant identification, wildlife observation, and geological instruction.

Tuition: five days, $400. Camping available at no fee to participants (bring your own equipment and food) at campgrounds throughout the park; nearby lodging is at your own expense.

NORDIC SKIING

The Balsams/ Wilderness

www.thebalsams.com
Dixville Notch, NH 03576
800/255–0600

This historic Grand Hotel resort on 15,000 acres, with 250 inches of snow annually, 95 km of groomed cross-country trails, and 30 km of backcountry trails, is, thankfully, uncrowded. Many instructors-guides are certified with Professional Ski Instructors of America; there's good telemark instruction and a snowboard halfpipe. You'll find other winter activities and evening entertainment here as well.

Mid-Dec.–late Mar.: midweek five-night package, $625–$725. Price includes lodging, breakfasts, dinners, use of both cross-country and alpine facilities, trail fee, and guided tours.

Boundary Country Trekking

www.boundarycountry.com
173 Little Ollie Rd.
Grand Marais, MN 55604
800/322–8327

The four cross-country trail networks include more than 200 km of ski trails—the 100-km Upper Gunflint Trail connects to the 29-km straight-run Banadad Trail and the 55-km Central Gunflint Trail. There are several lodges here; you can also indulge in a lodge-to-lodge or yurt-to-yurt self-guided trek. Boundary Country Trekking will instruct you on how to get from lodge to lodge.

Late Nov.–early Apr.: Nordic SkiVenture Package, six to seven nights, $660–$755; the larger the group, the lower the rate. Price includes lodging and meals, depending on the package. Banadad Deluxe Ski Adventure, two to three nights, including lodge and yurt accommodations and all meals, $280, two-person minimum; $375 for three nights. Other multiday packages can be arranged.

Country Inns Along the Trail

www.inntoinn.com
Box 59
Montgomery, VT 05470
800/838–3301, 802/326–2072

Ski from one charming Vermont inn to the next—on the Five Days in Colonial Inns trip—in the remote and beautiful Moosalamoo Recreation Area of the Green Mountain National Forest. Your bags get sent along and arrive at your destination at the end of the day, along with a cup of warm cider.

Jan.–early Mar.: five days, $695, including lodging, meals, and trail fees.

Izaak Walton Inn

www.izaakwaltoninn.com
Box 653
Essex, MT 59916
406/888–5700

If you're an experienced backcountry skier (or you bring a guide) you'll have plenty of options for exploring nearby Glacier National

Park. The terrain varies: steep descents; leisurely, relatively flat ski tours; and 33 km of groomed trails. Instructors are PSIA certified. The comfortable lodge is serviced directly by Amtrak—call beforehand and the inn's staff will pick you up. There are a few renovated turn-of-the-20th-century caboose cabins for the true train enthusiast here. Guided tours to nearby Autumn Creek and Snyder Lake will get you into the backcountry and into some sweet, waist-high powder.

Mid-Nov.–mid-Apr.: six nights, $1,427. Price includes two meals per day, lodging, and some guided tours.

Jackson Ski Touring Foundation

www.jacksonxc.org
Rte. 16
Box 216
Jackson, NH 03846
603/383–9355

More than 157 km of groomed trails and 90 km of backcountry trails that link with trails at Pinkham Notch and White Mountain National Forest span this large trail network. There's a courtesy patrol and rescue service, PSIA-certified instructors, and, nearby, cozy lodges and inns and two alpine ski areas: Wildcat and Black Mountain. An unusually high number of trails here are rated "most difficult." If you opt for the Inn Sampler Program, each innkeeper at the place you're staying shuttles you to a different trailhead each morning, and the next one picks you up in late afternoon.

Jackson Lodging Bureau, 800/866–3334. Mid-Dec.–late Mar.: trail fees $12–$14. Inn Sampler Program, midweek Jan. and Mar.: prices based on multiday customized packages. Individual inns also have custom multiday packages.

Lone Mountain Ranch

www.lmranch.com
Box 160069
Big Sky, MT 59716
800/514–4644

There are 75 km of groomed trails and myriad guided-backcountry possibilities in the rugged Montana Rockies. There are individual log cabins for guests as well as a central lodge for evening activities and dining. The ranch also offers guided cross-country tours in nearby Yellowstone National Park. If you want variety, the nearby downhill ski area, Big Sky Ski Resort, has some of the gnarliest terrain and deepest powder in the West.

Early Dec.–early Apr.: seven-day package, $3,202 per couple. Price includes, lodging, trail pass, and meals.

Maplelag

www.maplelag.com
30501 Maplelag Rd.
Callaway, MN 56521-9643
800/654–7711, 218/375–4466

This 600-acre maple syrup farm is a laid-back, all-inclusive destination resort, with Norwegian-style architecture, 53 km of groomed trails, PSIA instruction, children's programs, and 6 km of skating trails. Lucky, the resort's canine mascot, may follow you on your ski, or fireside to enjoy a cookie from the "bottomless cookie jar." The complex is large, with family-oriented lodging as well as smaller cabins.

Mid-Dec.–mid-Mar.: two nights, $180–$242 (extra nights $80). Price includes three meals a day; $15 surcharge for linens. Instruction costs extra.

Off the Beaten Path

www.offthebeatenpath.com
7 E. Beall St.
Bozeman, MT 59715
800/445–2995, 406/586–1311

An all-inclusive tour through Yellowstone National Park (Idaho and Wyoming), not exclusively a ski-touring adventure, incorporates horse-drawn sleds, cross-country skis, and snowshoes to get you off the beaten path and into Yellowstone's wilds, and you get to stay in a cozy lodge to boot. This outfit also customizes trips in the Canadian Rockies and Grand Tetons. On these trips you can pick your poison, be it 10 days of hard-core ski touring or a more mellow trip where you'll get a rest from time to time by taking horse-drawn sleds or snowmobiles.

Yellowstone Winter Discovery, Feb.: seven nights, $2,690. Price includes food and lodging.

Rendezvous Ski Tours

www.skithetetons.com
1110 Alta North Rd.
Alta, WY 83422
877/754–4887, 307/353–2900

This outfit's backcountry trips take place on the western slope of the Grand Tetons. Rendezvous operates three yurts, which provide access to the Jedediah Smith Wilderness Area and Grand Teton National Park. Their highly trained guides will bring you safely through this rugged region, which often receives up to 500 inches of snow annually.

Late Nov.–early Apr.: one to four days, $175–$640. Price includes food and lodging.

Royal Gorge Cross Country Ski Resort

www.royalgorge.com
Box 1100
Soda Springs, CA 95728
800/666–3871; 800/500–3871 outside northern California

America's largest cross-country ski resort has 330 km of groomed trails and four surface lifts to carry you home when your legs scream for mercy. Instructors are PSIA certified. About 400 inches of annual snowfall dump on California's ruggedly beautiful Sierra Nevada. You can either stay right out on the trails or at the bed-and-breakfast.

Mid-Nov.–mid-May: all-inclusive Wilderness Lodge package (you sleigh or ski in) includes lessons, trail passes, lodging, and three meals daily. Price per multi-day packages is based on $169 per night, based on two- or three-night minimum; longer packages are prorated. Rainbow Lodge bed-and-breakfast Midweek Special package, based on two- to five-night stays, costs about $183 per person for two nights and includes lessons, trail package, lodging, breakfast, trail passes, and standard group lesson.

Sun Mountain Lodge

www.sunmountainlodge.com
Box 1000
Winthrop, WA 98862
800/572–0493, 509/996–2211

More than 200 km of groomed trails wind through some of the Washington Cascades' most scenic terrain, and the lodge offers high-quality instruction and tours so you can explore the best of it. The Methow Valley Sports Trails Association, a local nonprofit, maintains nearly 200 km of cross-country trails here; it's one of the biggest Nordic ski centers in the country, and trails are unrepeated and machine-groomed. Nearby, the Loup is a decent downhill area.

Dec.–Apr.: three-night cross-country ski package, $336. Price includes meals, lodging and ski pass. Trail Pass $15.

Sun Valley Trekking

www.svtrek.com
Box 2200
Sun Valley, ID 83353
208/788–1966

This outfit's 10-day ski-mountaineering trek through Alaska's isolated and beautiful Saint Elias Range suits hard-core adventurers. The knowledgeable guides provide fine mountaineering instruction; advanced skiers and/or mountaineers who are ready to pioneer lines in one of North America's most remote wildernesses can expect many first ascent-descent opportunities. Good physical conditioning and strong intermediate backcountry skiing abilities are required. This operator, which has been guiding backcountry skiing and trekking trips since 1982, also runs trips in Wyoming and Idaho; most go from hut to hut or yurt to yurt.

Saint Elias Ski Mountaineering, May 17–26: 10-day tour, $1,575. Price includes ski rentals and food (you camp in tents).

10th Mountain Division Huts

www.paragonguides.com
Paragon Guides
Box 130
Vail, CO 81658
877/926–5299, 907/926–5299

With 24 huts linked by more than 480 km of trails, the 10th Mountain Division Hut system offers great backcountry options for experienced backcountry skiers. It's the country's most extensive system of ski-in huts and yurts, and it provides access to terrain in the White River, Arapaho, and San Isabel national forests. Note: due to the lightness of Colorado's "champagne powder" and its propensity to avalanche, you should use extreme caution in the backcountry.

Late Nov.–mid-Apr.: three to six days, $990–$1,860. Price includes food, lodging, and guide services. 10th Mountain Division Huts, 1280 Ute Ave., Suite 21, Aspen, CO 81612, 970/925–5775, www.huts.org. Reservations required ($22–$35 per night).

Trapp Family Lodge

www.trappfamily.com
700 Trapp Hill Rd.
Box 1428
Stowe, VT 05672
800/826–7000, 802/253–8511

This is the kingpin of all the cross-country ski centers around Stowe: it has 45 km of groomed trails and 100 km of backcountry trails. The lodge offers guided backcountry trips and instruction, as well as Tyrolean-style accommodations. You also have easy access to nearby downhill slopes.

Mid-Dec.–early Apr.: cross-country package, about $830–$890. Price includes breakfast, trail fee, one-hour private lesson for each adult, and rental equipment for three days, two nights. Packages can be created for longer stays.

Vista Verde Ranch

www.vistaverde.com
Box 465
Steamboat Springs, CO 80477
970/879–3858, 800/526–7433

Founded as a cattle ranch, this 540-acre spread offers views of the spectacular Routt National Forest and gives you access to virtually unlimited powder—PSIA-certified instructors will guide you to hip-high powder stashes and ensure your safety. Spanning the ranch are 30 km of groomed trails. Steamboat Springs, a top-notch ski area, is nearby.

Mid-Dec.–mid-Mar.: five-night package, $1,300–$1,500. Price includes food and instruction/guiding services.

Woodstock Ski Touring Center

www.woodstockinn.com
Woodstock Inn and Resort
14 The Green
Woodstock, VT 05091-1298
800/448–7900, 802/457–1100

This is a complete Nordic center, with 60 km of groomed trails on the golf course and centuries-old carriage roads. Also available are PSIA instruction, children's programs, tobogganing, snowshoeing, and downhill skiing at nearby Suicide Six.

Family Ski Week, Jan.–Feb.: three-night package, $389 per person, including lodging for two adults, lift tickets and rental equipment, one group lesson per person, breakfast, van service, and sleigh ride. Ski Vermont Free package (arrive Sun.–Thurs. mid-Dec.–early Apr.), $195–$589 daily rate, includes lodging, rental equipment, and trail fees.

RIVER RAFTING

Alaska Discovery

www.akdiscovery.com
5449-4 Shaune Dr.
Juneau, AK 99801
800/586–1911, 907/780–6226

Alaska's premier guide service, in business since 1972 (and now owned by Mountain Travel Sobek), runs an unparalleled 160-mi adventure on the legendary Tat, in southeastern Alaska. Using oar rafts (you help paddle while the guides row), you'll float by calving glaciers and through wonderful Class II–III rapids. On the terrific side hikes you're likely to see moose, bear, wolves, and bald eagles. This outfit pays attention to details and has expert Alaskan guides, as well as great food.

Rafting the Tatshenshini River, early July–early Sept.: 10 days, $1,850, including catered camping.

American River Touring Association (ARTA)

www.ARTA.org
24000 Casa Loma Rd.
Groveland, CA 95321
800/323–2782, 209/962–7873

Known as ARTA, this nonprofit corporation, in business since 1963, runs about 20 different trips in five western states. Trips accommodate people of all abilities, and the white water ranges from moderate Class III to big-water Class V. You travel in 14-ft paddle rafts or 18-ft oar boats and, on occasion, inflatable kayaks. ARTA has highly trained guides (averaging six years' experience) and well-maintained equipment, and the food is hearty but not fancy. You're free to help cook if you choose, but you're certainly expected to participate in basic camp chores, such as setting up your own tent and cleaning your dish.

Trips Apr.–Oct.: $105–$245 per day.

Dvorak's Kayak and Rafting Expeditions

www.dvorakexpeditions.
com
17921 U.S. 285
Suite F
Nathrop, CO 81236
800/824–3795, 719/539–6851

Family-owned by Bill and Jaci Dvořák since 1969, this is one of the country's premier operators, with expeditions to 10 western rivers. Besides rafting, they teach kayaking; guides have first-aid and swift-water rescue training. Desolation and Gray canyons are perfect places to hone your white-water skills. This trip's terrific: solitude, desert scenery, the chance to paddle your own inflatable kayak or ride in a raft, Class I to III+ rapids, and great side hikes.

Running the Green: White Water through Butch Cassidy Country (Utah), Apr.–Oct.: six days, $870, not including tent or sleeping bag. Prices for most trips average $145 per day, depending on which month you go.

ECHO: The Wilderness Company

www.echotrips.com
6529 Telegraph Ave.
Oakland, CA 94609
800/652–3246, 510/652–1600

Since 1971 Echo has been running three- and four-day family-, wine-tasting, fly-fishing-, and classical- and bluegrass-music trips on some of the best white-water rivers in the West. Trips include the Tuolomne in California, the Main and Middle Fork of the Salmon in Idaho, and a great run on Oregon's amazing Rogue River (Class III+ rapids).

The highly trained, experienced guides double as fine chefs, so you can expect, in addition to incredible white water and wilderness scenery, some fine camp cuisine.

Trip costs range from $170 to $250 a day. Rowdy Rogue trip (Oregon), June–Sept.: three to four days, starting at $600, including all meals and a less expensive camping option or a more expensive river-lodge option. Price does not include tent or sleeping bag.

Far Flung Adventures

www.farflung.com
Box 377
Terlingua, TX 79852
800/359–4138

Founded in 1975, Far Flung is best known for its Texas Rio Grande trips, especially the Lower Canyons trip through the Chihuahan Desert of Big Bend National Park. You'll see plenty of wildlife and wildflowers and ride mild rapids in 14- or 16-ft paddle or oar boats. An excellent trip on Arizona's Salt River includes desert scenery, great Class II–IV white water, and mild temperatures. There's also exceptional white water on the Rio

Grande in northern New Mexico. Guides are friendly, experienced, and well trained in first aid and swift-water rescue.

Monthly, year-round Rio Grande trip (best in spring/fall): seven days, $995. Early Feb.–mid-May Salt River trip: five days, $750. Prices include camping equipment (not sleeping bag) and food.

Grand Canyon Expeditions Company

www.gcex.com
Box 0
Kanab, UT 84741
800/544–2691, 435/644–2691

The Grand Canyon is arguably the greatest rafting expedition in the world. There are a plethora of outfitters offering varied trips, yet this outfitter has been called the Rolls-Royce of Colorado River companies: every detail of every trip is just a little bit better than on most other outfitters' excursions. You can opt for motorized raft runs that take 8 days, dory expeditions that take 14, or traditional unmotorized rafts that take up to 18 days. There are specialty trips for students of astronomy, geology, photography, and the like. Though the capacity of mo-

torized rafts is 20, there are never more than 14 people in a boat (4 in a dory).

8- to 18-day trips from $200 to $400 per day, with fine food and camping.

Hatch River Expeditions

www.hatchriver.com
Box 1150
Vernal, UT 84078
800/342–8243, 435/789–4316

Founded in 1929, this outfitter is one of the white-water pioneers in North America. A popular five-day trip (with good food and colorful guides) begins in remote northwestern Colorado and takes you along easy white water (Class II and III) through awe-inspiring canyons. Hatch River's fleet mainly includes oar boats, but paddle rafts are also available.

Floating the Green River through Dinosaur National Monument, mid-May–mid-Sept.: five days, $754. Price includes food but not tent or sleeping bag.

Holiday River Expeditions

www.bikeraft.com
544 E. 3900 S
Salt Lake City, UT 84107
800/624–6323, 801/266–2087

Founded in 1966, this operator runs trips on eight rivers in three western states, including the infamous Salmon, Colorado, and Green rivers. Oar and paddle boats as well as inflatable kayaks are available on most trips. The guides are an experienced and highly diverse lot, with rescue and first-aid skills. Guides set up camp and cook the meals—you're only responsible for setting up your own tent.

May–Sept., trips average $180 per day for multiday trips; four to seven trips on various rivers, about $700–$1,400. Camping equipment (but not tent) and food included.

Hughes River Expeditions

www.hughesriver.com
Box 217
Cambridge, ID 83610
208/257–3477

Family owned and operated by Jim Hughes for nearly 30 years, this outfit operates primarily in Idaho and eastern Oregon on the Salmon and Snake rivers. Trips are best described as luxurious white-water expeditions. Oar boats, paddle boats, or inflatable kayakers are available on most trips. Savvy, ex-perienced guides (most in their thirties and forties) attend to every detail, including preparing delicious hors d'oeuvres. Food includes halibut, steak, and lobster tail, with fresh baked goods from the Dutch Oven.

Trips start at about $200 per day and can be up to twice that depending on the services you choose.

Mountain Travel Sobek

www.mtsobek.com
6420 Fairmount Ave.
El Cerrito, CA 94530-3606
510/527–8100, 800/227–2384

Born high in the snowy Sawtooth Mountains of Idaho, the Salmon River has 200 mi of fabulous white water. Protected under the federal government's Wild and Scenic River Act, it's one of the most sought-after white-water runs in North America. Of the three forks, the Middle is widely considered to be the most scenic and to offer the most punch. There are almost 100 rapids in as many miles, ranging from Class II to class IV. On this exceptional six-day adventure down the Middle Fork, you can ride along on an oar boat, crew one of the paddle boats, or, if you're truly adventurous, try an inflatable kayak. If you're seeking big water, book your trip in late May or early June, when the river peaks. (Novice and intermediate paddlers, go July–September.) Guides with this established, high-end operation are highly experienced, the equipment and meals impeccable.

Middle Fork of the Salmon River: Whitewater and Mountain Wilderness, six days, $1,690, all inclusive.

Outdoor Adventure River Specialists (OARS)

www.oars.com
Box 67
Angels Camp, CA 95222
800/346–6277, 209/736–4677

Running rivers since 1968, OARS offers excellent adventures from Alaska to Mexico. Popular trips include Idaho's Salmon, Utah's Green River, and the Grand Canyon leg of the Colorado River. Guides are experienced and have extensive rescue and first-aid training. On the three-day trip down the San Juan, a tributary of the Colorado River, there are no rapids above Class II, which makes it great for families and novice rafters. Expect to see petroglyphs of the Ancestral Pueblan (Anasazi) people and incredible geology. On the 75-mi Grande Ronde wilderness adventure in northeast Oregon (on dorries), you'll get solitude and gentle rapids (Class II with one Class III).

Prices average $200 per day for most trips. Petroglyphs and Pottery Shards: Floating the San Juan (Utah), late Mar.–Aug.: three days, $598; price doesn't include tent. Grande Ronde (northeast Oregon), May–June: three to four days, from $613.

Sheri Griffith Expeditions

www.griffithexp.com
Box 1324
Moab, UT 84532
800/332–2439, 435/259–8229

To experience five days of desert wilderness and heart-stopping rapids deep in Canyon Lands National Park, you travel by 18-ft oar boats rowed by expert guides. You'll learn about natural history and archaeology and will see lots of wildlife; expect big rapids and cold water in May and June, moderate rapids and warmer temperatures in July and August. Camps are usually on sandy beaches, and cuisine is best described as western barbecue.

The Colorado River through Cataract Canyon, May–mid-Sept.: five days, $1,043. Price includes flight and ground transportation from take-out to Moab. Tent not included.

Unicorn Expeditions

www.unicornraft.com
Box T
Brunswick, ME 04011
800/864–2676, 207/725–2255

In business since 1979, this outfit runs one- to five-day trips on Class III, IV, and V sections of the Penobscot. Trips are suitable for both advanced paddlers and novices and families. Excellent white water and great wilderness make this a run you won't soon forget.

Mid-June–early Sept.: two days, $225.

SAILING SCHOOLS

Annapolis Sailing School

www.annapolissailing.com
601 6th St.
Box 3334
Annapolis, MD 21403
800/638–9192

At one of oldest and largest sailing schools in the coun-

try, you'll spend 80%–90% of your time on the water, under sail. The student–instructor ratio is 4:1, and they offer two-, three-, and five-day beginner courses in 24- to 50-ft boats; cruising and advanced bareboat certification courses are also available. Other schools are in St. Petersburg, Florida, and St. Croix, United States Virgin Islands.

Apr.–Oct.: two-day beginner course, $295; three days, $425; five days, $575; four-part beginner course, $295; two-day advanced beginner course, $450; five-day cruising course on 30-ft boat, $2,325, for up to six students; five-day cruising course on 37-ft boat, $2,570, for up to six students. Longer trips offer onboard lodging but no provisioning.

Bay Island Sailing School

www.sailme.com
120 Tillson Ave.
Rockland, ME 04841
800/421–2492, 207/596–7550

Coed classes take place in Penobscot Bay, where 100% of the instruction is on board. Boats (19 to 29 ft) are under sail 80% of the time, and the student–instructor ratio 4:1. There's a 16-hour weekend beginner course and a five-day, 20-hour combination beginner and coastal cruising class; intermediate, advanced cruising, and bareboat certification courses are also available.

June–mid-Sept.: five-day beginner class, $800; two-day beginner class, $435; five-day bareboat course, $1,000; or weekend coastal cruising course, $435; private lessons $100 per hour with two-hour minimum. Longer trips offer onboard lodging but no provisioning.

BaySail on the Chesapeake

www.baysail.net
Tidewater Marina Bldg.
100 Bourbon St.
Havre de Grace, MD 21078
800/526–1528, 410/939–2869

Expect to spend 85%–90% of your hands-on time on the water, in 22-ft boats, at this recreational- and racing-oriented school. The student–instructor ratio is 4:1. There's a three-day weekend or weekday basic sailing course; graduates receive a 15% discount coupon for their first boat rental. Cruising, bareboat charter certification, and racing courses are available.

Apr.–Oct.: basic three-day course, $400–$450; three-day Learn to Charter course, $550–$650; five-day Ocean Cruising course, $995–$1,230; three-day race/performance course, $650–$750. Provisioning not included for any class.

Blue Water Sailing School

www.bwss.com
940 N.E. 20 Ave.
Fort Lauderdale, FL 33304
800/255–1840, 954/763–8464

If you want rigorous, coed courses to learn extended offshore sailing, this is the place. Boats are under sail 70%–80% of the time during the 9-to-5 day, and all instruction takes place on board. The student–instructor ratio 4:1. Six-day beginners courses to the Florida Keys or the Bahamas are in 35- to 40-ft boats; repeat students receive a $150 discount. Cruising, passage-making, and catamaran courses are available; schools also are in Newport, Rhode Island, and St. Thomas, United States Virgin Islands.

Year-round: all six-day courses, $1,365 with provisioning.

Chapman School of Seamanship

www.chapman.org
4343 S.E. St. Lucie Blvd.
Stuart, FL 34997
772/283–8130, 800/225–2841

This outfit is geared to serious recreational or marine career-oriented students. The hands-on time spent sailing is 85%–90%, with a student–instructor ratio of 4:1. Two-day beginner courses take place on 36- to 40-ft boats; coastal cruising and offshore passage-making courses are available.

Year-round: two-day certification course, $340, no provisioning; three-day basic coastal cruising course, $430 without provisioning; seven-day offshore sailing course, $1,410 plus port fees of $20–$30 with provisioning; private lessons $80 per hour.

Club Nautique

www.clubnautique.net/
index_JS.html
1150 Ballena Blvd.
Suite 161
Alameda, CA 94501
800/343–7245, 510/865–4700

The four-day, 32-hour beginner course (coed) is given in two formats: two consecutive weekends or weekdays Tuesday–Friday. You get 80%–90% on-water instruction in 23- to 26-ft boats, and the student–instructor ratio is 4:1. Basic cruising, bareboat certification, and offshore passage-making courses are available; classes may be split between three locations—Marina del Rey, Newport Beach, and San Francisco Bay.

Year-round: basic keelboat, $895; basic cruising, $995; bareboat cruising, $1,195; advanced coastal cruising, $895; coastal navigation, $595; offshore passage-making, $1,495; all without provisioning; special rates and packages are often offered.

Coastline Sailing School

Eldridge Yard
Marsh Rd.
Noank, CT 06340
800/749–7245, 860/536–2680

Classes are oriented to beginning sailors who want to charter boats for sailing vacations. Boats are under sail 80% of the time during the 12-hour beginner weekend course. The student–instructor ratio is 4:1, and up to 20 students are admitted per class. Instruction is on 30-ft boats. There are two- to five-day cruising and five-day bareboat chartering certification courses as well as a six-day sailing vacation to Martha's Vineyard and/or Nantucket.

Mid-Apr.–mid-Oct.: Weekender course, $325 ($45 extra to stay on board Sat. night); two- to five-day coastal cruising course starts at $425 without lodging or provisioning; five-day bareboat chartering course, $1,265; six-day vacation course, $2,650 per couple, provisioning included.

Florida Sailing and Cruising School

www.flsailandcruiseschool.
com
3444 Marinatown La. NW
North Ft. Myers, FL 33903
239/656–1339, 800/262–7939

Come here for coed sailing and cruising on 20- to 30-ft boats around the southwest coast, including around the islands. About 85%–90% of your time is on the water, under sail, and the student–instructor ratio is between 2:1 and 4:1. There's a two-day basic sailing course to start; bareboat charter and offshore passage-making courses are also available.

Year-round: two-day basic sailing, $395; three-day basic sailing and coastal cruising, $795; three-day bareboat

charter, $795; four-day basic sailing and coastal cruising, $895; five-day bareboat chartering and coastal cruising, $1,295; 12-day offshore passage-making, $2,795. Prices do not include provisioning.

J World

www.jworldschool.com
Box 1509
Newport, RI 02840
401/849–5492, 800/343–2255

Only sailors who are serious about learning and getting certified take these performance-oriented recreational and racing classes, where 84%–92% of the time is spent sailing. The student–instructor ratio is 4:1. There are three beginner courses: two-day, 13-hour weekend; five-day, 34-hour weekday; and six-day, 39-hour consecutive weekends. Instruction is on 24- to 40-ft boats; racing and cruising courses are available. The school is also in Key West, Florida, from October to May.

Newport Rhode Island, mid-May–Sept.: five-day course, $845; weekend course, $425; three-day live-aboard course, $1,200. Breakfast, lunch, and some dinners provided. Prices are the same for the Key West school.

Miami Sailing Club

www.miamisailing.org
Box 331748
Coconut Grove, FL 33569
305/858–1130

This outfit offers coed recreational and career-oriented courses, during which 85%–90% of the time you're on water under sail. The student–instructor ratio is 4:1 on the three-day, 20-hour and four-day, 28-hour basic sailing courses for catamarans and monohulls respectively (in 14- to 56-ft boats). Intermediate and advanced coastal cruising, racing and bareboat certification, piloting, navigational, instrument, and captain's license courses are available.

Year-round: five-day Advanced Sailing, $950; seven-day Coastal Cruising Course, $3,400 including food and board; seven-day Offshore Cruising Course, $4,600. Prices include food and onboard lodging.

Milwaukee Community Sailing Center

www.sailingcenter.org
1450 N. Lincoln Memorial Dr.
Milwaukee, WI 53202
414/277–9094

Between 70% and 80% of instruction at this coed, private nonprofit school is on the water, and the student–instructor ratio is 4:1. An eight-session, 24-hour beginner course is held weeknights or weekends; expect to sail in 14- to 24-ft boats. Former students are eligible to use the center's boats (for a membership fee). The center runs intermediate and advanced courses, day sailing, racing, and adaptive sailing courses for the physically challenged.

May–Oct.: intensive weekend beginner course, $250 plus $250 membership fee for singles, $350 for couples.

Offshore Sailing School

www.offshore-sailing.com
16731 McGregor Blvd.
Ft. Myers, FL 33908
800/221–4326, 941/454–1700

This coed, large school serves 3,000 students annually. About 75% of hands-on time is on the water, and the student–instructor ratio is 4:1. Beginners learn-to-sail classes are in two formats: three-day or five-day; boats are 26 ft. Intermediate and advanced, cruising, bareboat certification, passage-making, and racing courses are available. Seasonal instruction May–October takes place in

Newport, Rhode Island; Stamford, Connecticut; Jersey City, New Jersey; and Chicago, Illinois. Year-round instruction is in Jacksonville, St. Petersburg, Duck Cay, and Captiva Island in Florida and Tortola, British Virgin Islands.

Year-round: three-day day-sailing courses start at $895 without accommodations or provisioning; three-day bareboat courses start at $995; five-day bareboat charter course, $1,295 with accommodations, including provisioning.

Oyster Bay Sailing School

www.oysterbaysailing.com
Box 187
West End Ave.
Oyster Bay, Long Island, NY 11771
516/922–7245

Small coed classes are the draw here. About 75% of instruction is on board and under sail, in 23-ft boats, and the student–instructor ratio is 3:1. There's a four-day, 28-hour basic sailing course; graduates get four hours' free sailing time plus a lifetime membership that permits chartering of the school's day sail fleet any-

time. Cruising and bareboat certification courses are available, as are vacation packages for cruising the British Virgin Islands (for school graduates).

May–mid-Oct.: four-day basic sailing course, $450 weekdays, $450 weekends; two-day coastal cruising course, $450 without meals, but no extra charge for sleeping on board; three-day bareboat course, $595, including meals.

Sailboats, Inc.

www.sailboats-inc.com
250 Marina Dr.
Superior, WI 54880
800/826–7010, 715/392–7131

The focus here is coed recreational courses, with 85% of instruction on the water and a student–instructor ratio of 4:1. The three-day beginner learn-to-sail and cruise "mini-vacation" takes place at seven locations in the Great Lakes area, on 28- to 40-ft boats. Former students receive a 5% discount on charters at any Stardust Yacht Charters locations worldwide.

July–Sept: three-day Learn to Sail and Cruise, $795, without provisioning.

San Juan Sailing

www.sanjuansailing.com
1 Squalicum Harbor
Esplanade
Bellingham, WA 98225
800/677–7245, 360/671–4300

Classes here are coed, and 80%–90% of instruction is on the water. The student–instructor ratio is 4:1, and instruction is on 33- to 40-ft boats. There are three levels of weekend beginner courses and a six-day Learn-n-Cruise course; intermediate and advanced courses are also available.

Year-round: two-day weekend courses, $199–$289 without provisioning; six-day course, $975 with provisioning.

Santa Barbara Sailing Center

www.sbsailctr.com
133 Harbor Way
Santa Barbara, CA 93109
800/350–9090, 805/962–2826

In the coed recreational courses, 90% of instruction is on the water. The student–instructor ratio can be 1:1, 2:1, or 4:1, and boats are between 21 and 24 ft. A four-day, 20-hour weekday or weekend beginner course is available, as are intermediate and advanced cruising, bareboat certification, and

passage-making. Club membership includes discounts on charter rentals.

Year-round: basic four-day course, one person $800, two persons $550, four persons $350; 2½-day basic coastal cruising, two persons $625, four persons $480; four-day bareboat chartering, two persons $1,300, four persons $1,030. Meals not included.

School of Sailing & Seamanship

www.occsailing.com
Orange County College
1801 W. Coast Hwy.
Newport Beach, CA 92663
949/645–9412

This large, public boating education program offers 80% of instruction on the water and a student–instructor ratio between 2:1 and 4:1. Beginner courses take two formats: three-hour classes over five weekend days or four-hour classes over four Fridays; 14-ft boats are standard. Intermediate and advanced cruising, bareboat certification, and racing courses are available.

Year-round: bareboat cruising course to Catalina Island, two days $270, three days $415; Channel Islands Cruise, five days $625, no provisioning included.

Sea Sense

www.seasenseboating.com
25 Thames St.
New London, CT 06320
203/444–1404, 800/332–1404

Women-taught, women-only classes are on live-aboard 35-ft to 45-ft boats. On the three-, five-, and seven-day courses, for all skill levels, you sail to different ports each night within the region where the school is located; schools are also in Milwaukee, Wisconsin; St. Petersburg, Sarasota, and Ft. Myers, Florida; Annapolis, Maryland; and Anacortes, Washington. Cruising destinations include British Virgin Islands, St. Maarten/St. Martin, Bahamas, Greece, and France.

May–Sept.: three-day course, $775; five days, $1,225; seven days, $1,525; private lessons on your boat, $400 a day, plus transportation. Seven-day cruising packages to Europe or Caribbean start at $1,650. Prices include provisioning and lodging on board.

Texas Sailing Academy

www.texassailing.com
103-B Lakeway Dr.
Austin, TX 78734
512/261–6193, 800/864–7245

Classes—private or group instruction—are coed, and 80% of the time is spent on board under sail, on 23-ft boats. The student–instructor ratio is 1:1, 2:1, or 4:1. Cruising and bareboat charter courses are available, as are intermediate and advanced cruising, bareboat certification, and offshore passage-making.

Year-round: basic keelboat 30-hour beginner sailing, $1,195 (five six-hour days; no provisioning, but you can sleep on the boat); two-day charter plus eight hours' instruction, $670, no provisioning; two-day coastal cruising, $1,280, no provisioning; three-day bareboat certification, $2,300, no provisioning.

WaterWays

www.sailwaterway.com
Box 872
Wrightsville Beach, NC 28480
910/256–4282, 800/562–7245

This group offers coed recreational classes, with 80% of the instruction on the water, under sail, on 25- to 30-ft boats. The student–instructor ratio is 4:1. There's a four-day beginner course and intermediate and advanced coastal cruising and bareboat certification. Refresher and sail-vacation packages are also available.

Apr.–Nov.: two-day basic keelboat sailing course, $425; two-day basic coastal cruising, $525; 2½-day bareboat chartering course, $625 with provisioning; six-day crash course in bareboat chartering, $1,275 without provisioning; seven-day live-aboard, $1,625 with provisioning; coastal navigation correspondence course, $225; advanced course in coastal cruising, $775 with provisioning.

Womanship

www.womanship.com
137 Conduit St.
Annapolis, MD 21401
800/342–9295, 410/267–6661

Although classes are women-taught and women-only, men can join as part of a customized couples course. Boats are under sail 80% of the time, and all instruction takes place on board. The student–instructor ratio is from 2:1 to 4:1. There are two- and three-day beginners courses, on 39- to 45-ft boats; cruising, passage-making, mother-daughter courses, and vacation sailing to foreign destinations are available. Schools also in San Diego, New England, the Florida Keys, the British Virgin Islands, and Vancouver, British Columbia.

Apr.–Nov.: two-day day-sailing course, $400, no meals; three-day day-sailing course, $545, no meals; three-day live-aboard course, $785 (includes provisioning); five days, $1,235 (includes provisioning); seven days, $1,585 (includes provisioning).

Women for Sail

537 Edgwater Ave.
Oceanside, CA 92057
800/346–6404, 619/631–2860

On these women-taught, women-only classes, expect to spend 80% of your time on water, under sail. The student–instructor ratio is 3:1. The three-, five-, and seven-day live-aboard courses take place on a 43-ft boat. The company also teaches in Key West, San Diego, Annapolis, the Virgin Islands, and in southern Europe and Thailand. Bareboat certification is offered.

Year-round: three- to seven-day cruises range from $1,695 to $2,995 with provisioning, depending on location.

Women's Sailing Adventures

39 Woodside Ave.
Westport, CT 06880
800/328–8053, 203/227–7413

Women-taught, women-only classes, on 25-ft boats, are standard. All instruction takes place on board, and boats are under sail 75% of the time. The student–instructor ratio is from 2:1 to 4:1. There's a four-day, 20-hour beginner course, as well as seven-day beginner and intermediate cruising courses in the San Juan Islands, Maine's Penobscot Bay, and the British Virgin Islands.

May–Sept.: 20-hour, four-day beginner course, $540; seven-day course, $1,695. Price includes all provisioning during the seven-day course.

SCUBA DIVING

Bamboo Reef

www.bambooreef.com
584 4th St.
San Francisco, CA 94107
415/362–6694

Bamboo Reef has classrooms and pool facilities in San Francisco and Sonoma, so you can enjoy San Francisco's hills and restaurants or Sonoma's vineyards after class. Open-water dives take place in Monterey's Marine Sanctuary, among kelp forests, brilliant orange garibaldis (California's official state fish), seals, and sea lions. Sea stars, urchins, and anenomes cluster on the bottom while sea otters populate the surface. Water temperature ranges between 50°F and 55°F with visibility best in October and November—or, if the winter has been dry, February and March.

Four-day course, $950. Price includes purchase of mask, fins, and snorkel.

Cape Ann Divers

www.capeanndivers.com
Cape Anne Marketplace
127 Eastern Ave.
Gloucester, MA 01930
978/281–8082

Gloucester is the heart of New England diving. At Cape Anne Divers, all instruction is one instructor per student. Confined-water training is done in the ocean. Entry into the underwater world is typically down huge sloping slabs of granite. Among the large boulders farther out, you'll see brightly colored northern starfish, sea cucumbers, lobster, and cunner. Water temperature ranges from 40 to 65 degrees. This area has plenty of other leisure activities—you can bike ride along country roads, kayak in marshes, or take a whale-watching cruise.

Apr.–Oct.: four-day course, $1,000. Price includes purchase of mask, fins, mitts, and snorkel.

Catalina Divers Supply

www.catalinadiverssupply.com
On the Pier
Box 126
Avalon, CA 90704
800/353–0330, 310/510–0330

This dive shop has been on Avalon's pier since 1958. The waters around Catalina are a National Marine Sanctuary, so marine life is protected—you'll find urchins, abalone, and sea stars clinging to ancient lava flows. Golden garibaldi, sheephead, and barracuda swim above grazing bottom-fish, such as scorpionfish and bat rays. Sea lions are plentiful here. The island has wonderful hiking, and Avalon is a sailing port with plenty of watering holes. Kayaking, sailing, and deep-water fishing are also popular. Water temperature

ranges from 55 to 68 degrees; visibility is best in October and November.

Four-day course, $650 for two to six students, $950 for private class. Price includes mask, fins, and snorkel.

Copamarina Beach Resort

www.copamarina.com
Rte. 333, Km 6.5
Box 805
Puerto Rico 00653
800/468–4553, 787/821–0505

Southern Puerto Rico's dive spots aren't as crowded as those on the north coast or other Caribbean Islands. Open-water boat dives take you to coral reefs and to the continental shelf drop-off, a spectacular marine wall with a series of slopes and sheer drop-offs from 30 ft to 120 ft before disappearing into a 2,000-ft drop. Dive Copamarina has exclusive rights to its dive sites, so you won't see other divers—just unspoiled reef and wall life. Water temperature averages 80 degrees. This resort offers all-inclusive packages, so when you sign up for your class, ask about lodging deals.

Five-day course, $300. Price covers the rental of all equipment.

Lahaina Reef Diving

www.lahainadivers.com
143 Dickenson St.
Lahaina, Maui, HI 96761
800/998–3483

Lahaina Divers is in the heart of Old Lahaina, a 19th-century whaling village. Class size depends on how many sign up but shouldn't be more than six students. On your checkout dive, you'll see tropical fish, rays, octopus, and eels frolicking in and around jagged volcanic flows. To allow maximum time for diving, you're expected to get the textbook and complete a required reading and study assignment before the course starts. The company has facilities for handicapped divers. Water temperature is in the 80s.

Three-day course, $350. Price includes rental of all equipment and the purchase of course materials.

Lost Reef Adventures

www.lostreefadventures.
com
261 Margaret St.
Key West, FL 33040
800/952–2749, 305/296–9737

You'll quickly see why Hemingway loved the Keys. Choose either PADI or NAUI certification; check-out boat dives take you 6–12 mi out to the world's third-largest barrier coral reef. Visibility is best if you come in September or October. Water temperature averages 80°F.

Four-day certification course, $425. Price includes rental of all equipment. The dive shop can arrange a good rate on rooms at the diver-owned Eaton Manor, a converted conch house.

Moss Bay Divers

www.mossbaydivers.com
Box 3421
Kirkland, WA 98083
425/827–6584

This club matches you with instructors for individualized certification anywhere on Washington's Puget Sound, a favorite dive site for the Cousteau family. Visibility is best from October to March. Water temperature ranges from 48 to 53°F. Open-water dives to the wall where the continental shelf abruptly drops hundreds of feet. This area of cool, nutrient-rich water hosts prehistoric-looking ratfish, big skates, and sixgill sharks. Keep an eye out for the giant Pacific octopus, a curious, gentle, and intelligent creature that can grow to more than 20 ft.

Four-day course, $250. Price includes all rental equipment.

Neptune Divers

www.neptunedivers.net
2445 South 900 E
Salt Lake City, Utah 84106
801/466–9630

Open-water dives take place at Bonneville Seabase, a warm springs-fed artificial aquarium stocked with fish from around the world. Seabase is a microcosm of the world's oceans—in the form of a 150- by 600-ft lake. Tiny angelfish, puffers, lobsters, and 6-ft nurse sharks all from different ocean environments live together in this peaceable underwater kingdom surrounded by snowcapped mountains. Water temperature ranges from 70 to 80°F.

Three-week course, $500. Price includes purchase of mask, fins, and snorkel.

Red Sail Sports

www.redsail.com
Hilton Waikoloa Village
425 Waikoloa Beach Dr.
Kamuela, HI 96743
877/735–7245, 808/885–2876

Although housed at the Hilton, Red Sail Sports accepts students from any nearby hotel. Open-water dives visit white-tip reef sharks (who will ignore you unless offered food), sea turtles, eels, and myriad schools of tiny, colorful fish all swimming among strange shapes and tubes formed by recent lava flows. Water temperature is in the 80s.

NAUI or PADI four-day course, $395 for two to four students, $650 for private class. Price includes rental of all equipment and purchase of course materials.

Rollins Scuba Association

owscuba@aol.com
68 Washington Ave.
South Portland, ME 04104
207/799–7990

Instructors at Rollins are both professional divers and instructors, so you get the best of both worlds, and your class will be tailored just for you. If you have a preference, you can choose certification by the YMCA, NAUI, or PADI. Even though the water temperature ranges from 36 to 62 degrees, courses are taught year-round; visibility is best in January and February. Open-water dives are usually at Kettle Cove, with rocky areas full of lobsters, sea stars, scallops, and flounder. The large (18-inch) pre-historic-looking sea raven might kiss you on the cheek if you pet it. Divers with handicaps are welcome.

Five-day course, $650; three-week course, $500.

Scuba Sports

www.scuba-sports.com
1196 Hwy. 248
Branson, MO 65616
417/334–9073

Get certified in the heart of the Ozark Mountains and explore the underwater town—flooded by the creation of a reservoir—on your open-water dives. Vehicles have been sunk to add to the interest. Water temperature ranges from 50 to 75 degrees. In town you'll find live performances at night in the 40 theaters and dozens of entertainment centers.

Four-day course, $600. Price includes purchase of mask, fins, and snorkel.

Scubawest

www.divescubawest.com
330 Strand St.
Frederiksted, St. Croix
USVI 00840
800/352–0107, 340/772–3701

This dive center is on the quiet side of St. Croix;

confined-water training takes place in the shallow water of the harbor, a popular site for underwater photographers. The open-water checkout dives are around and under the Frederiksted Pier, rich in sea life. You'll see seahorses, octopus, lobsters, rays, sea stars, and urchins. Other residents include sea slugs, trumpet fish, gigantic parrot fish, eels, scorpion fish, and other Caribbean reef fish. Water temperature averages 80°F.

Four-day course, $350. Price includes rental of all equipment.

Tarpoon Diving Center

www.tarpoondivecenter.com
300 Alton Rd.
Miami Beach, FL 33139
305/532–1445

This 50-year-old business is now run by the founder's two daughters. You'll get your own instructor for the five-day certification course. After class, you can hang at the marina or enjoy trendy South Beach with its pastel deco architecture and beautiful people. Open-water dives include visits to coral reefs and wrecks, both of which abound in the waters off Miami. Water temperature averages 80°F.

Five-day certification course, $500. Price includes purchase of mask, fins, and snorkel.

TL Sea Diving

www.tlsea.com
23405 Pacific Hwy. S
Des Moines, WA 98198
888/448–5733, 206/824–4100

All instruction is personalized here—you can pick your instructor, if you like, according gender and age. TL Sea offers dry-suit diving, which warms you with a layer of air, not water. Controlled-water dives are in the ocean. The open-water dives explore the sea life in the protected waters of the docks, where you'll see gunnels, sun stars, plumose anemones, and nudibranchs (sea snails).

Four-day course, $250. Price includes all rental equipment.

SEA KAYAKING

Alaska Discovery

www.akdiscovery.com
5310 Glacier Hwy.
Juneau, AK 99801
800/586–1911, 907/780–6226

After 30 years of guiding wilderness outings, these guys know what they're do-

ing: they hold the exclusive concession for sea-kayaking trips in Glacier Bay National Park, in southeastern Alaska. One eight-day trip involves 60 mi of rigorous paddling along the east arm of the bay. When planning, remember that June gets 18 hours of light, but August gets the northern lights. Expect wildlife and rain. You get two guides for a maximum of 10 paddlers. Energetic beginners will be fine: you just need to be fit because on some days you paddle 10–15 mi daily to reach the campsites.

One-day trips, $125; multi-day trips, 3–10 days, $500–$3,000. Glacier Bay expedition, June–Aug., eight days, $2,195; price includes float-plane air charter (from Glacier Bay to Gustavus) and first night's inn lodging, camping equipment (sleeping bags optional), and meals.

Blue Moon Explorations

home.cio.net/bluemoon
4658 Blank Rd.
Sedro Woolley, WA 98284
360/856–5622

In 1988 Blue Moon's Kathleen Grimbly combined her interest in cultural anthropology and nature studies with kayaking. Beginners take tours in two-person kayaks; experienced kayakers can refine technique and learn navigation and forecasting of tide, weather, and currents. Blue Moon specializes in customized tours, including corporate retreats and women's workshops, to the San Juan Islands, Vancouver Island, Hawaii, and Baja, California.

From $105 per day in San Juan Islands to about $1,000 for a week paddling in Hawaii; prices include breakfast and dinner (lunch upon request), and all gear except sleeping bag and pad.

Florida Bay Outfitters

www.kayakfloridakeys.com
104050 Overseas Hwy.
Key Largo, FL 33037
305/451–3018

In operation for a decade, Florida Bay gears all of its trips to paddlers of all abilities; it runs multiday trips throughout the Keys. On the five-day Florida Keys trip you'll cruise from Key Largo to Key West and explore John Pennekamp State Park, Indian and Lignumvitae Key State parks, Great White Heron Wildlife Refuge, and Bahia Honda State Park. This cruise of the Conch Island Republic includes a stop in Old Key West.

Mid-Nov.–mid-Apr., Florida Keys: five days. Trips from two to seven days, $275–$1,050; one-day tours, $95. Prices include most meals, campground or resort lodging, equipment, gear, and park fees.

Kayak and Canoe Institute

www.umdoutdoorprogram.org
University of Minnesota
Outdoor Program
121 Sports and Health
Center
10 University Dr.
Duluth, MN 55812-2496
218/726–6533

Serving students and other interested kayakers for 19 years, this program runs tours along the shores of Lake Superior and courses in sea-kayaking skills. As you travel along the Apostle Islands National Seashore around Lake Superior (Wisconsin), the world's largest freshwater lake, the kayaking experience is varied: still waters, wind and waves, fog and rain. On this trip six paddlers maximum, in rigid single or double

kayaks, paddle 10–15 mi
daily.

July–Aug.: four days, $390.

Kayak Kauai Outbound

www.kayakkauai.com
Box 508
Hanalei
Kauai, HI 96714
800/437–3507, 808/826–9844

This outfit, founded in 1984,
runs short tours and weeklong adventures. On the Na
Pali Coast tour, in Kauai,
you kayak 6 mi daily to
semi-remote, gleaming
beaches and into sea caves
that open into vaults of light.
Count on ocean swells and
surf, however, so if you're
prone to seasickness or don't
like eating sand, avoid this
trip. On this trip (12 paddlers maximum, two guides)
you also camp, snorkel, and
hike. Fit beginners will do
fine.

May–Sept.: seven days,
$1,550. Price includes trans-
port to and from Hanalei
headquarters.

Maine Island Kayak Company (MIKCO)

www.maineislandkayak.
com
70 Luther St.
Peaks Island, ME 04108
800/796–2373, 207/766–2373

Founded in 1986, MIKCO
offers island-camping trips
and conducts sea-kayak
training sessions from 12-
year-old novices to expert
kayakers training to be
guides. The group's emphasis
is on acquiring solid paddling skills and on understanding the marine
environment. Trips take
place along the Maine Island
Trail and in Nova Scotia;
guides are BCU-trained and
Registered Maine Guides.
A popular three-day trip
from the fishing port of
Stonington to Acadia
National Park suits athletic
beginners. The Down East
Maine trip—from the coast
into Canada's maritime
provinces—is rugged and
remote; the going is difficult,
so you need endurance and
strong paddling skills.

Half-day to five-day trips,
$60–$895. Stonington, June–
Sept.: three days, $495.
Down East Maine, July–
Sept.: five days, $895.
Multiday trips include
meals, gear, and camping
equipment (not sleeping
bags or pads).

Outward Bound

www.outwardbound.org
100 Mystery Point Rd.
Garrison, NY 10524
845/424–4000, 888/882–6863

If you don't mind the constant emphasis on team-building and community, Outward Bound programs offer some of the best paddling-skills workshops and trips in the country. Be aware, however, that having fun is often second on the agenda, and food is even lower still. Outward Bound runs sea-kayaking programs in Colorado, Florida, Maine, Minnesota, North Carolina, and Washington. The outfit's eight-day trip in North Carolina's Outer Banks, for example, teaches you compass-reading and navigation; you're also left alone for 24 hours at the end to test your survival skills.

Eight-day Outer Banks trip in May, Sept., and Oct., $1,195.

Sea Quest Expeditions

www.sea-quest-kayak.com
Zoetic Research
Box 2424
Friday Harbor, WA 98250
360/378–5767

Founded in 1992 and run by a marine biologist, Sea Quest knows the best places to spot whales. For five days in the San Juan Islands you paddle five to six hours daily, looking for orcas (killer whales). Despite their nickname and their size (up to 25 ft long), they've never been known to so much as dump a kayaker. There's a maximum of eight clients per guide paddle in rigid double kayaks.

June-Oct.: five days, $549, including all equipment, tents, and meals.

Sierra Club

www.sierraclub.org
85 2nd St.
2nd floor
San Francisco, CA 94105
415/977–5500

There are only about 10 sea-kayaking trips to choose from, and destinations, itineraries, and even leaders change. However, this established organization (founded 1901) almost always runs trips to Alaska and Lake Tahoe (California) and along the Suwannee River of Georgia and Florida, and the Midwest—such as the Apostle Islands in Wisconsin. Camping out and participating as a group in camp chores are the operative protocols, and costs are low to moderate.

Trips from six to eight days, from $650 to $1,000, including equipment, food, and lodging.

Southwind Kayak Center

www.southwindkayaks.com
17855 Sky Park Cir.
Suite A
Irvine, CA 92714
800/768–8494, 949/261–0200

Founded in 1987, this extremely well run operation emphasizes training and skills for both beginner and advanced paddlers. A five-day inland sea-kayaking trip on the Green River brings you through 70 mi of beautiful red rock canyons. Alternatively, on a two- or three-day offshore cruise to southern California's Catalina Islands you paddle into the caves and tunnels of Santa Cruz Island. All kinds of kayaks are available, so if you are shopping for a kayak you can try a wide variety of models to find one that suits you best.

Green River, five days, $1,525, including airfare from Orange County, and camping and food ($1,450 if you bring your own kayak). Catalina Islands, two days, $255; three days, $325, including permits, paddling gear, transportation from coast to island, and equipment; food and camping gear not included.

Wilderness Inquiry, Inc.

www.wildernessinquiry.org
808 14th Ave. SE
Minneapolis, MN 55414
612/676–9400, 800/728–0719

Founded 1978 as a nonprofit, the company runs trips that tend to have a diverse mix of people. Two guides accompany 10–12 paddlers in triple kayaks; groups paddle 5–15 mi (four to six hours) daily; people with disabilities may also be included. If you're a beginning kayaker, you'll be able to handle the 186-mi-long Lake Powell in Utah. Plan for heat and sun and know that shade is hard to find. You paddle into shallow, narrow, out-of-the-way caves, coves, and beaches along the lake's 1,960 mi of shoreline.

Lake Powell, Apr. and Oct.: six days, $750; other trips (nationwide) from $350 for three-day trip to $695 for a week. Trips are all-inclusive, with camping, gear, and food.

SKI SCHOOLS

Boyne USA Resorts

www.boynemountain.com
Boyne Mountain
Boyne Falls, MI 49713
616/549–6000

This is one of the Midwest's best ski schools, with clinics for racers, women, and aspiring carvers (carving is a new style of skiing with shaped, parabolic skis; a true carver inclines much more while skiing, using the shape of the ski rather than a huge weight transfer to make the turn). The private instruction includes video analysis, and the majority of instructors are PSIA certified. The Super-Five Ski Week Package gives you instruction for five days at bargain-basement prices. Unlike most mountains in the West, which have about 3,000 ft of vertical drop (from the top of the mountain to the very bottom), Boyne has only 500 ft of vertical drop.

Boyne Highlands, Harbor Springs, MI 49740, 231/549–6065 or 800/462–6963. Super Five Ski Week Package: $110. (Price includes eight hours of lessons, a race, and an awards presentation.)

Crested Butte, Club Mediterranée

www.clubmed.com
Club Mediterranée
500 Gothic Rd.
Mt. Crested Butte 81225
888/932–2582, 970/349–8700

Crested Butte is one of the gnarliest, steepest mountains in the United States; thankfully, weeklong all-inclusive stays include ski instruction by a well-trained international staff. Club Med is also an excellent place for families: there are kids' programs daily, and the instruction and facilities are first-rate.

Seven nights, $1,490, including airfare from certain U.S. cities, all meals, lift tickets, and instruction.

Grand Targhee

www.grandtraghee.com
Box SKI
Alta, WY 83422
800/827–4433, 307/353–2300

There's excellent instruction for beginners to advanced skiers at this ski resort, which gets 500 inches of snow annually. Yes, this is powder central. Snow-Cat tours are offered, or you can hire a guide-instructor to take you to the lift-serviced, inbounds secret powder stashes. Three-day backcountry and telemark clinics are offered throughout the season.

Backcountry clinic, Mar.: $290. Price includes breakfast, lift tickets, and airport shuttle. Telemark clinics, Dec.–Apr.: $515. Price includes lodging, lift tickets, and video analysis.

Keystone

www.keystoneresort.com
Mahre Training Center
Keystone Resort
Box 38
Keystone, CO 80435
800/255–3715, 970/496–4170

It's no minor opportunity to ski with former Olympians Steve and Phil Mahre. The three- to five-day intensive ski camps include evening lectures, video analysis, and instruction supervised by two of America's best skiers. Though Keystone lacks the super-steeps of some Colorado mountains, it's an awesome family resort, with good grooming and some fun bump-and-bash runs in the back.

Dec.–Feb.: three-day program, $540; five-day, $825. Price includes lift tickets.

Killington

www.killington.com
4763 Killington Rd.
Killington, VT 05751
800/923–9444, 802/422–6201

Perfect Turn instruction at the ski school here will, supposedly, help align your inner energy with the flow of the mountain. It helps, too, that there are plenty of ways to glide down the mountain—this is the East's largest ski resort, with seven mountains, 200 trails, and 31 lifts. The terrain, across which PSIA-certified instructors will guide you, includes everything from steep mogul runs to long, groomed cruisers. Killington offers a Learn to Ski Week (from two to seven days) for first-timers. The five-day Mountain Masters' Program (maximum five people) is best if you want to hone your technical skills. There are also children's programs and weeklong racing clinics, which are held throughout the year.

Oct.–June: five-day Learn to Ski, starting at $355 per person, in early or late season. Price includes five nights lodging starting Sun. night, half-day Discovery Center Program on first day and two-hour lessons each following day, specially designed learning equipment, limited lift tickets on days one and two, and unlimited lift tickets from day three onward. Five-day Mountain Masters' Program, Mon.–Fri., including five-day lift ticket, free Sun.-afternoon lift ticket and one-day demo ski rental, and three hours coaching daily (plus video analysis). Call for prices. Meals are not included in any package.

The Magic of Skiing, Aspen

www.aikiworks.com
Magic of Skiing
Aiki Works, Inc.
Box 7845
Aspen, CO 81612
970/925–7099, 716/924–7302

A weeklong course overseen by Aikido master and PSIA-certified instructor Thomas Crum, the Magic of Skiing focuses on developing a mind-body relationship to bring students to their ultimate performance levels. More than just a ski school, this Zen-inspired, new-agey course has daily seminars that focus on conflict resolution and relaxation techniques.

In 2003, Jan. 11–18, Feb. 1–8: seven days, $2,295. Price includes lodging, breakfasts, video analysis, and lift tickets.

Mammoth Mountain

www.mammothmountain.com
Box 24
Mammoth Lakes, CA 93546
800/626–6684, 760/934–2571

A long ski season, an 11,053-ft-high mountain, and tons of snow (a whopping 383 inches annually) bring in skiers of every fashion—from raw novices to outright experts. If you want a guide to take you to the local powder stashes, or if you're simply itching to ski during the outer limits of the ski season, Mammoth Mountain may be the place to book a trip, though you'll have to arrange your own package based on a daily rate. It's worth it, however, as long as you don't mind mixing with the many locals who drive up for shorter stays. as the name implies, it's one of California's biggest resorts.

Nov.–May: Stay and Ski Free program, packages start at $129 per person, including two nights lodging and two days lift tickets.

Okemo

www.okemo.com
Okemo Mountain Resort
77 Okemo Ridge Rd.
Ludlow, VT 05149
800/786–5366, 802/228–4041

Specialized clinics include Dan Egan's Kid's Big Air Camp and Couple's-only Ski Clinic, and Women's Spree, a five-day women's clinic. These clinics, except for the Kid's Big Air Camp, are for skiers of all levels and ages. Okemo is a small resort, with only 2,150 ft of vertical drop, making for some icy, crowded slopes.

Women's Spree, Jan.–Mar.: five days, $525; Big Air, Dec.–Feb.: two days, $189. Price includes lift ticket (for Women's Spree), breakfasts, lunches, welcome party, and video analysis.

Park City Ski Area Ski School

www.parkcitymountain.com
Box 39
Park City, UT 84060
435/649–8111, 800/227–2754

This is an all-around fine ski school on a great ski mountain. The school offers Performance Series workshops for advanced skiers; these classes take you out to the mountain's extreme side and address specific skills, like powder skiing or banzai mogul bashing.

For lodging, Park City Ski Holidays will set you up with any type of accommodation, 800/222–7275. Performance Series workshop, $65 (does not include lift ticket).

Smugglers' Notch

www.smuggs.com
4323 Vermont Rte. 108 S
Smugglers' Notch, VT
05464-9537
800/451–8752

An excellent all-around ski school called Snow Sport University takes place at this 1,000-acre resort, widely hailed as one of the East's best family resorts. Graduation does not guarantee tight turns on double-diamond steeps, but it sure is fun. The kids' programs are renowned and popular. Weeklong kids' camps are held throughout the year; packages are available for adults who want in-depth instruction.

Dec.–Mar.: Weeklong Family Fest kids' camp package, $483, seven days (age 3 to 14), day camp from 9–4, including hot lunch, rental skis, and evening family programs, and two free dinners at Mountain Grill restaurant when dining with their parents. Dec.–Mid-Apr.: Weeklong package for two adults, $1,526. Price includes seven nights in efficiency during a non-holiday week, daily lessons, daily lift passes, and use of resort facilities. Ski rentals cost $215 extra for the week.

Squaw Valley, Lake Tahoe

www.squaw.com
Squaw Valley Ski School
Box 2007
Olympic Valley, CA 96146
800/403–0206, 530/583–6955

The Squaw Valley Ski School's five-day Advanced Skiing Clinic (ASC) has been dubbed Marine Corps Boot Camp Revisited. Despite the hard-browed teaching techniques, the program has received serious accolades and yields top-notch results. Squaw is one of California's best resorts.

Dec.-Mar.: five days, $855. Price includes lunches, video analysis, and lift tickets.

Steamboat

www.steamboat.com
Billy Kidd Center for
Performance Skiing
Steamboat Ski School
2305 Mt. Werner Cir.
Steamboat Springs, CO
80487
800/299–5017

The Billy Kidd Center for Performance Skiers is where world-class instructors bring out the full potential of their clients. The program relies heavily on video analysis and uses the same training techniques that gave Billy Kidd the silver in the 1964 Olympic slalom. Steamboat is a world-class resort with excellent all-around skiing and some of Colorado's deepest powder. On select Sundays, Olympic bronze medalist Nelson Carmichael gives free bump lessons on his namesake run.

Early Dec.–early Apr.: $199 per day. Price includes lunch and lift ticket. Free instruction from Nelson Carmichael select Sundays.

Stowe

www.stowe.com
Stowe Mountain Resort
5781 Mountain Rd.
Stowe, VT 05672
800/253–4754, 802/253–3000

Adults' and kids' programs are taught by an experienced staff, many with PSIA certification. Women in Motion Clinics focus on women-specific ski techniques and are a good time to just hang out with the girls. They are held throughout the winter. With more than 400 acres of skiing and a 2,360-ft vertical drop, Stowe offers plenty of terrain options to practice your turns, and the five-day Stowe for Starters is a great program for novices.

In 2003: Women in Motion Clinics: Jan. 13–15, Feb. 3–5, Mar. 3–5, $60 per day. Lessons $35–$72. Five-day Stowe for Starters $464.

Stratton

www.stratton.com
Stratton Mountain Resort
Box 145
Stratton Mountain, VT
05155-9406
800/787–2886, 802/297–4000

You'll find PSIA-certified instructors and specialized clinics here, such as Mike Nick's Skiboard Camp, where aspiring big-air artists (mostly under the age of 20) learn the tricks of the trade; women's ski clinics and racing clinics are also offered. An innovative Crossroads program focuses on building not only skiing skills but also social skills and spiritual health for kids.

Classes and clinics, one day, $20–$89.

Sugarbush

www.sugarbush.com
Sugarbush Resort
R.R. 1
Box 350
Warren, VT 05674
800/537–8427, 888/651–4827

Tons of clinics for every type of skier are held at this mega-resort, which has six mountains and more than 4,000 acres of skiable terrain. There are clinics for everyone from never-evers to experienced mogul thrashers

looking to nail their first mid-run heli. Adventure-skiing legend John Egan hosts small weekend clinics for intermediate and advanced skiers (during the holiday season only). Beginners can organize Learn to Turn packages for up to a week's stay.

John Egan Clinics: begins Dec. 29, $110 daily, per person. Learn to Turn Package: six days, starting at $1,100 (includes six nights lodging at inn during peak season, restricted lift tickets, lessons, equipment, and breakfasts).

Sunday River

www.sundayriver.com
Sunday River Resort
Box 450
Bethel, ME 04217
800/543–2754, 207/824–5959

The Perfect Turn program here is taught by PSIA-certified instructors. There are also special women's classes on weekends, a weekend Black Diamond Club for advanced skiers, a Mogul Munchkins kids' program, and freestyle classes. Sunday River has a vertical drop of 2,340 ft, gets 155 inches of snow annually, and is serviced by 18 lifts.

Nov.–May: one day, $75, including lift tickets.

Taos Ski Valley

www.skitaos.org
Box 90
Taos Ski Valley, NM 87525
800/776–1111, 505/776–2291

The intense, weeklong clinics here are designed to help you reach your ultimate potential. They cater to Masters (50 years and older), women, and telemarkers, and have video analysis and expert instruction. Taos has a 2,700-ft vertical drop and is one of the most charming ski resorts in the States. Snowboarding is not allowed at Taos.

Dec.–Mar.: five or six days, $375–$450 for Ski Better Weeks, $692 for Super Ski Weeks. Price includes lift tickets.

Timberline

www.timberlinelodge.com
Timberline Atomic Summer Ski Race Camp
Timberline Lodge, OR 97028
503/622–7979, 503/231–5402

These super-intense, week-long camps focus on dynamic racing technique. There is a Master's series for grown-ups in August, while the majority of campers are in the 18-and-under crowd during the early summer months.

Late June–Aug.: seven-day camp, $1,095–$1,295. Price includes lodging, meals, video analysis, and lift tickets.

Vail

www.wedelweeks.com
Pepi's Wedel Weeks
231 E. Gore Creek Dr.
Vail, CO 81657
800/610–7374, 970/476–5626

Work on the short, choppy turns often used on steep terrain and in moguls—known as wedel (pronounced *vay*-del) turns—at Pepi's Wedel Week, led by former Austrian National Ski Team Member Pepi Gramshammer and Franz Fuchsberger, a two-time World Powder 8 champion. These clinics will not only teach you to wedel like Chubby Checker but will also make you into a great all-around skier. Vail also has one of the world's best ski schools (800/475–4532, www.vail.com); they run shorter, multiday lesson and have excellent kids' programs and specialized clinics.

Pepi's Wedel Week, Nov.–Jan.: seven days, $2,380–$2,635. Price includes lodging, breakfasts, three dinners, and lift tickets.

Winter Park

www.nscd.org
www.skiwinterpark.com
National Sports Center for
the Disabled
Winter Park Resort
239 Winter Park Dr.
Winter Park, CO 80482
970/726–1540

This is the best "adaptive"
program (adapting to special
needs) in the world, with
highly experienced instructors, equipment, and facilities for people with any kind
of disability. Winter Park itself is a great ski area and
has terrain for all sorts of
skiers, as well as some of
Colorado's best bump runs.

Central Reservations, 800/
979–0332. Nov.–Apr.; call
for special package deals, as
rates vary.

Women's Ski Adventures

www.skiwithkim.com
Box 697
Crested Butte, CO 81224
888/444–8151

Kim Reichhelm, two-time
World Women's Extreme
Skiing Champion, person-
ally runs clinics geared to
women's needs and physical
abilities. Her goal is to enable women of all ages to ski
with confidence and enjoy-

ment. All students, from
first-timers to advanced, will
learn to ski more aggres-
sively in all conditions.
Clinic sites change each
year; most years there are
clinics in Aspen, Crested
Butte, and possibly Big Sky
Montana or even Alaska's
famed Alyeska area.

Mid-Dec.–Mar.: five-day
clinics, $1,528–$2,995. Price
includes luxury accommo-
dations, skiing clinics with
video analysis, airport transfers, welcome and awards
dinners, fashion shows, fun
races and awards, lift tickets,
breakfast and lunch, product
demos, and après-ski parties.

X-Team Advanced Ski Clinics

www.skiclinics.com
Box 988
Campton, NH 03223
800/983–2670, 603/726–9931

The Des Lauriers and Egan
brothers—perennially top-
ranked extreme skiers and
genuine ski movie stars—run
hard-core extreme-skiing
schools at several resorts
worldwide throughout the
year. The goal: to ski as many
different types of terrain and
snow conditions (including
off-piste, or extreme, skiing)
that the mountain has to offer, focusing on the specific

skills and technique required. Intensive sessions emphasize balance and body position, speed acceptance, visualization, and such disciplines as mogul, "air," and powder skiing. These clinics—held around the world in such steep-and-deep areas as Big Sky, Montana; Chamonix, France; and Squaw Valley, California—are for experts only. Bringing a go-big-or-go-home attitude (as well as a helmet) is recommended. The areas change each year, so call ahead to make your plans.

Mid-Dec.–Mar. and Aug.: seminar in South America, $989–$2,775. Three- to eight-day clinics, including lodging, lift tickets, clinics with video analysis, welcome party, awards ceremony (everyone gets one).

SURFING SCHOOLS

Hans Hedemann Surfing School

www.hhsurf.com
2947 Kalakaua Ave.
No. 105
Honolulu, HI 96815
808/924–7778

Hedemann, a well-known former pro surfer from Hawaii, gears his camp to people of all ages. This camp has the advantage of having accommodations at the Diamond Head Beach Hotel, right on the beach at Waikiki. You can learn to surf with a view of world-famous Diamond Head, a mountainlike volcanic landmark that looms over a beach where Hawaiians have been surfing since the very beginning of the sport. Besides having a good reputation, this camp offers more flexibility in terms of when you come and how long you stay than many others.

Year-round surf camp, including lodging at the Diamond Head Beach Hotel and Continental breakfast, $150 per day for as many days as you can handle. The surf camp is ongoing, and you can enroll at any time.

Kauai Surf School

www.kauaisurfschool.com
Box 220
Koloa
Kauai, HI 96756
808/332–7411

Surf at Poipu beach on Hawaii's "Garden Isle," so called because of its lush vegetation and super-relaxed atmosphere. Because Kauai is less visited than the other Hawaiian islands, classes at this school tend to be smaller and more personalized. After a few days, if you reach a comfortable level of competence, the instructors will take you on excursions to other beaches on their island to broaden your surfing experience.

All ages (eight and up) year-round: seven-day, all-inclusive (all meals and apartment lodging, space limited) surf clinics, $200 per day.

Lou Maresca's Central Florida Surf School

www.surfschoolcamp.com
1085 Morningside Dr.
Vero Beach, FL 32963
561/231–3265

Four-day (ages eight and up) camps and private lessons can be arranged every week of the year. This is the only surf school approved to operate on Florida State Beach Parks; lessons are given in the gentle waves at Fort Pierce Inlet State Recreation Area. The school also runs all-inclusive weeklong Learn to Surf adventures in Costa Rica.

Four-day camps, $325, food and lodging not included. Some lodging available at the owner's house, Osprey's Nest, for $65 per night, breakfast and dinner included.

Nancy Emerson Surf School

www.surfclinics.com
Box 463
Lahaina
Maui, HI 96767
808/244–7873

"If a dog can surf, so can you," claims Emerson, who taught her dog to ride waves to shore (no kidding—check out the photos in her ads). Since 1973, Emerson—a pioneer in women's professional surfing—has taught celebrities, pro surfers, and one World Champion surfer the principles of the sport. Surf camps take place in Maui, but this school also arranges surf clinics–surfaris to Australia and Fiji.

Five-day camp, $740, food and lodging not included.

Paskowitz Surfing Camps

www.paskowitz.com
Paskowitz Productions
Box 522
San Clemente, CA 92674
949/361–9283

Founded in 1972, this was the first surf camp in the country. The Paskowitz family is well respected in the surfing community. Octogenarian "Doc" Paskowitz, the family patriarch and school founder, has been introducing people to the surfing lifestyle since the late 1930s; he was also the first person to introduce surfing to Israel. His son runs the school now, but Doc still occasionally shows up for a surf. The camp curriculum he developed has become the industry standard. The five-day coed youth (10 to 17) camps run all season; five-day adult camps (18 and up) are at the end of the season. The outfit also arranges weeklong surf camps in Cabo San Lucas, Mexico.

June–Sept.: all five-day camps, $990, including meals and lodging at Campland by the Bay in San Diego. Year-round lessons are available.

Richard Schmidt Surf Camp

www.richardschmidt.com
236 San Jose Ave.
Santa Cruz, CA 95060
831/423–0928

Santa Cruz is a surf town nestled on a partially rocky coastline among redwood trees. The surf spots are all part of the Monterey Bay National Marine Sanctuary. The camp's namesake is a well-known big-wave surfer who has been teaching surfing since 1983 and has earned a reputation as a patient, enthusiastic instructor. Camps also include visits to a Marine Biology laboratory, elephant seal hike, and a visit to the Santa Cruz Surf Museum and the Arrow Surfboard Factory for an up-close look at how surfboards are shaped.

June–Aug.: five-day camp, $900. Private lessons available year-round.

Surf Diva Surf School

www.surfdiva.com
2160 Avenida de la Playa
La Jolla, CA 92037
858/454–8273

This popular place—the first all-women surf school—has been teaching women to surf since 1996. Surf clinics take place at La Jolla Shores beach, a scenic beach at the northern portion of La Jolla Cove, near San Diego. Five-day camps are at South Carlsbad State Beach, just north of San Diego. The most popular packages are the all-women weekend surf clinics. The outfit also offers five-day "boarding school" surf camps as well as weeklong women-only trips to Mexico.

Year-round weekend clinics: Level 1, $115; Level 2, $80 (instruction only). June–Aug.: five-day Teen (12 to 17) and Adult (18 and up) camps, $850, including food and tent lodging at South Carlsbad State Beach near San Diego.

Surf Sessions

www.atlanticbreezes.com/
surfcamp.htm
Rte. 3
Box 275 D
Fenwick Island, DE 19944
302/539–2126

Of the five-day overnight camps, most are for kids, and one is for adults. The school's director, a middle-school teacher, works with children and young adults year-round. There's an emphasis on water time here. You can surf for as long as your paddling muscles hold out or until it gets dark, whichever comes first.

June–Sept.: five-day camp, $500, including meals and bunk-bed accommodations in a beach cottage 50 yards from the water.

TENNIS CAMPS

Gardiner's Resort & Tennis Ranch

www.tennis-ranch.com
Box 228
Carmel Valley, CA 93924
800/453–6225, 831/659–2207

In this plush, traditional setting, with fine dining, two heated swimming pools, an outdoor whirlpool, a fitness room, and spa services (golf nearby), expect to see many celebrities and politicians tuning up their strokes. You get 10 championship courts and 2 teaching courts. The student–instructor ratio is 3:1. Most attendees range in age from 35 to 65.

Late Mar.–late Nov.: five days, $1,925–$2,250, including five hours' instruction daily, lodging in homes or guest rooms, and all meals.

Gunterman Tennis School at Stratton

www.greattennis.com
Box 1633
Manchester Center, VT 05255
800/426–3930, 802/297–4230

In addition to 19 courts (15 outdoor, 4 indoor), Gunterman has lots of dining and lodging options. The fitness center has racquetball, a pool, steam rooms, aerobics classes, and a spa. You'll also find trails for hiking, mountain biking, and horseback riding; Stratton is in the heart of Vermont's lovely Green Mountains.

May–early Oct.: five days, $355–$395, including three-hour clinic daily, individualized instruction on fourth day, and unlimited access to courts; price doesn't include dinners or accommodations.

The John Newcombe Tennis Ranch

www.newktennis.com
Box 310469
New Braunfels, TX 78131
830/625–9105, 800/444–6204

There are 28 courts (8 lighted and 4 covered) here, in Texas hill country, and a decent 4:1 student–instructor ratio. Teaching includes a combination of drills, strategy sessions, and supervised match play; the staff are fun and gregarious. There are scores of food options, and parties, dancing, and live entertainment in the evenings. When you're not swinging the bat, you can go river rafting or bungee jumping, play golf, or indulge in a massage.

Year-round: five days, $635–$788, including full-day instruction, accommodations, and buffet meals.

Killington Tennis

www.killingtontennis.com
Cortina Inn & Resort
Killington, VT 05751
802/773–3333, 800/451–6108

This place emphasizes ball control, pace, and spin. There are round-robin and mixed-doubles tournaments, and 12 courts (8 clay, 4 hard indoor) to play them on. The student–instructor ratio is 4:1. Hiking, mountain biking, and multiple 18-hole golf courses are nearby.

Late May–late Sept.: five days, $1,000, including five hours' instruction daily, optional hitting sessions with pros, lodging at resort, and three meals daily.

Litchfield Racquet Club & Tennis School

www.litchfieldbeach.com
Litchfield Beach & Golf Resort
Drawer 320, Hwy. 17
Pawleys Island, SC 29585
800/845–1897, 843/237–3411 ext. 2

You get unlimited court time on 17 Har-Tru courts (4 lighted) and are taught by USPTA- and USPTR-certified tennis professionals at this fancy resort on the Carolina coast. There are daily round robins and stroke-of-the-day clinics. The club is in the vicinity of Myrtle Beach golfing areas; on-site you have access to a health club, pool, and hot tub.

Year-round: four days, $225, including three hours' instruction daily. Price doesn't include accommodations or meals.

Nick Bollettieri Tennis Academy at IMG Academies

www.imgacademies.com
5500 34th St. W
Bradenton, FL 34210
800/872–6425, 941/755–1000

This place, a famous breeding ground for most top American pros, is serious about tennis. There are a whopping 71 courts of all surfaces (4 indoor) on which you partake in intensive drills and conditioning exercises. They teach both recreational and advanced players here; extras include a million-dollar fitness center, a private pool, a sauna, and massage therapy.

Year-round: five days, $838, including four hours' instruction daily, accommodations in lodge or villa, and all meals.

Nike Tennis Camp at Amherst, Massachusetts

www.ussportscamps.com
4470 Redwood Hwy.
San Rafael, CA 94903
415/451–2201, 800/645–3226

Nike has 36 courts; open sessions (basics and beyond); and singles, doubles, and advanced clinics focusing on strokes and strategy. Instructors include USPTA players, college tennis instructors, and foreign pros; attendees include young professionals and repeat students.

Mid-June–mid- or late Aug.: five days, $695, including dorm lodging and three buffet-style meals daily, five hours' instruction daily, and three private lessons.

Saddlebrook Tennis Center

www.saddlebrookresort.com
5700 Saddlebrook Way
Wesley Chapel, FL 33543-4499
813/907–4214 ext. 4211, 800/729–8383

This is the official resort of the Women's Tennis

Association; many top pros have trained here. There are 45 courts of all surface types, a 4:1 student–instructor ratio, and a physically and mentally demanding program. You can relax in the swimming pool or the European-style spa or play golf on the two Arnold Palmer–designed courses. An elaborate fitness center is on-site, as well as jogging and bicycle trails.

Year-round: five days, $1,058–$1,590, including hotel accommodations and meals, five hours of drills and fitness-agility training.

Sugarbush Tennis School

www.sugarbush.com
R.R. 1
Box 350
Warren, VT 05674
802/583–2391, 800/537–8427

This relatively small school has six courts (three lighted), a 4:1 student–instructor ratio, and a lovely view of the mountains. Attendees fall anywhere in the beginner-to-advanced range; round-robin tournaments are popular. For recreation, there are swimming pools, fitness rooms, racquetball courts, steam baths, and saunas.

Mid-May–late Sept.: five days, $565, including three hours' instruction in morning, unlimited court time in afternoon, lodging in inn or condos, and breakfast (no lunches or dinners).

Swarthmore Tennis Camp in Pennsylvania

www.
swarthmoretenniscamp.com
444 E. 82nd St.
Suite 31D
New York, NY 10028
800/223–2442, 212/879–0225

The focus here is on game-sharpening drills and strategy; the student–instructor ratio is 4:1. In the package you get a few private lessons and videotaping. There are 12 outdoor all-weather courts and 6 indoor courts (3 use a cushioned surface called Rebound Ace). You also get indoor and outdoor pools, an outdoor track, and massages, as well as healthy, hearty meals. This program, 12 mi from Philadelphia on Swarthmore's lovely, woodsy campus, is popular with singles.

Mid-June–mid-Aug.: five days, $850, including lodging in Strathaven Victorian stone mansion, all meals, five hours of instruction daily, three half-hour private lessons, and supervised matches.

Total Tennis

www.totaltennis.com
Box 28
Saugerties, NY 12477
845/247–9177, 800/221–6496

Beginners should expect to learn the fundamentals, and advanced players to play a smarter, tougher game. There are 25 courts (11 red clay, 7 hard, 2 artificial grass, 5 indoors), which you can use on off-hours. The student–instructor ratio is 4:1. The focus is on improving your game, not on changing the way you play. Attendees are pretty evenly split between single and married types. There's a DJ on Saturdays and a pool, hot tub, fitness center, and gym (and fine dining; after all, you work the calories off). The school, in upstate New York, is within driving distance of Manhattan and Boston.

Early June–Labor Day; seven days, $850, including five hours' instruction daily, half-hour private lesson, and accommodations in lodge with private bathroom.

Van der Meer Tennis

www.vdmtennis.com
Box 5902
Hilton Head Island, SC 29938
800/845–6138, 843/785–8388

Geared toward intermediate and advanced players, this school focuses on consistency, agility, footwork, and mental concentration. There are 28 courts (8 lighted and 4 covered) and a 5:1 student–instructor ratio.

Year-round: five days, $269–$429 ($100 more for clinics personally led by Dennis Van der Meer), including up to six hours' instruction daily. Price does not include accommodations (there are special rates at five nearby hotels) or meals.

Vic Braden Tennis College

www.vicbradentennis.com
1871 W. Canyon View Dr.
St. George, UT 84770
800/237–1068, 435/628–8060

Mental strategies are the focus here, and the facilities are extensive and sophisticated. There are 19 courts (4 indoors) and a 5:1 student–instructor ratio. Attendees tend to be between the ages of 35 and 65. The school is a two-hour drive from Las

Vegas. There are indoor and outdoor pools, basketball courts, and a fancy spa.

Year-round: five days, $600, including five hours' instruction daily. Price does not include lodging or meals.

WILDERNESS AND SURVIVAL SCHOOLS

Boulder Outdoor Survival School

www.boss-inc.com
Box 1590
Boulder, CO 80306
303/444–9779

Courses emphasize knowledge and technique, not modern technology. Typical gear includes a blanket, poncho, and knife and minimal food. Seven-day Skills Courses teach traditional skills in a primitive base camp; 7- to 28-day Field Courses take place on a trail and are physically challenging; 7- to 10-day Explorer Courses are like Field Courses minus the challenging impact phase. Field and Explorer courses have 9–12 participants; Skills have up to 15. There are three instructors per course. Field and most Explorer courses have solo.

Field and expedition courses, 7–28 days, $875–$3,075.

Headwaters Outdoor School

www.hwos.com
Box 1698
Santa Cruz, CA 95061-1698
530/938–1304

This outfit runs mainly one-week courses (winter class 11 days) around Mt. Shasta/northern California. The group teaches the skills you need to survive, including nature awareness. Programs have 12–24 participants, three to six staff, plus apprentices. Ages 14 and up are permitted, younger if with a family. You get a 10% discount if you sign up three months or more in advance.

One week, about $675, winter $775.

National Outdoor Leadership School

www.nols.edu
284 Lincoln St.
Lander, WY 82520-3140
307/332–5300

The focus here is on outdoor skills and leadership. Students are trained to take others into backcountry responsibly, avoiding survival situations. Domestic courses are 2–12 weeks. Twelve students and two to four instructors are typical.

$2,000–$10,000 per course, $105 per day average.

Outward Bound

www.outwardbound.org
Rte. 9D
R2, Box 280
Garrison, NY 10524-9757
888/882–6863

Outward Bound is known for helping people discover their personal potential and face the unfamiliar in a wilderness experience. All courses include solo, a community service project, a personal challenge (usually physical), and a group expedition in which participants take the lead. Courses run nationwide, 4–28 days. Courses are for teens, college students, and adults; there are also special courses for families, women, those in life changes, and specific age groups. There are 7 to 10 per group plus two instructors.

4–28 days, and semester-long courses, $700–$8,000 per course, $100–$125 per day.

Reevis Mountain School

www.reevismountain.org
HCO2
Box 1534
Roosevelt, AZ 85545
480/961–0490

On the seven-day Desert Course, offered once or twice annually (usually in spring), you can expect to learn desert survival skills in Superstition Wilderness (Arizona); the course emphasizes edible/useful/medicinal plants and natural healing. There are up to 25 participants, two primary instructors, and assistants; you must be a teen or older.

Desert Course, seven days, $775, including three meals daily. Camping is free; rental cabins $12 nightly or dorm-style yurt $5 nightly.

Tom Brown's Tracker School

www.trackerschool.com
Box 173
Asbury, NJ 08802
908/479–4681

Tracking, nature awareness, and the "ancient philosophy of the earth" characterize the courses here. The one-week Standard Course is requisite before taking others; it involves tracking, nature observation, survival skills, and Native American lifestyles. There are 70–75 students per course, six instructors, and 15–20 volunteers. You must be 18 or older, unless you're taking a family course.

Standard Course: $700 in New Jersey, $800 in California or Florida.

Wilderness Awareness School

www.wildernessawareness. org
Box 5000
PMB 137
Duvall, WA 98019
425/788–1301

Programs run one week, for ages 18 and up. The Art of Mentoring (Washington, Vermont, California) focuses on awakening your connection to nature and preparing you to work with youth; 40–50 participants average, 15–25 staff. Wolf tracking (Idaho) has 35 participants max, 15 staff (age 18 and up).

Mentoring $625, wolf tracking $745.

WINDSURFING SCHOOLS

ABK Sports

www.abksports.com
914 Mission Ave.
4th floor
San Rafael, CA 94901
415/451–1935, 800/996–2267

This is the oldest professionally run windsurfing school in the country. Its teaching method has been developed and refined by professionals in windsurfing, World Cup racing, and equipment technology. Perhaps the best part, though, is that ABK comes to you—they have about 16 multiday camp destinations throughout the summer.

Rates are about $385–$600 for three or four days, depending on location, lodging, and what's included.

AccesSport America

www.accessportamerica.com
119 High St.
Acton, MA 01720
866/457–7678, 978/264–0985

Using a teaching style a little unusual among windsurfing schools, to say the least, instructors here adapt and teach sailboarding and other high-challenge sports to adults and children with disabilities. They have seven locations in New England and Florida.

Fees based on sliding scales, $15 to $100 per session.

Banana River Windsurfing Resort

www.bananariverresort.com
3590 S. Atlantic Ave.
Cocoa Beach, FL 32931
321/784–0166

This resort has everything: accommodations, lessons, rentals, and activities for nonsailors. Its owners have a combined 35 years' experience, and they have coached everyone from beginners to athletes training for the Olympics. Packages are individually tailored.

Daily rates from $110 (campsite) to $325 (riverview suite). Prices do not include meals. Single rooms and suites have access to a large community kitchen.

Club Med

www.clubmed.com
75 Valencia Ave.
9th floor
Coral Gables, FL 33134
800/258–2633

Its 120 villages worldwide, from Mexico to the Caribbean to the Mediterranean, offer beginner, intermediate, and advanced windsurfing lessons in all-inclusive packages. Personal equipment such as booties and wet suits are about the only thing you are asked to bring.

Year-round, weekdays 6 AM–6 PM Pacific time, weekends 6:30–3: $973–$1,148. Prices are all-inclusive: lessons; accommodations; all meals; unlimited beer, wine, and soft drinks with lunch and dinner; gratuities; most additional sports (such as snorkeling or tennis); and nightly shows. Air transfers are included when you book airfare through Club Med.

Vela Windsurf Resorts

www.velawindsurf.com
351C Foster City Blvd.
Foster City, CA 94404
800/223–5443, 415/525–2070

In business for more than 15 years, this established outfit has schools in seven locations: Aruba; Baja, Mexico; Cabarete Bay, Dominican Republic; Los Roques Marine National Park and Margarita and Coche Islands, Venezuela; and Maui. The group offers all levels of instruction.

Prices range from about $330 to $1,741 a week, depending on which Vela property you go to. Prices include equipment, lodging, hotel taxes, and some meals.